Rick.

SNAPSHOT

Norway

CONTENTS

INTRODUCTION

This Snapshot guide, excerpted from my guidebook *Rick Steves' Scandinavia,* introduces you to a land with immigrant roots, modern European values, and the great outdoors like nowhere else—Norway.

Start in Oslo, Norway's sharp capital city, with its historic and walkable core, mural-slathered City Hall, and inspiring Nobel Peace Center. Oslo's excellent museums are dedicated to Norwegian art, the paintings of Edvard Munch, Viking ships, traditional folk life, Norway's WWII resistance, and more. Ogle the celebration-of-humanity statues at Vigeland Park, and relive Olympic memories at Holmenkollen Ski Jump.

Then head for Norway's countryside for a dose of natural wonder. The famous "Norway in a Nutshell" ride—by train, ferry, and bus—showcases the scenic splendor of the country, from snowcapped mountains to the striking Sognefjord. Choose a cozy fjordside hamlet (such as Balestrand, Solvorn, or Aurland) as your home base for touring mighty glaciers and evocative stave churches. Explore the Gudbrandsdal Valley, Lillehammer's superb open-air folk museum, and the impressive Jotunheimen Mountains.

Dip into Bergen, Norway's salty port town, with its lively fish market, colorful Hanseatic quarter, and a funicular to the top of Mount Fløyen. You can round out your Norwegian experience in the lively city of Stavanger, the time-passed Setesdal Valley, and resorty Kristiansand.

To help you have the best trip possible, I've included the following topics in this book:

• **Planning Your Time,** with advice on how to make the most of your limited time

• **Orientation,** including tourist information (abbreviated as TI), tips on public transportation, local tour options, and helpful hints

- **Sights** with ratings:
  - ▲▲▲—Don't miss
  - ▲▲—Try hard to see
  - ▲—Worthwhile if you can make it
  - No rating—Worth knowing about
- **Sleeping** and **Eating,** with good-value recommendations in every price range
- **Connections,** with tips on trains, buses, and driving
- **Practicalities,** near the end of this book, has information on money, phoning, hotel reservations, transportation, and more, plus Norwegian survival phrases.

To travel smartly, read this little book in its entirety before you go. It's my hope that this guide will make your trip more meaningful and rewarding. Traveling like a temporary local, you'll get the absolute most out of every mile, minute, and dollar.

Ha en god tur! Happy Travels!

NORWAY

NORWAY

Norge

 Norway is stacked with superlatives—it's the most mountainous, most scenic, and most prosperous of all the Scandinavian countries. Perhaps above all, Norway is a land of intense natural beauty, its famously steep mountains and deep fjords carved out and shaped by an ancient ice age.

Norway is also a land of rich harvests—timber, oil, and fish. In fact, its wealth of resources is a major reason why Norwegians have voted *"nei"* to membership in the European Union. They don't want to be forced to share fishing rights with EU countries.

The country's relatively recent independence (in 1905, from Sweden) makes Norwegians notably patriotic and proud of their traditions and history.

Norway's Viking past (c. A.D. 800–1050) can still be seen today in the country's 28 remaining stave churches—with their decorative nods to Viking ship prows—and the Viking artifacts housed in Oslo's Viking Ship Museum.

The Vikings, who also lived in present-day Denmark and Sweden, were great traders, shipbuilders, and explorers. However, they are probably best known for their infamous invasions, which terrorized much of Europe. The sight of their dragon-prowed ships on the horizon struck fear into the hearts of people from Ireland to the Black Sea.

Named for the Norse word *vik*, which means fjord or inlet, the Vikings sailed their sleek, seaworthy ships on extensive voyages, laden with amber and furs for trading—and weapons for fighting. They traveled up the Seine and deep into Russia, through the Mediterranean east to Constantinople, and across the Atlantic to Greenland and even "Vinland" (Canada). In fact, they touched the soil of the Americas centuries before Columbus, causing proud "ya sure ya betcha" Scandinavian immigrants in the US to display bumper stickers that boast, "Columbus used a Viking map!"

Both history and Hollywood have painted a picture of the Vikings as fierce barbarians, an image reinforced by the colorful names of leaders like Sven Forkbeard, Erik Bloodaxe, and Harald Bluetooth. Unless you're handy with an axe, these don't sound

NORWAY

like the kind of men you want to hoist a tankard of mead with. They kept slaves and were all-around cruel (though there is no evidence that they forced their subjects to eat lutefisk). But the Vikings also had a gentle side. Many were farmers, fishermen, and craftsmen who created delicate works with wood and metal. Faced with a growing population constrained by a lack of arable land, they traveled south not just to rape, pillage, and plunder, but in search of greener pastures. Sometimes they stayed and colonized, as in northeast England, which was called the "Danelaw," or in northwest France, which became known as Normandy ("Land of the North-men").

The Vikings worshipped many gods and had a rich tradition of mythology. Epic sagas were verbally passed down through generations or written in angular runic writing. The sagas told the heroic tales of the gods, who lived in Valhalla, the Viking heaven, presided over by Odin, the god of both wisdom and war. Like the

Norway Almanac

Official Name: Kongeriket Norge—"The Kingdom of Norway"—or simply Norge (Norway).

Population: Norway's 4.6 million people (about 30 per square mile) are mainly of Nordic and Germanic heritage, with a small population of indigenous Sami people in the north. The rapidly growing immigrant population is primarily from Pakistan, Sweden, Denmark, Iraq, Vietnam, and Somalia. Most Norwegians speak one of two official forms of Norwegian (Bokmål and Nynorsk), and the majority speak English as a second language. While church attendance is way down, the vast majority of Norwegian Christians consider themselves Lutheran.

Latitude and Longitude: 62°N and 10°E, similar latitude to Canada's Northwest Territories.

Area: 148,900 square miles, slightly larger than New Mexico.

Geography: Sharing the Scandinavian Peninsula with Sweden, Norway also has short northern borders with Finland and Russia. Its 51,575-mile coastline extends from the Barents Sea in the Arctic Ocean to the Norwegian Sea and North Sea in the North Atlantic. Shaped by glaciers, Norway has a rugged landscape of mountains, plateaus, and deep fjords. In the part of Norway that extends north of the Arctic Circle, the sun never sets at the height of summer, and never comes up in the deep of winter.

Biggest Cities: Norway's capital city, Oslo, has a population of 580,000; over a million live in its metropolitan area.

Economy: The Norwegian economy grows around 4 percent each year, contributing to a healthy $215 billion Gross Domestic Product and a per capita GDP of $46,200. Its

Egyptians, the Vikings believed in life after death, and chieftains were often buried in their ships within burial mounds, along with prized possessions such as jewelry, cooking pots, food, and Hagar the Horrible cartoons.

Like the Greeks and Etruscans before them, the Vikings never organized on a large national scale and eventually faded away due to bigger, better-organized enemies and the powerful influence of Christianity. By 1150, the Vikings had become Christianized and assimilated into European society. But their memory lives on in Norway.

Beginning in the 14th century, Norway came under Danish rule for more than 400 years, until the Danes took the wrong side in the Napoleonic Wars. The Treaty of Kiel forced Denmark to cede Norway to Sweden in 1814. Sweden's rule of Norway lasted until 1905, when Norway voted to dissolve the union. Like many European countries, Norway was taken over by Germany during

primary export is oil—Norway ranks behind only Saudi Arabia and Russia in the amount of oil exported, making it one of the world's richest countries. Thanks to this oil wealth, and the country's generally prudent approach to debt, the recent economic crisis has been relatively easy on Norway.

Currency: 6 Norwegian kroner (kr) = about $1.

Government: As the leader of Norway's constitutional monarchy, King Harald V has largely ceremonial powers. The head of state since October 2005 has been Prime Minister Jens Stoltenberg, who survived a narrow election in 2009. The legislative body is the Stortinget, with 169 members elected for four-year terms. The Labor Party currently holds 61 seats, followed by the Progress Party with 38, the Conservative Party with 23, and the Socialist Left Party with 15. The remaining seats are divided among smaller political parties.

Flag: The Norwegian flag is red with a blue Scandinavian cross outlined in white.

The Average Norwegian: The average Norwegian is 38 years old, has 1.78 children, and will live to be 79. One in three Norwegians is employed in the service sector, one in four in industry, and only 4 percent in agriculture.

World War II. April 1940 marked the start of five years of Nazi occupation, during which a strong resistance movement developed and hindered some of the Nazi war efforts.

Each year on May 17, Norwegians celebrate their ill-fated but idealistic 1814 constitution with fervor and plenty of flag-waving. Men and women wear folk costumes *(bunads)*, each specific to a region of Norway. Parades are held throughout the country. The parade in Oslo marches past the Royal Palace, where the royal family waves to the populace from their balcony. While the king holds almost zero political power (Norway has a parliament chaired by a prime minister), the royal family is still highly revered and respected.

Four holidays in early summer disrupt transportation schedules: Constitution Day (May 17, mentioned above), Ascension Day (May 13 in 2010, June 2 in 2011), and Whitsunday and Whitmonday (a.k.a. Pentecost and the following day, May 23–24 in 2010, June 12–June 13 in 2011).

High taxes contribute to Norway's high standard of living. Norwegians receive cradle-to-grave social care: university education, health care, nearly yearlong maternity leave, and an annual six weeks of vacation. Norwegians feel there is no better place than home. Norway regularly shows up in first place on the annual UN Human Development Index.

Visitors enjoy the agreeable demeanor of the Norwegian people—friendly but not overbearing, organized but not uptight, and with a lust for adventure befitting their gorgeous landscape. Known for their ability to suffer any misfortune with an accepting (if a bit pessimistic) attitude, Norwegians are easy to get along with.

Despite being looked down upon as less sophisticated by their Scandinavian neighbors, Norwegians are proud of their rich folk traditions—from handmade sweaters and folk costumes to the small farms that produce sweet goat cheese, called *geitost.* Less than 7 percent of the country's land is arable, resulting in numerous small farms. The government recognizes the value of farming, especially in the remote reaches of the country, and provides rich subsidies to keep this tradition alive. These subsidies would not be allowed if Norway joined the European Union—yet another reason the country remains an EU holdout.

Appropriate for a land with countless fjords and waterfalls, Norway is known for its pristine water. Norwegian bottled artisan water has an international reputation for its crisp, clean taste. Although the designer Voss water (www.vosswater.com)—the H_2O of choice for Hollywood celebrities—comes with a high price tag, the blue-collar Olden is just as good. (The tap water is actually wonderful, too—and much cheaper.)

While the Norwegian people speak a collection of mutually understandable dialects, the Norwegian language has two official forms: *bokmål* (book language), and *nynorsk* (New Norse). During the centuries of Danish rule, people in Norway's cities and upper classes adopted a Danish-influenced style of speech and writing (called Dano-Norwegian), while rural language remained closer to the Old Norse. After independence, Dano-Norwegian was renamed *bokmål,* and the rural dialects were formalized as *nynorsk,* as part of a nationalistic drive for a more purely Norwegian language. Despite later efforts to combine the two forms, *bokmål* remains the most commonly used, especially in urban areas, books, newspapers, and government agencies. Students learn both.

The majority of the population under 70 years of age also speak English, but a few words in Norwegian will serve you well. For starters, see the Norwegian Survival Phrases on page 185. If you visit a Norwegian home, be sure to leave your shoes at the door; indoors is usually meant for stocking-feet only. At the end of a meal, it's polite to say "Thanks for the food"—*"Takk for maten"* (tahk for MAH-ten). Norwegians rarely feel their guests have eaten enough food, so be prepared to say *"Nei, takk"* (nigh tahk; "No, thanks"). You can always try *"Jeg er met"* (yigh ehr met; "I am full"), but be careful not to say *"Jeg er full"*—"I am drunk."

Stave Churches

Norway's most distinctive architecture is the stave church. These medieval houses of worship—tall, skinny, wooden pagodas with  dragon's-head gargoyles—are distinctly Norwegian and palpably historic, transporting you right back to the Viking days. On your visit, make it a point to visit at least one stave church.

Stave churches are the finest architecture to come out of medieval Norway. Wood was plentiful and cheap, and locals had an expertise with woodworking (from all that boat-building). In 1300, there were as many as 1,000 stave churches in Norway. After a 14th-century plague, Norway's population dropped and many churches fell into disuse or burned down. By the 19th century, only a few dozen stave churches survived. Fortunately, they became recognized as part of the national heritage and were protected. Virtually all of Norway's surviving stave churches have been rebuilt or renovated, with painstaking attention to the original details.

A distinguishing feature of the "stave" design is its frame of tall, stout vertical staves (Norwegian *stav*, or "staff"). The churches typically sit on stone foundations, to keep the wooden structure away from the damp ground (otherwise it would rot). Most stave churches were made of specially grown pine, carefully prepared before being felled for construction. As the trees grew, the tips and most of the branches were cut off, leaving the trunks just barely alive to stand in the woods for about a decade. This allowed the sap to penetrate the wood and lock in the resin, strengthening the wood while keeping it elastic. Once built, a stave church was slathered with black tar to protect it from the elements.

Stave churches are notable for their resilience and flexibility. Just as old houses creak and settle over the years, wooden stave churches can flex to withstand fierce winds and the march of time. When the wind shifts with the seasons, stave churches groan and moan for a couple of weeks...until they've adjusted to the new influences, and settle in.

Even after the Vikings stopped raiding, they ornamented

the exteriors of their churches with warlike, evil spirit–fighting dragons reminiscent of their ships. Inside, a stave church's structure makes you feel like you're huddled under an overturned ship. The churches are dark, with almost no windows (aside from a few small "portholes" high up). Typical decorations include carved, X-shaped crossbeams; these symbolize the cross of St. Andrew (who was crucified on such a cross). Round, Romanesque arches near the tops of the staves were made from the "knees" of a tree, where the roots bend to meet the trunk (typically the hardest wood in a tree). Overall, these churches are extremely vertical: the beams inside and the roofline outside both lead the eye up, up, up to the heavens.

Most surviving stave churches were renovated during the Reformation (16th and 17th centuries), when they acquired more

horizontal elements such as pews, balconies, pulpits, altars, and other decorations to draw attention to the front of the church. In some (such as the churches in Lom and Urnes), the additions make the church feel almost cluttered. But the most authentic (including Hopperstad near Vik) feel truly medieval. These time-machine churches take visitors back to early Christian days: no pews (worshippers stood through the service), no pulpit, and a barrier between the congregation and the priest, to symbolically separate the physical world from the spiritual one. Incense filled the church, and the priest and congregation chanted the service back and forth to each other, creating an otherworldly atmosphere that likely made worshippers feel close to God. (If you've traveled in Greece, Russia, or the Balkans, Norway's stave churches might remind you of Orthodox churches, which reflect the way all Christians once worshipped.)

When traveling through Norway, you'll be encouraged to see stave church after stave church. Sure, they're interesting, but there's no point in spending time seeing more than a few of them. Of Norway's 28 remaining stave churches, seven are described in this book. The easiest to see are the ones that have been moved to open-air museums in Oslo and Lillehammer. But I prefer to appreciate a stave church in its original fjords-and-rolling-hills setting. My two favorites are both near Sognefjord: Borgund and Hopperstad. They are each delightfully situated, uncluttered by more recent additions, and evocative as can be. Borgund is in a pristine wooded valley, while Hopperstad is situated on a fjord. Borgund comes with the only good adjacent stave church museum. (Most stave churches on the Sognefjord are operated by the same preservation society; for more details, see www .stavechurch.com.)

Other noteworthy stave churches include the one in Lom, near the Jotunheimen Mountains, which is one of Norway's biggest, and is indeed quite impressive. The Urnes church, across from Solvorn, is technically the oldest of them all—but it's been thoroughly renovated in later ages (it is still worth considering, however, if only for its exquisite carvings and the fun excursion to get to it; see the "More on the Sognefjord" chapter). The Fantoft church, just outside Bergen, recently burned down, and the replica built to replace it has none of the original's magic. The stave church in Undredal (see the "Norway in a Nutshell" chapter) advertises itself as the smallest. I think it's also the dullest, and unless you're in tiny Undredal with time to kill, I recommend skipping it.

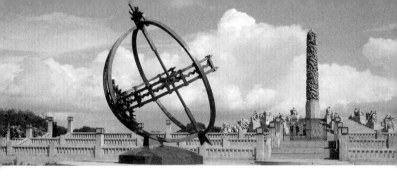

OSLO

While Oslo is the smallest and least earth-shaking of the Scandinavian capitals, this brisk little city offers more sightseeing thrills than you might expect. As an added bonus, you'll be inspired by a city that simply has its act together.

Sights of the Viking spirit—past and present—tell an exciting story. Prowl through the remains of ancient Viking ships, and marvel at more peaceful but equally gutsy modern boats (the *Kon-Tiki*, *Ra*, and *Fram*). Dive into the traditional folk culture at the Norwegian open-air folk museum, and get stirred up by the country's heroic spirit at the Norwegian Resistance Museum.

For a look at modern Oslo, tour the striking City Hall, take a peek at sculptor Gustav Vigeland's people pillars, climb the newly rebuilt Holmenkollen Ski Jump (opening in spring of 2010), walk all over the new Opera House, and then celebrate the world's greatest peacemakers at the Nobel Peace Center.

Situated at the head of a 60-mile-long fjord, surrounded by forests, and populated by more than a half-million people, Oslo is Norway's cultural hub. For 300 years (1624–1924), the city was called Christiania, after Danish King Christian IV. With independence, it reverted to the Old Norse name of Oslo. As an important port facing the Continent, Oslo has been one of Norway's main cities for a thousand years and the de facto capital since around 1300. Still, Oslo has always been small by European standards; in 1800, Oslo had 10,000 people, while cities such as Paris and London had 50 times as many.

Today the city sprawls out from its historic core to encompass over a million people in its metropolitan area, about one in

five Norwegians. Oslo's port hums with international shipping and a sizeable cruise industry. Its waterfront, once traffic-congested and slummy, is undergoing a huge change: Cars and trucks now travel in tunnels, a string of upscale condos and restaurants is taking over, and the neighborhood has a splashy new Opera House. Oslo is full of rich Norwegians and is, understandably, expensive. Its streets are a mix of grand Neoclassical facades and boxy 60s-style modernism. But overall, the feel of this major capital is green and pastoral—spread out, dotted with parks and lakes, and surrounded by hills and forests. For the visitor, Oslo is an all-you-can-see *smörgåsbord* of historic sights, trees, art, and Nordic fun.

Planning Your Time

Oslo offers an exciting two-day slate of sightseeing thrills. Ideally, spend two days, and leave on the night boat to Copenhagen or on the scenic "Norway in a Nutshell" train to Bergen the third morning. Spend the two days like this:

Day 1: Take my self-guided introductory walk. Tour the Akershus Fortress and the Norwegian Resistance Museum. Catch the City Hall tour. Spend the afternoon at the National Gallery and at the Holmenkollen Ski Jump and museum.

Day 2: Ferry across the harbor to Bygdøy and tour the *Fram, Kon-Tiki,* and Viking Ship museums. Spend the afternoon at the Norwegian Folk Museum. Finish the day at Frogner Park, enjoying the Vigeland statues (two recommended restaurants are nearby).

Orientation to Oslo

Oslo is easy to manage. Its sights cluster around the main boulevard, Karl Johans Gate (with the Royal Palace at one end and the train station at the other), and in the Bygdøy district, a 10-minute ferry ride across the harbor.

The monumental, homogenous city center contains most of the sights, but head out of the core to see the more colorful neighborhoods. Choose from Majorstuen and Frogner (chic boutiques, trendy restaurants), Grünerløkka (bohemian cafés, hipsters), and Grønland (multiethnic immigrants' zone).

Tourist Information

Oslo has two TIs: The **Oslo Information Center** faces City Hall (June–Aug daily 9:00–19:00, shorter hours and closed Sat–Sun off-season, Fridtjof Nansens Plass 5, www.visitoslo.com, info @visitoslo.com). Another TI is in front of the **train station** (Mon–Fri 7:00–20:00; Sat–Sun 8:00–18:00, until 20:00 May–Sept). Go early or late to avoid lines; otherwise, grab a number as you enter and wait. They answer the phone only on weekdays from 9:00 to 16:00 (tel. 24 14 77 00).

At either TI, pick up these freebies: an Oslo map, the helpful public transit map, the annual *Oslo Guide* (with plenty of details on sightseeing, shopping, and eating), the *What's On in Oslo* monthly (for the most accurate listing of museum hours and special events), and *Streetwise* magazine (an insightful, worthwhile student guide that's fun to read and full of offbeat ideas). If you're traveling on, pick up the *Bergen Guide* and information for the rest of Norway. The annual *Fjord Norway Travel Guide* is very useful. Consider buying the Oslo Pass (described below), unless you get the Oslo Package, which includes your hotel accommodation and an Oslo Pass (described under "Sleeping in Oslo," page 56).

Use It, a hardworking information center, is officially geared for those under age 26 but is generally happy to offer anyone its solid, money-saving, experience-enhancing advice (July–mid-Sept daily 9:00–18:00; off-season Mon–Fri 11:00–17:00, closed Sat–Sun; Møllergata 3, look for *Ungdomsinformasjonen* sign, tel. 24 14 98 20, www.unginfo.oslo.no). They can find you the cheapest beds in town (no booking fee), and offer free Internet access (30-min limit, may have to wait for a computer). Their free *Streetwise* magazine—packed with articles on Norwegian culture, ideas on eating and sleeping cheap, good nightspots, the best beaches, and so on—is a must for young travelers and worthwhile for anyone curious to probe the Oslo scene.

Oslo Pass: This pass covers the city's public transit, ferry boats, and entry to nearly every major sight—all described in a useful handbook (220 kr/24 hours, 320 kr/48 hours, 410 kr/72 hours; kids ages 4–15 and seniors over age 67 save 30 percent). Do the arithmetic carefully before buying; add up the individual costs of the sights you want to see to determine whether an Oslo Pass will save you money. (Here are some sample charges: 8-ride transit pass-180 kr, Nobel Peace Center-80 kr, three boat museums at Bygdøy-140 kr, National Gallery-free. These sights alone justify the cost of a 48-hour pass). Students with an ISIC card may be better off without the Oslo Pass. The TI's Oslo Package (see "Sleeping in Oslo," page 56) includes an Oslo Pass with your discounted hotel room.

Entertainment Listings: The periodical *What's On in Oslo* has an extensive listing of happenings every day. Pick it up free at the TI, and review the busy lineup of special events, tours, and concerts. *Streetwise* magazine is also good.

Arrival in Oslo

By Train

The central train station (Oslo Sentralstasjon, or "Oslo S" for short) is slick and helpful. You'll find Internet cafés, ATMs, and a Forex exchange desk. The station is plugged into a lively modern shopping mall called Byporten (Mon–Fri 10:00–21:00, Sat 10:00–18:00, closed Sun). You'll also find a Bit sandwich shop with seating for a cheap meal, an ICA supermarket (near the escalator, Mon–Fri 7:00–21:00, Sat–Sun 9:00–18:00), and a Vinmonopolet liquor store (Oslo's most central place to buy wine or liquor, sold only at Vinmonopolet stores). The TI is across the square in front of the station.

For tickets and train info, you can go to the station's ticket office (Mon–Fri 6:30–19:00, Sat 7:00–18:00, Sun 10:00–18:00) or to the helpful train office at the National Theater railway and T-bane station, which can have shorter lines (Mon–Fri 7:00–21:00, Sat–Sun 10:00–19:00, Ruseløkkveien, southwest of National Theater). There's also an after-hours full-service ticket desk at the train station, located between tracks 8 and 9 (open until 23:15). At each office, you can buy domestic, international, and Norway in a Nutshell tickets, and pick up leaflets on the Flåm and Bergen Railway. The TI also sells train tickets—likely friendlier and faster—for the same price.

By Plane

Oslo Airport: Oslo Lufthavn, also called Gardermoen, is about 30 miles north of the city center and has a helpful 24-hour information center (www.osl.no). For SAS, dial tel. 05400.

The speedy **Flytoget** train zips travelers between the airport and the central train station in 20–25 minutes (170 kr, less for students and seniors, 4/hr, runs roughly 5:00–24:00, not covered by railpasses, buy and validate ticket before boarding, keep it to exit, tel. 81 50 07 77, www.flytoget.no). Note that Flytoget trains alternate between those that go only to the central train station, and others that also continue on through Oslo, stopping at the National Theater station (which is closer to some recommended hotels and uses the same ticket).

Local trains cost less than Flytoget and take only a little longer (102 kr, hourly, 40 min, covered by railpasses, some also serve National Theater station). You'll save about 50 percent on this trip with an Oslo Pass because the pass covers transportation within Oslo; you only need to pay the fare for the stretch between the airport and the edge of town.

To reach the Flytoget and local train counters at the airport, exit right after you leave customs, and walk all the way to the far corner; you'll see two separate ticket counters (one for Flytoget,

NSB for the cheaper local trains) and separate TV screens showing the timetables for Flytoget and the "lokal–InterCity–fjerntog" trains.

Flybus airport buses stop directly outside the arrival hall and make several downtown stops, including the central train station (140 kr one-way, 4/hr, 40 min).

Taxis run to and from the airport (670-kr fixed rate, confirm price before you commit, some companies have cheaper special deals). If you start your ride after 17:00, there's a 200-kr extra charge (get in at 17:01 and suddenly it costs 870 kr). I prefer the slick and faster Flytoget train, but the taxi can be a good value for families and those with lots of luggage.

Sandefjord Airport Torp: Ryanair and other discount airlines use this airport, 70 miles sounds of Oslo (trains run hourly between Sandefjord station and Oslo, fewer Sat–Sun, 1.75 hours, www.nsb.no; 219-kr train fare includes shuttle bus between airport and Sandefjord station—2/hr, 4 min). Airport info: tel. 33 42 70 00, www.torp.no.

Helpful Hints

Pickpocket Alert: They're a problem in Oslo, particularly in crowds on the street and in subways and buses. Always wear your money belt. To call the police, dial 112.

Street People and Drug Addicts: Oslo's street population loiters around the train station. While a bit unnerving to some travelers, locals consider this rough-looking bunch harmless. The police have pretty much corralled them to the square called Christian Frediks Plass, south of the station.

US Embassy: It's the big place behind all the fortifications (passport services open Mon–Fri 9:00–12:00, Henrik Ibsens Gate 48, tel. 22 44 85 50, norway.usembassy.gov).

Currency Exchange: Banks don't change money. Use ATMs or Forex exchange offices (outlets near City Hall at Fridtjof Nansens Plass 6, at train station, and at Egertorget at the crest of Karl Johans Gate, hours vary by location but generally Mon–Fri 9:00–18:00, Sat 9:00–16:00, closed Sun).

Internet Access: You have two options at the train station. **Sidewalk Express,** the budget choice, has locations on the mezzanine level under the escalators and near the city center entrance (29 kr/1.5 hours, open 24/7, coin-op). **@rctic Internet Café,** in the station's main hall and above track 13, is quieter but pricey (60 kr/hr, daily 9:00–22:00, sells international phone cards).

Post Office: It's in the train station.

Pharmacy: Jernbanetorgets Vitus Apotek is open 24 hours daily (across from train station on Jernbanetorget, tel. 23 35 81 00).

Laundry: Selva Laundromat is on the corner of Wessels Gate and Ullevålsveien at Ullevålsveien 15, a half-mile north of the train station (daily self-serve 8:00–21:00, full-serve 10:00–19:00, walk or catch bus #37 from station, tel. 41 64 08 33).

Bike Rental: Bikes are tough to rent in Oslo. A public system lets you grab simple city bikes out of locked racks at various points around town (80 kr/24 hours, rent card at TI, must leave credit-card number as deposit). A more expensive conventional bike rental company delivers bikes to your hotel (details at TI).

Getting Around Oslo

By Public Transit: Commit yourself to taking advantage of Oslo's excellent transit system, made up of buses, trams, ferries, and a subway (*Tunnelbane,* or T-bane for short). Use the TI's free public transit map to navigate. The system runs like clockwork, with schedules clearly posted and followed. Many stops have handy electronic reader boards showing the time remaining before the next tram arrives (usually less than 10 min). **Trafikanten,** the public-transit information center, faces the train station under the glass tower (same building as TI; Mon–Fri 7:00–20:00, Sat–Sun 8:00–20:00, tel. 177 or 81 50 01 76, www.trafikanten.no).

Individual **tickets** work on buses, trams, ferries, and T-bane for one hour (25 kr if bought at a Narvesen kiosk/convenience store, or 36 kr if bought on board). Other options include the **Flexicard** (180 kr for 8 rides, shareable, can buy from driver), the 24-hour **Dagskort Tourist Ticket** (65 kr, pays for itself in three rides), and the **Oslo Pass** (free run of entire system; pass described earlier).

By Taxi: Taxis come with a 105-kr drop charge that covers you for three or four kilometers—about two miles (134 kr on evenings and weekends). To get a taxi, wave one down, find a taxi stand, or call 02323.

Tours in Oslo

By Boat, Bus, and Foot

Oslo Fjord Tours—A fascinating world of idyllic islands sprinkled with charming vacation cabins is minutes away from the Oslo harborfront. For locals, the fjord is a handy vacation getaway. Tourists can get a glimpse of this island world by public ferry or tour boat. Cheap ferries regularly connect the nearby islands with downtown (covered by Oslo Pass or transit pass).

Several tour boats leave regularly from pier 3 in front of City Hall. Båtservice has a relaxing and scenic 50-minute mini-cruise, with a live-but-boring multilanguage commentary, that departs on the hour (130 kr, daily late May–June 10:00–16:00, July–Aug until 19:00, no boats Sept–late May, tel. 23 35 68 90, www.boat sightseeing.com). They won't scream if you bring something to munch. They also offer two-hour fjord tours (230 kr, 3–4/day late April–Sept) and a "Summer Evening on the Fjord" dinner cruise (390 kr; joyride without narration that includes a "shrimp buffet"—just shrimp, bread, and butter; daily late June–mid-Sept 19:00–22:00). The 72-hour Oslo Pass gets you Båtservice's two-hour lunch cruise for free (normally costs 390 kr, 10:30–12:30 summer only, seats limited so reserve far in advance).

Bus Tours—Båtservice, which runs the harbor cruises (above), also offers three-hour bus tours of Oslo, with stops at the ski jump, Bygdøy museums, and Frogner Park (380 kr, 2/day late May–Aug, departs from ticket office on pier 3, longer tours also available, tel. 23 35 68 90, www.boatsightseeing.com). HMK also does daily city bus tours (215 kr/2 hours, 300 kr/3 hours, departs from TI across from City Hall, tel. 22 78 94 00, www.hmk.no). While there is a hop-on, hop-off bus service for Oslo (225 kr/24 hours), the city doesn't really work well with this kind of tour bus. Again, commit yourself to public transit to save lots of time, and try the self-guided tram tour described below.

Guided Walking Tour—The local guides' union offers 90-minute historic "Oslo Promenade" walks (from 100 kr, free with Oslo Pass; Mon, Wed, Fri at 17:30 in summer; leaves from sea side of City Hall, confirm departures at TI, tel. 22 42 70 20, www.guide service.no).

Local Guide—To hire a private guide, call the guides' association at tel. 22 42 70 20 (1,150 kr/2 hours, www.guideservice.no). Another local guide bureau is at tel. 22 42 28 18.

Self-Guided Tram Tour

Tram #11/#12: A Hop-On, Hop-Off Introduction to Oslo

Tram #12, which becomes tram #11 halfway through its loop (at Majorstuen), circles the city from the train station, lacing together many of Oslo's main sights. Apart from the practical value of being able to hop on and off as you sightsee your way around town (trams come by at least every 10 minutes), this 40-minute trip gives you a fine look at parts of the city you wouldn't otherwise see.

The route starts at the main train station, at the traffic-island tram stop located immediately in front of the transit office tower. The route finishes at Stortorvet (the cathedral square), making 90 percent of a circle, and dropping you a three-minute walk from where you began the tour. Confirm with your driver that the tram #12 you're boarding becomes tram #11, and finishes at Stortorvet. Here's what you'll see and ideas on where you might want to hop out:

From the **station,** you'll go through the old grid streets of 16th-century Christiania, King Christian IV's planned Renaissance town. After the city's 17th fire, in 1624, the king finally got fed up. He decreed that only brick and stone buildings would be permitted in the city center, with wide streets to serve as fire breaks.

You'll turn a corner at the **fortress** (Christiana Torv stop; get off here for the fortress and Norwegian Resistance Museum), then head for **City Hall** (Rådhus stop). Next comes the harbor and upscale **Aker Brygge** waterfront neighborhood (jump off at the Aker Brygge stop for the harbor and restaurant row). Passing the harbor, you'll see on the left a few old shipyard buildings that still survive. Then the tram goes uphill, past the **House of Oslo** (a mall of 20 shops highlighting Scandinavian interior design; Vikatorvet stop) and into a district of ugly 1960s buildings (when elegance was replaced by "functionality"). The tram then heads onto the street Norwegians renamed **Henrik Ibsens Gate** in 2006 to commemorate the centenary of Ibsen's death, honoring the man they claim is the greatest playwright since Shakespeare.

After Henrik Ibsens Gate, the tram follows Frognerveien through the chic **Frogner neighborhood.** Behind the fine old facades are fancy shops and spendy condos. Here and there you'll see 19th-century mansions built by aristocratic families who wanted to live near the Royal Palace. Today many of these house foreign embassies. Turning the corner, you roll along the edge of **Frogner Park,** stopping at its grand gate (hop out at the Vigelandsparken stop for Frogner Park and Vigeland statues).

Ahead on the left, a statue of 1930s ice queen Sonja Henie marks the arena where she learned to skate. Turning onto Bogstadveien, the tram becomes #11 at the Majorstuen stop. **Bogstadveien** is lined with trendy shops, restaurants, and cafés—it's a fun place to stroll and window-shop. (You could get out here and walk along this street all the way to the Royal Palace park and the top of Karl Johans Gate.) The tram veers left before the palace, passing the **National Historical Museum** and stopping at the **National Gallery** (Tullinløkka stop). As you trundle along, you may notice that lots of roads are ripped up for construction. It's too cold to fix the streets in the winter, so, when possible, that work is done in the summer. Jump out at **Stortorvet** (a big square filled with flower stalls and fronted by the cathedral and the big GlasMagasinet department store). From here, you're a three-minute walk from the station, where this tour began.

OSLO

Hello Oslo Walk

1. Trafikanten Tower & TI
2. Byporten Mall
3. Oslo Sweater Shop
4. Oslo Cathedral
5. Stortorvet Square
6. Crest of Karl Johans Gate
7. Heimen Husfliden Shop
8. Grand Hotel & Café
9. Parliament Building
10. National Theater
11. City Hall
12. Harbor View
13. Nobel Peace Center

Self-Guided Walk

▲▲Hello Oslo

This stroll covers the heart of Oslo—the zone most tourists find themselves walking—from the train station, up the main drag, and past City Hall to the harborfront. It takes a brisk 30 minutes if done nonstop.

Train Station: Start at the main entrance of Oslo's central train station (Oslo Sentralstasjon)—still marked *Østbanehallen,* or "East Train Station," from when Oslo had two stations. The statue of the tiger commemorates the 1,000th birthday of Oslo's founding, celebrated in the year 2000. The statue alludes to the town's nickname of Tigerstaden ("Tiger Town"). In the 1800s, Oslo was considered an urban tiger, leaving its mark on the soul of simple country folk who ventured into the wild and crazy New York City of Norway. (These days, the presence of so many beggars, or *tigger,* has prompted the nickname "Tiggerstaden.")

With your back to the train station, look for the glass Trafikanten tower that marks the **public transit office** (and TI);

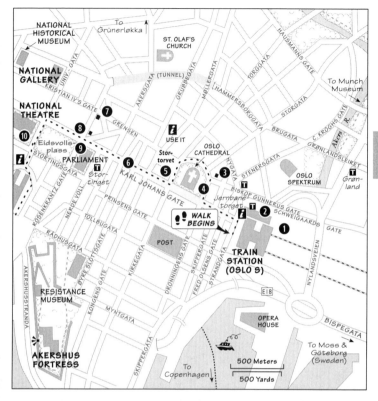

from here, trams zip to City Hall (harbor, boat to Bygdøy), and the underground subway (T-bane, or *Tunnelbane*—look for the *T* sign to your right) goes to Frogner Park (Vigeland statues) and Holmenkollen. Tram #12—featured in the self-guided tram tour described above—leaves from directly across the street.

The green building behind the Trafikanten tower is a shopping mall called **Byporten** (literally, "City Gate," see big sign on rooftop), built to greet those arriving from the airport on the shuttle train. Oslo's 37-floor pointed-glass **skyscraper,** the Radisson/SAS Plaza Hotel, looms behind that. Its 34th-floor pub welcomes the public with air-conditioned views and pricey drinks (daily 16:00–24:00). The tower was built with reflective glass so that, from a distance, it almost disappears. The area behind the Radisson—the lively and colorful "Little Karachi," centered along a street called Grønland—is where most of Oslo's immigrant population settled. It's become a vibrant nightspot, offering a fun contrast to the predictable homogeneity of Norwegian cuisine and culture (see "Immigration in Norway" sidebar).

Oslo allows hard-drug addicts and prostitutes to mix and mingle in the station area. (While it's illegal to buy sex in Norway, those who sell it are not breaking the law.) Troubled young people come here from small towns in the countryside for anonymity and community. The two cameras near the top of the Trafikanten tower monitor drug deals. Signs warn that this is a "monitored area," but victimless crimes proceed while violence is minimized.

• *Turn your attention to Norway's main drag...*

Karl Johans Gate: This grand boulevard leads directly from the train station to the Royal Palace. The street is named for the French prince Jean Baptiste Bernadotte, who was given a Swedish name, established the current Swedish dynasty, and ruled as a popular king (1818–1844) during the period after Sweden took Norway from Denmark.

Walk three blocks up Karl Johans Gate. This stretch is referred to as **"Desolation Row"** by locals because it has no soul. (Shoppers can detour to the recommended Oslo Sweater Shop, a block to the right down Skippergata, at Biskop Gunnerusgata 3.)

• *Hook around the curved old brick structure of an old market and walk to the...*

Oslo Cathedral (Domkirke): This Lutheran church, from 1697, is where Norway celebrates and mourns its royal marriages and deaths. The most recent royal wedding here was of Crown Prince Håkon Magnus and commoner Mette-Marit Tjessem Høiby—an unwed mom—in August 2001. Her father was a pensioner, poor enough to be a cheap source of gossip for the tabloids. It's a win-win situation, since locals enjoyed all the blather...and he got new teeth and a free mobile phone paid for by Oslo's tabloids.

Look for the cathedral's cornerstone (right of entrance), a thousand-year-old carving from Oslo's first and long-gone cathedral showing how the forces of good and evil tug at each of us. Step inside beneath the red, blue, and gold seal of Oslo and under an equally colorful ceiling. The box above on the right is for the royal family. Back outside, notice the tiny square windows midway up the copper cupola—once the lookout quarters of the fire watchman.

Walk behind the church. The **courtyard** is lined by a circa-1850 circular row of stalls from an old market. Rusty meat hooks now decorate the lamps of a peaceful café, which has quaint tables around a fountain. The atmospheric **Café Bacchus,** at the far left end of the arcade, serves food outside and in a classy café downstairs (light 120-kr meals, Mon–Sat 11:00–22:00, closed Sun, salads, good cakes, coffee, tel. 22 33 34 30).

• *The big square that faces the cathedral is called...*

Stortorvet: In the 17th century, when Oslo's wall was about here, this was the point where farmers were allowed to enter and

Immigration in Norway

Oslo has a big and growing immigrant community. About 10 percent of today's Norwegians are not ethnic Norwegians, and one in four of Oslo's residents is an immigrant. The border was closed to immigration in 1975. But because immigrants already in Norway have been allowed to sponsor relatives—and because Norway still allows refugees to enter for humanitarian reasons (for instance, Iranians can claim they are gay and can't safely return)—its immigrant population continues to grow.

These "new Norwegians" have provided a much-needed and generally appreciated labor force, filling jobs that wealthy Norwegians would rather not do. Immigrants are critical in the booming construction industry. Cab companies, restaurants, and hotels employ large numbers of immigrant workers. And entrepreneurial immigrants have opened wonderful ethnic restaurants, literally adding spice to the otherwise pretty drab local cuisine.

But in some parts of Oslo (such as near the train station), you'll see some of the downside of a country that is disinclined to be a melting pot. There have been scuffles between gangs and immigrant groups. Locals complain that the Norwegian government gives refuge to various ethnic groups who are historic enemies and then houses them side by side. Another source of friction is the tough love Norwegians feel they get from their government compared to the easy ride offered to needy immigrants: "They even get pocket money in jail!"

While Norway is a leader among rich nations in per-capita giving to the developing world, the immigrant issue is an awkward one for locals to discuss. While many aren't eager to have their country become the next melting pot, they're also careful not to object too strenuously, wary of being labeled racist.

sell their goods. Today it's still lively as a flower and produce market (Mon–Fri). The statue shows Christian IV, the Danish king who ruled Norway around 1600, dramatically gesturing that-a-way. He named the city, immodestly, Christiania. (Oslo took back its old Norse name only in 1924.) Christian was serious about Norway. During his 60-year reign, he visited it 30 times (more than all other royal visits combined during 300 years of Danish rule). The big GlasMagasinet department store is a landmark on this square.

• *Return to Karl Johans Gate, and continue up the boulevard past street musicians, cafés, shops, and hordes of people. Kongens Gate leads left, past the 17th-century grid-plan town to the fortress. Continue hiking straight up to the crest of the hill, pausing to enjoy some of the street musicians along the way. If you're here early in the morning (Mon–Fri) you may see a commotion at #14. This is the studio of a big TV station (channel 2) where the Norwegian version of the* Today *show is taped, and as in New York, locals gather here, clamoring to get their mug on TV.*

The Crest of Karl Johans Gate: Look back at the train station. A thousand years ago, the original (pre-1624) Oslo was located at the foot of the wooded hill behind the station. Now look ahead to the Royal Palace in the distance, which was built in the 1830s "with nature and God behind it and the people at its feet." If the flag flies atop the palace, the king is in the country. Karl Johans Gate is a parade ground from here to the palace—the axis of modern Oslo. Each May 17th, Norway's Independence Day, an annual children's parade turns this street into a sea of marching student bands and costumed young flag-wavers, while the royal family watches from the palace balcony. Since 1814, Norway has preferred peace. Rather than celebrating its military on the national holiday, it celebrates its children.

King Harald V and Queen Sonja moved back into the palace in 2001, after extensive (and costly) renovations. To quell the controversy caused by this expense, the public is now allowed inside to visit each summer with a pricey one-hour guided tour (95 kr, daily late June–mid-Aug at 14:00, Mon–Thu and Sat also at 12:00, buy tickets in advance at any post office or by calling 81 53 31 33, www .kongehuset.no).

From here, the *T* sign marks a stop of the T-bane (Oslo's subway). Let W. B. Samson's bakery tempt you with its pastries (and short cafeteria line; WC in back). Next to that, David Andersen's jewelry store displays traditional silver art and fine enamel work. Inside, halfway down the wall on the right (next to the free water dispenser), is a display of Norwegian folk costumes *(bunader)* with traditional jewelry—worn on big family occasions and church holidays. From here, the street called Akersgata kicks off a worthwhile stroll past the national cemetery and through a park-like river gorge to the trendy Grünerløkka quarter (an hour-long walk).

People-watching is great along Karl Johans Gate, but remember that if it's summer, half of the city's regular population is gone—vacationing in their cabins or farther away—and the city center is filled mostly with visitors.

Hike two blocks down Karl Johans Gate, past the big brick Parliament building (on the left). In this section, the sidewalk is heated so it won't be icy in the frigid winter. On the right is a statue of the painter Christian Krohg. Farther down Karl Johans Gate, just past the Freia shop (Norway's oldest and best chocolate), the venerable **Grand Hotel** (Oslo's celebrity hotel—Nobel Peace Prize winners sleep here) overlooks the boulevard.

• *Ask the waiter at the Grand Café if you can pop inside for a little sightseeing (he'll generally let you).*

Grand Café: This historic café was for many years the meeting place of Oslo's intellectual and creative elite. The playwright Henrik Ibsen was a regular here. Notice the photos and knick-knacks on the wall. At the back of the café, a mural shows Norway's literary and artistic clientele—from a century ago—enjoying this fine hangout. On the far left, find Ibsen, coming in as he did every day at 13:00. Edvard Munch is on the right, leaning against the window, looking pretty drugged. Names are beneath the mural.

OSLO

• *For a cheap bite with prime boulevard seating, continue next door to Deli de Luca, a convenience store with a super selection of take-away food and a great people-watching perch. Across the street, a little park faces Norway's…*

Parliament Building (Stortinget): Norway's Parliament meets here (along with anyone participating in a peaceful protest outside). Built in 1866, the building seems to counter the Royal Palace at the other end of Karl Johans Gate. If the flag's flying, Parliament's in session. Today the king is a figurehead, and Norway is run by a unicameral Parliament and a prime minister. Guided tours of the Stortinget are offered for those interested in Norwegian government (free; mid-June–Aug Mon–Fri at 10:00, 11:30, and 13:00; enter on Karl Johans Gate side, tel. 23 31 35 96, www.stortinget.no).

• *Continue walking toward the palace through the park, past the fountain, to the…*

Statue of Wergeland: The poet Henrik Wergeland helped inspire the movement for Norwegian autonomy. In the winter, the pool here is frozen and covered with children happily ice-skating. Across the street behind Wergeland stands the **National Theater** and statues of Norway's favorite playwrights: Ibsen and Bjørnstjerne Bjørnson. Across Karl Johans Gate, the pale yellow building is the first university building in Norway, dating from 1854. A block behind that is the National Gallery, with Norway's best collection of paintings (free entry).

• *Follow Roald Amundsens Gate left, to the towering brick…*

City Hall (Rådhuset): Built in the 1930s with contributions from Norway's leading artists, City Hall is full of great art and is

worth touring. The mayor has his office here (at the base of one of the two 200-foot towers), and every December 10, this building is where the Nobel Peace Prize is presented. For the best exterior art, circle the courtyard clockwise, studying the colorful woodcuts in the arcade. Each shows a scene

Oslo at a Glance

▲▲▲**Frogner Park** Sprawling park with works by Norway's greatest sculptor, Gustav Vigeland, and the studio where he created them (now a museum). **Hours:** Park—always open; Museum—June-Aug Tue-Sun 10:00-17:00, closed Mon; Sept-May Tue-Sun 12:00-16:00, closed Mon. See page 39.

▲▲▲**Norwegian Folk Museum** Norway condensed into 150 historic buildings in a large open-air park. **Hours:** Daily mid-May–mid-Sept 10:00-18:00, off-season park open daily 11:00-15:00 but most historical buildings closed. See page 45.

▲▲▲**City Hall** Oslo's artsy 20th-century government building, lined with huge, vibrant, municipal-themed murals, best visited with included tour. **Hours:** Daily 9:00-18:00; tours daily at 10:00, 12:00, and 14:00, no tours Sat-Sun in winter. See page 27.

▲▲▲**National Gallery** Norway's cultural and natural essence, captured on canvas. **Hours:** Tue–Fri 10:00-18:00, Thu until 19:00, Sat-Sun 11:00-17:00, closed Mon. See page 31.

▲▲**Norwegian Resistance Museum** Gripping look at Norway's tumultuous WWII experience. **Hours:** June-Aug Mon-Sat 10:00-17:00, Sun 11:00-17:00; Sept-May Mon-Fri 10:00-16:00, Sat-Sun 11:00-16:00. See page 30.

▲▲**Viking Ship Museum** An impressive trio of ninth-century Viking ships, with exhibits on the people who built them. **Hours:** Daily May–Sept 9:00-18:00, Oct-April 11:00-16:00. See page 46.

▲▲*Fram* **Museum** Captivating exhibit on the Arctic exploration ship. **Hours:** Daily June-Aug 9:00-18:00, May and Sept 10:00-17:00, Oct-April 10:00-16:00. See page 47.

▲▲**Holmenkollen Ski Jump and Ski Museum** Dizzying vista and schuss through skiing history. **Hours:** Reopens spring of 2010 after big rebuild; museum open daily June-Aug 9:00-20:00, May and Sept 10:00-17:00, Oct-April 10:00-14:00. See page 48.

from Norwegian mythology, well-explained in English: Thor with his billy-goat chariot, Ask and Embla (a kind of Norse Adam and Eve), Odin on his eight-legged horse guided by ravens, the swan maidens shedding their swan disguises, and so on. Circle around City Hall on the right to the front. The statues (especially the six laborers on the other side of the building, facing the harbor, who seem to guard the facade) celebrate the nobility of the working class.

▲▲*Kon-Tiki* **Museum** Adventures of primitive *Kon-Tiki* and *Ra II* ships built by Thor Heyerdahl. **Hours:** Daily June–Aug 9:30–17:30, April–May and Sept 10:00–17:00, Oct–March 10:30–16:00. See page 48.

▲**Nobel Peace Center** Exhibit celebrating the ideals of the Nobel Peace Prize and the lives of those who have won it. **Hours:** June–Aug daily 10:00–18:00; Sept–May Tue–Sun 10:00–18:00, closed Mon. See page 29

OSLO

▲**Akershus Fortress Complex and Tours** Historic military base and fortified old center, with guided tours, a ho-hum castle interior, and a couple of museums (including the excellent Norwegian Resistance Museum, listed above). **Hours:** Park open daily 6:00–21:00; 45-minute tours of the grounds generally offered May–Aug Mon–Fri at 11:00, 12:00, 13:00, 14:00, and 15:00, Sat–Sun at 13:00 and 15:00, no tours off-season. See page 30.

▲**Norwegian Holocaust Center** High-tech walk through rise of anti-Semitism, the Holocaust in Norway, and racism today. **Hours:** Daily summer 10:00–18:00, off-season 11:00–16:00. See page 47.

▲**Norwegian Maritime Museum** Dusty cruise through Norway's rich seafaring heritage. **Hours:** Mid-May–Aug daily 10:00–18:00; Sept–mid-May daily 10:30–16:00, Thu until 18:00. See page 48.

▲**Edvard Munch Museum** Works of Norway's famous Expressionistic painter. **Hours:** June–Aug daily 10:00–18:00; Sept–May Tue–Fri 10:00–16:00, Sat–Sun 11:00–17:00, closed Mon. See page 49.

▲**Opera House** Stunning performance center that's helping revitalize the harborfront. **Hours:** Mon–Fri 10:00–23:00, Sat 11:00–23:00, Sun 12:00–22:00. See page 29.

▲**Grünerløkka** Oslo's bohemian district, with bustling cafés and pubs. **Hours:** Always open. See page 51.

• *Walk to the...*

Harbor: A few years ago, you would have dodged several lanes of busy traffic to get to the harborfront. But in Oslo today, most cars cross the city underground in tunnels. The city has made its town center relatively quiet and pedestrian-friendly by levying a traffic-discouraging 25-kr toll for every car entering town. (This system, like a similar one in London, subsidizes public transit and the city's infrastructure.)

Browsing

Oslo's pulse is best felt by strolling. Three good areas are along and near the central Karl Johans Gate, which runs from the train station to the palace (see my self-guided walk); in the trendy harborside Aker Brygge mall, a glass-and-chrome collection of sharp cafés, fine condos, and polished produce stalls (really lively at night, trams #10 and #12 from train station); and along Bogstadveien, a lively shopping street with no-nonsense modern commerce, lots of locals, and no tourists (T-bane to Majorstuen and follow this street back toward the palace and tourist zone). While most tourists never get out of the harbor/Karl Johans Gate district, the real, down-to-earth Oslo is better seen elsewhere, such as Bogstadveien. The bohemian, artsy Grünerløkka district is good for a daytime wander.

At the water's edge, find the shiny metal plaque (just left of center) listing the contents of a time capsule planted in the harbor for 1,000 years. You can see the little lighthouse in the harbor ahead. Go to the end of the stubby pier (on the right). This is the ceremonial "enter the city" point for momentous occasions. One such occasion was in 1905 when Norway gained its independence from Sweden, and a Danish prince sailed in from Copenhagen to become the first modern king of Norway. Another milestone event occurred at the end of World War II, when the king returned to Norway after the country was liberated from the Nazis.

• *Stand at the harbor and give it a sweeping counterclockwise look.*

Harborfront Spin-Tour: Oslofjord is a playground, with 40 city-owned, park-like islands. Big white cruise ships—a large part of the local tourist economy—dock just under the Akershus Fortress on the left. Just past the fort's impressive 13th-century ramparts, a statue of FDR grabs the shade. He's here in gratitude for the safe refuge the US gave to members of the royal family (including a young prince who is now Norway's king) during World War II—while the king and his government-in-exile waged Norway's fight against the Nazis from London.

Enjoy the grand view of City Hall. The yellow building farther to the left was the old West Train Station; today it houses the Nobel Peace Center, which celebrates the work of Nobel Peace Prize winners. The next pier is the launch pad for harbor boat tours and the shuttle boat to the Bygdøy museums. A fisherman often moors his boat here, selling shrimp from the back. Shrimp doesn't get fresher: He catches them, and while making the four-hour sail back into Oslo, cooks them up (40 kr/half-liter, 80 kr/liter, Tue–Sat from 8:00 until sold out; no fishing allowed on weekends so closed Sun–Mon). He often sells smaller shrimp for about 25 percent less; they're considered tastier, but you'll find them less easy to shell. At the other end of the harbor, shipyard buildings (this was the heart of Norway's once important ship-building industry) have been transformed into Aker Brygge—Oslo's thriving restaurant/shopping/nightclub zone (see "Eating in Oslo").

• *From here, you can tour City Hall (cheap lunches Mon–Fri 12:30–13:30 only), visit the Nobel Peace Center, hike up to Akershus Fortress, take a harbor cruise (see "Tours in Oslo," earlier), or catch a boat across the harbor to the museums at Bygdøy (from pier 3). The sights just mentioned are described in detail in the following section.*

Sights in Oslo

Near the Harborfront

▲▲▲**City Hall (Rådhuset)**—In 1931, Oslo tore down a slum and began constructing its richly decorated City Hall. It was

finished—after a WWII delay—in 1950 to celebrate the city's 900th birthday. Norway's leading artists all contributed to the building, an avant-garde thrill in its day.

City halls, rather than churches, are the dominant buildings in Scandinavian capitals. The prominence of this building on the harborfront makes sense in this most humanistic, yet least churchgoing, end of the Continent. Up here, people pay high taxes, have high expectations, and are generally satisfied with what their governments do with their money.

At Oslo's City Hall, the six statues facing the waterfront—dating from a period of Labor Party rule in Norway—celebrate the nobility of the working class. The art implies a classless society, showing everyone working together. The theme continues inside, with 20,000 square feet of bold and colorful Social Realism murals showing town folk, country folk, and people from all walks of life working harmoniously for a better society. The huge murals take you on a voyage through the collective psyche of Norway, from its simple rural beginnings through the scar tissue of the Nazi occupation and beyond. Filled with significance and symbolism—and well-described in English—they become more meaningful only with the excellent, 50-minute guided **tours** (free tours daily at 10:00, 12:00, and 14:00, no tours Sat–Sun in winter).

The main hall feels like a temple to good government, with its altar-like mural celebrating "work, play, and civic administration."

The mural emphasizes Oslo's youth participating in community life—and rebuilding the country after Nazi occupation. Across the bottom, the slum that once cluttered up Oslo's harborfront is being cleared out to make way for this building. Above that, scenes show Norway's pride in its innovative health care and education systems. Left of center, near the top, Mother Norway rests on a church—reminding viewers that the Lutheran Church of Norway (the official state religion) provides a foundation for this society. On the right, four forms represent the arts; they illustrate how creativity springs from children. And in the center, the figure of Charity is surrounded by Culture, Philosophy, and Family.

The "Mural of the Occupation" lines the left side of the hall. It tells the story of Norway's WWII experience. Looking left to right, you'll see the following: The German blitzkrieg overwhelms

the country. Men head for the mountains to organize a resistance movement. Women huddle around the water well, traditionally where news is passed, while Quislings (traitors named after the Norwegian fascist who ruled the country as a Nazi puppet) listen in. While Germans bomb and occupy Norway, a family gathers in their living room. As a boy clenches his fist (showing determination) and a child holds the beloved Norwegian flag, the Gestapo steps in. Columns lie on the ground, symbolizing how Germans shut down the culture by closing newspapers and university. Two resistance soldiers are executed. A cell of resistance fighters (wearing masks and using nicknames so if tortured they can't reveal their compatriots' identities) plan a sabotage mission. Finally, prisoners are freed, the war is over, and Norway celebrates its happiest day: May 17, 1945—the first Independence Day after five years under Nazi control.

While gazing at these murals, keep in mind that the Nobel Peace Prize is awarded in this central hall each December (though the general Nobel Prize ceremony occurs in Stockholm's City Hall). You can see videos of the ceremony and acceptance speeches in the adjacent Nobel Peace Center (see below).

City Hall is free and open daily (9:00–18:00; enter on Karl Johans Gate side, tel. 23 46 12 00). There's a free WC and a wonderful budget lunch cafeteria downstairs that offers a simple hot meal and salad bar at a no-profit price; it's primarily for the building's workers, but the public is also welcome (Mon–Fri 12:30–13:30 only).

Fans of the explorer Fridtjof Nansen might enjoy a coffee or beer across the street at Fridtjof, an atmospheric bar filled with memorabilia from Nansen's Arctic explorations (Mon–Sat 12:00 until late, Sun 14:00–22:00, Nansens Plass 7, near Forex).

▲**Nobel Peace Center (Nobels Fredssenter)**—This thoughtful and thought-provoking museum, housed in the former West Train Station (Vestbanen), poses the question, "What is the opposite of conflict?" It celebrates the 120-some past and present Nobel Peace Prize winners with engaging audio and video exhibits and high-tech gadgetry (all with good English explanations). Allow time for reading about past prizewinners and listening to acceptance speeches by recipients from President Carter to Mother Theresa. Check out the interactive book detailing the life and work of Alfred Nobel, the Swedish inventor of dynamite, who initiated the prizes—perhaps to assuage his conscience (80 kr; June–Aug daily 10:00–18:00; Sept–May Tue–Sun 10:00–18:00, closed Mon; included guided tours at 11:00, 12:00, and 15:00; Brynjulfs Bulls Plass 1, tel. 48 30 10 00, www.nobelpeacecenter.org).

▲**Opera House**—Opened in 2008, Oslo's striking Opera House is the talk of the town and a huge hit. The Opera House rises from

the water on the city's eastern harbor, across the highway from the train station. Its boxy, low-slung, glass center holds a state-of-the-art, 1,400-seat main theater. The jutting white marble planes of its roof double as a public plaza. When visiting, you feel a need to walk all over it. The Opera House is part of larger harbor redevelopment that includes rerouting traffic into tunnels and turning a once-derelict industrial zone into an urban park.

In summer, the Opera House offers guided tours of the auditorium and backstage area (daily at 14:00, 100 kr) and foyer concerts (daily at 13:00, 50 kr). For tours, reserve by email at omvis

ninger@operaen.no, or use the website, www.operaen.no (foyer and café/restaurant open Mon–Fri 10:00–23:00, Sat 11:00–23:00, Sun 12:00–22:00, just a short walk via a sky-bridge from train station, tel. 21 42 21 00).

▲Akershus Fortress Complex

This park-like complex of sights scattered over Oslo's fortified old center is still a military base. But as you dodge patrol guards and vans filled with soldiers, you'll see the castle, a prison, war memorials, the Norwegian Resistance Museum, the Armed Forces Museum, and cannon-strewn ramparts affording fine harbor views and picnic perches. There's an unimpressive changing of the guard daily at 13:30 (at the parade ground, deep in the castle complex). The park is open daily 6:00–21:00. From the harbor, follow the stairs (which lead past the FDR statue) to the park.

Fortress Visitors Center: Located immediately inside the gate, the information center has an interesting exhibit tracing the story of Oslo's fortifications from medieval times through the environmental struggles of today. Stop here to pick up a castle overview booklet, quickly browse through the museum, watch the quick video, and consider catching a tour (see below; museum entry free, mid-June–mid-Aug Mon–Fri 9:00–18:00, Sat–Sun 11:00–17:00, shorter hours off-season, tel. 23 09 39 17, www.mil.no/felles/ak).

▲Fortress Tours—The free 45-minute, English-language walking tours of the grounds help you make sense of the most historic piece of real estate in Oslo (generally offered May–Aug Mon–Fri at 11:00, 12:00, 13:00, 14:00, and 15:00; Sat–Sun at 13:00 and 15:00; no tours off-season; depart from Fortress Visitors Center, call center in advance to confirm times, phone number above).

Akershus Castle—Although it's one of Oslo's oldest buildings (c. 1300), the castle overlooking the harbor is mediocre by European

standards; the big, empty rooms recall Norway's medieval poverty. From the old kitchen, where the ticket desk and gift shop are located, you'll follow a one-way circuit of rooms open to the public. Descend through a secret passage to the dungeon, crypt, and royal tomb. Emerge behind the altar in the chapel, then walk through echoing rooms including the Daredevil's Tower, Hall of Christian IV, and Hall of Olav I. The castle is more interesting with the included tour (65 kr, sparse English descriptions throughout; May–Aug Mon–Sat 10:00–16:00, Sun 12:30–16:00; castle tours in English Mon–Sat at 11:00, 12:00, 13:00, 14:00, and 15:00; Sun at 13:00 and 15:00; closed Sept–April except tours in English Thu at 12:00, 13:00, and 14:00; tel. 22 41 25 21). There are terrific harbor views from the rampart just outside.

▲▲Norwegian Resistance Museum (Norges Hjemmefrontmuseum) —This fascinating museum tells the story of Norway's WWII experience: appeasement, Nazi invasion (they made Akershus their headquarters), resistance, liberation, and, finally, the return of the king. It's a one-way, chronological, can't-get-lost route—enter through the 1940 door.

You'll see propaganda posters attempting to get Norwegians to join the Nazi party, and the German ultimatum to which the king gave an emphatic "No." Various displays show secret radios, transmitters, underground newspapers, crude but effective home-made weapons, and the German machine that located clandestine radio stations. Exhibits explain how the country coped with 350,000 occupying troops; how airdrops equipped a home force of 40,000 ready to coordinate with the Allies when liberation was imminent; and the happy day when peace and freedom returned to Norway.

The museum is particularly poignant because many of the patriots featured inside were executed by the Germans right outside the museum's front door. (At war's end, the traitor Vidkun Quisling was also executed here.) With good English descriptions, this is an inspirational look at how the national spirit can endure total occupation by a malevolent force.

Cost, Hours, Location: 50 kr, 100-kr family ticket covers two adults plus one or two kids; June–Aug Mon–Sat 10:00–17:00, Sun 11:00–17:00; Sept–May Mon–Fri 10:00–16:00, Sat–Sun 11:00–16:00; next to castle, overlooking harbor, tel. 23 09 31 38, www.mil.no/felles/nhm.

Armed Forces Museum (Forsvarsmuseet) —Across the fortress parade ground, a too-spacious museum traces Norwegian military history from Viking days to post–World War II. The early stuff is sketchy, but the WWII story is compelling (free, May–Aug Mon–Fri 10:00–17:00, Sat–Sun 11:00–17:00, shorter hours and closed Mon off-season, tel. 23 09 35 82).

▲▲▲National Gallery (Nasjonalgalleriet)

While there are many schools of painting and sculpture displayed in Norway's National Gallery, focus on what's uniquely Norwegian.

Paintings come and go in this museum, but you're sure to find plenty that showcase the harsh beauty of Norway's landscape and people. A thoughtful visit here gives those heading into the mountains and fjord country a chance to pack along a little of Norway's cultural soul. Tuck these images carefully away with your goat cheese—they'll sweeten your explorations.

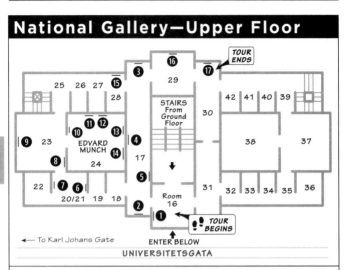

National Gallery—Upper Floor

OSLO

❶ MUNCH—Self-Portrait After the Spanish Influenza

❷ DAHL—Stalheim

❸ FEARNLEY—Waterfall

❹ DAHL—From Hjelle in Valdres

❺ TIDEMAND & GUDE—The Bridal Voyage

❻ TIDEMAND—Low Church Devotion

❼ PETERSSEN—Christian II

❽ WERENSKIOLD—A Peasant Burial

❾ KROHG—Albertine to See the Police Surgeon

❿ MUNCH—Self-Portrait with a Cigarette

⓫ MUNCH—The Sick Child

⓬ MUNCH—Madonna

⓭ MUNCH—The Scream

⓮ MUNCH—Dance of Life

⓯ KROHG—A Sick Girl

⓰ ARBO—The Wild Hunt of Odin

⓱ SOHLBERG—Winter Night in the Mountains

The gallery also has several Picassos, a noteworthy Impressionist collection, and some Vigeland statues. Its many raving examples of Edvard Munch's work, including one of his famous *Scream* paintings, make a trip to the Munch Museum unnecessary for most.

Cost, Hours, Location: Free, Tue–Fri 10:00–18:00, Thu until 19:00, Sat–Sun 11:00–17:00, closed Mon, chewing gum prohibited, Universitets Gata 13, tel. 22 20 04 04, www.national museum.no. The 25-kr audioguide covers 15 paintings, has a poetic narrative with quotes from artists, and forces you to linger at each work of art—but doesn't have much more information than my tour below.

Self-Guided Tour

This easy-to-handle museum gives an effortless tour back in time and through Norway's most beautiful valleys, mountains, and fjords, with the help of its Romantic painters (especially Johan Christian Dahl). The paintings are organized roughly chronologically, from 1814 through 1950.

• *Go up the stairs into Room 16, where you're treated to a nibble of the misery that was Munch.*

❶ Munch—*Self-Portrait After the Spanish Influenza* **(1919):** Norway's long, dark winters and social isolation have produced many gloomy artists, but none gloomier than Edvard Munch (1863–1944). Here he paints himself suffering from the effects of the devastating influenza pandemic that ravaged the globe at the end of World War I, killing tens of millions. Drained, rigid, and glassy-eyed, Munch personifies the weary disillusionment of postwar Europe.

• *We'll get back to Munch later. But for now, let's head somewhere more idyllic. Enter Room 17.*

Landscape Paintings and Romanticism

Landscape painting has always played an important role in Norwegian art, perhaps because Norway provides such an awesome and varied landscape to inspire artists. The style reached its peak during the Romantic period in the late 1800s, which stressed the beauty of unspoiled nature. (This passion for landscapes sets Norway apart from Denmark and Sweden.) After 400 years of Danish rule, the soul of the country was almost snuffed out. But with semi-independence and a constitution in the early 1800s, there was a national resurgence. Romantic paintings featuring the power of Norway's natural wonders and the toughness of its salt-of-the-earth folk came in vogue.

❷ Johan Christian Dahl—*Stalheim* **(1842):** This painting epitomizes the Norwegian closeness to nature. It shows the same view 21st-century travelers enjoy on their Norway in a Nutshell

excursion: the mountains at the head of the Sognefjord as seen from the venerable Stalheim Hotel. Painted in 1842, it's textbook Romantic style. Nature rules—the background is as detailed as the foreground, and you are sucked in.

Johan Christian Dahl (1788–1857) is considered the father of Norwegian Romanticism. Romantics such as Dahl (and Turner, Beethoven, and Lord Byron) put emotion over rationality. They reveled in the power of nature—death and pessimism ripple through their work. The rainbow says it all: This is God's work. Nature is big. God is great. Man is small...and he's gonna die. The birch tree—standing boldly front and center—is a standard symbol for the politically downtrodden Norwegian people: hardy, cut down, but defiantly sprouting new branches. The tiny folks are in traditional dress. In the mid-19th century, Norwegians were awakening to their national identity. Throughout Europe, nationalism and Romanticism went hand in hand.

Find four typical Norse farms. They remind us that these are hardworking, independent, small landowners. There was no feudalism in medieval Norway. People were poor...but they owned their own land. You can almost taste the *geitost*.

• *Look at the other works in Room 17 (the biggest room in the gallery). Dahl's paintings and those by his Norwegian contemporaries, showing heavy clouds and glaciers, repeat these same themes—drama over rationalism, nature pounding humanity. Human figures are melancholy. Norwegians, so close to nature, are fascinated by those plush, magic hours of dawn and twilight. The dusk makes us wonder: What will the future bring?*

In particular, focus on....

❸ **Thomas Fearnley—*Waterfall* (1817):** Man cannot control nature or his destiny. Lumberjacks are working. But the eagle says, "While you can cut these logs, they'll always be mine."

❹ **Dahl—*From Hjelle in Valdres* (1851):** Another typical Dahl setting: romantic nature and an idealized scene. The characters are wearing the *bunad* (national folk costume of Norway). This isn't everyday work wear, but it fits just fine in this nationalistic tableau.

❺ **Adolph Tidemand and Hans Gude—*The Bridal Voyage* (1848):** This famous painting shows the ultimate Norwegian scene: a wedding party with everyone decked out in traditional garb, heading for the stave church on the quintessential fjord (Hardanger). It's a studio work (not real) and a collaboration: Hans Gude painted the landscape, and Adolph Tidemand painted the people. Study their wedding finery. This work trumpets  the greatness of both the landscape and Norwegian culture.

• *Continue through Rooms 18 and 19 to Room 20.*

The Photographic Eye

At the end of the 19th century, Norwegian painters traded the emotions of Romanticism for more slice-of-life detail. This was the end of the Romantic period and the beginning of Realism. With the advent of photography, painters went beyond simple realism and into extreme realism.

❻ **Tidemand—*Low Church Devotion* (1848):** This scene shows a dissenting Lutheran church group (of which there were many in the 19th century) worshipping in a smokehouse. The light of God powers through the chimney, illuminating salt-of-the-earth people with strong faiths. Rather than accept the Norwegian king's "High Church," they worshipped in their homes in a more ascetic style. Later, many of these people emigrated to America for greater religious freedom.

❼ **Eilif Peterssen—*Christian II* (1875):** The Danish king signs the execution order for the man who'd killed the king's beloved mistress. With camera-like precision, the painter captures the whole story of murder, anguish, anger, and bitter revenge in the king's set jaw and steely eyes.

• *Enter Room 23 and browse the paintings.*

Modern Life

In the 1880s, Europe's artistic community (which included a few Norwegians) turned to Paris. Impressionism took the art world by storm. French artists abandoned reality, using the physical object only as a rack upon which to hang light and color—their true subject matter. Inhibited Norwegians couldn't go quite that far. While their Naturalism (parallel to Impressionism) came with a new appreciation of light, their subjects remained real things.

❽ **Erik Werenskiold—*A Peasant Burial* (1885):** While Monet and the Impressionists were busy abandoning the realistic style, Norwegian artists continued to embrace it. In this painting, you're invited to participate. The poor man's funeral is attended by not many more than his family, the preacher, and the gravediggers. Your presence completes the half-circle at the grave site. The simple scene is set before a majestic, perfectly lit mountain backdrop that dwarfs the deceased man's legacy. Rough Impressionistic brush strokes have replaced the tedious detail of earlier Romantic Age painters, but you still have earthy people immersed in nature. Their hands speak volumes about the life of toil here. A common thread in Norwegian art is the cycle—the tough cycle—of life. There's also an interest in everyday experiences.

❾ **Christian Krohg—*Albertine to See the Police Surgeon* (c. 1885–1887):** Christian Krohg (1852–1925) is known as Edvard Munch's inspiration, but to Norwegians, he is famous in his own right for his artistry and giant personality. Krohg had a sharp interest in social justice. In this painting, Albertine, a sweet girl from the countryside, has fallen into the world of prostitution in the big city. She's the new kid on the red light block in the 1880s,

Edvard Munch
(1863-1944)

Edvard Munch (pronounced "moonk") is Norway's most famous and influential painter. His life was rich, complex, and sad. His father was a doctor who had a nervous breakdown. His mother and sister both died of tuberculosis. He knew suffering. And he gave us the enduring symbol of 20th-century pain, *The Scream*.

He was also Norway's most forward-thinking painter, a man who traveled extensively through Europe, soaking up the colors of the Post-Impressionists and the curves of Art Nouveau. He helped pioneer a new style—Expressionism—using lurid colors and wavy lines to "express" inner turmoil and the angst of the modern world.

After a nervous breakdown in 1908, Munch emerged less troubled—but a less powerful painter. His late works were as a colorist: big, bright, less tormented...and less noticed.

as Oslo's prostitutes are pulled into the police clinic for their regular checkup. Note her traditional dress and the disdain she gets from the more experienced girls. Krohg has buried his subject in this scene. His technique requires the viewer to find her, and that search helps humanize the prostitute.

• *Continue into Room 24, the Munch room.*

Turmoil

Room 24 is filled with works by Norway's single most famous painter, Edvard Munch (see sidebar). Munch infused his work with emotion and expression at the expense of realism. After viewing the paintings in general, take a look at these in particular (listed in clockwise order).

❿ **Edvard Munch**—*Self Portrait with a Cigarette* (1895): In this self-portrait, Munch is spooked, haunted—an artist working, immersed in an oppressive world. Indefinable shadows inhabit the background. His hand shakes as he considers his uncertain future. (Ironic, considering he created his masterpieces during this depressed period.) After a 1909 visit to a Danish clinic, he found peace—and lost his painting power. Afterward, Munch never again painted another strong example of what we love most about his art.

⓫ Munch—*The Sick Child* (1896): The death of Munch's sister in 1877 due to tuberculosis likely inspired this painting. The girl's face melts into the pillow. She's becoming two-dimensional, halfway between life and death. Everything else is peripheral, even her despairing mother saying good-bye. You can see how Munch scraped and repainted the face until he got it right.

⓬ Munch—*Madonna* (1894–1895): Munch had a tortured relationship with women. He never married. He dreaded and struggled with love, writing that he feared if he loved too much, he'd lose his painting talent. This painting is a mystery: Is she standing or lying? Is that a red halo or some devilish accessory? Munch wrote that he would strive to capture his subjects at their holiest moment. His alternative name for this work: *Woman Making Love.* What's more holy than a woman at the moment of conception?

⓭ Munch—*The Scream* (1893): Munch's most famous work shows a man screaming, capturing the fright many feel as the human "race" does just that.  The figure seems isolated from the people on the bridge—locked up in himself, unable to stifle his scream. Munch made four versions of this scene, which has become *the* textbook example of Expressionism. On one, he graffitied: "This painting is the work of a madman." He explained that the painting "shows today's society, reverberating within me... making me want to scream." He's sharing his internal angst. In fact, this Expressionist masterpiece is a breakthrough painting; it's angst personified.

⓮ Munch—*Dance of Life* (1899–1900): In this scene of five dancing couples, we glimpse Munch's notion of femininity. To him, women were a complex mix of Madonna and whore. We see Munch's take on the cycle of women's lives: She's a virgin (discarding the sweet flower of youth), a whore (a jaded temptress in red), and a widow (having destroyed the man, she is finally alone, aging, in black). With the phallic moon rising on the lake, Munch demonizes women as they turn men into green-faced, lusty monsters.

• *Go back through Room 23 to reach Room 28.*

Vulnerability

Death, disease, and suffering were themes seen again and again in art from the late 1800s. The most serious disease during this period was tuberculosis (which killed Munch's mother and sister).

⓮ Krohg—*A Sick Girl* (1880): This extremely realistic painting shows a child dying of tuberculosis, as so many did in Norway in the 19th century. The girl looks directly at you. You can almost feel the cloth, with its many shades of white.

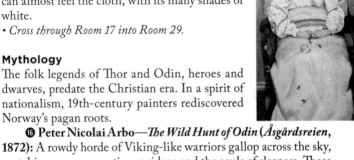

• *Cross through Room 17 into Room 29.*

Mythology

The folk legends of Thor and Odin, heroes and dwarves, predate the Christian era. In a spirit of nationalism, 19th-century painters rediscovered Norway's pagan roots.

⓯ Peter Nicolai Arbo—*The Wild Hunt of Odin (Åsgårdsreien,* 1872): A rowdy horde of Viking-like warriors gallop across the sky, snatching up unsuspecting maidens and the souls of sleepers. These supernatural hunters of folklore, led by Odin (the king of the gods, in billowing cape), represent the uncontrolled life force of Nature that fights the encroachment of civilization. Lit by moonlight and a fiery sunset, the huge band blends into the cloudy distance, suggesting the wild party goes on forever.

• *Continue to Room 30.*

Atmosphere

Landscape painters were often fascinated by the phenomena of nature, and the artwork in this room takes us back to this ideal from the Romantic Age. Painters were challenged by capturing atmospheric conditions at a specific moment, since it meant making quick sketches outdoors, before the weather changed yet again.

⓰ Harald Sohlberg—*Winter Night in the Mountains* (1914): Harald Sohlberg was inspired by this image while skiing in the mountains in the winter of 1899. Over the years, he attempted to re-create the scene that inspired this remark: "The mountains in winter reduce one to silence. One is overwhelmed, as in a mighty, vaulted church, only a thousand times more so."

Near the National Gallery

National Historical Museum (Historisk Museum)—Directly behind the National Gallery and just below the palace is a fine Art Nouveau building offering a free and easy (if underwhelming) peek at Norway's history. The ground floor offers a walk through

OSLO

the local history from prehistoric times. It includes the country's top collection of Viking artifacts, displayed in low-tech, old-school exhibits with barely a word of English to give it meaning. There's also some medieval church art. The museum's highlight is upstairs: an exhibit (well-described in English) about life in the Arctic for the Sami people (also previously known to outsiders as Laplanders). In this overview of the past, a few Egyptian mummies and Norwegian coins through the ages are tossed in for good measure. The museum offers free 45-minute Viking tours daily at noon in the summer (free; mid-May–mid-Sept Tue–Sat 10:00–17:00, Sun 11:00–16:00, closed Mon; mid-Sept–mid-May Tue–Sun 11:00–16:00, closed Mon; Frederiks Gate 2, tel. 22 85 99 12, www.khm.uio.no).

▲▲▲Frogner Park

This 75-acre park contains a lifetime of work by Norway's greatest sculptor, Gustav Vigeland (see sidebar on next page). In 1921, he made a deal with the city. In return for a great studio and state support, he'd spend his creative life beautifying Oslo with this sculpture garden. From 1924 to 1943 he worked on-site, designing 192 bronze and granite statue groupings—600 figures in all, each nude and unique. Vigeland even planned the landscaping. Today the park is loved and respected by the people of Oslo (no police, no fences, and

no graffiti). The garden is always open and free (buses #20 and #45, and trams #12 and #19 all stop immediately in front of the main entry; or T-bane: Majorstuen and a 5-min walk). The Frognerbadet swimming pool is also at Frogner Park. The park is safe (cameras monitor for safety) and lit in the evening.

Vigeland's park is more than great art: It's a city at play. Appreciate its urban Norwegian ambience. The park is huge, but this visit is a snap. Here's a quick, four-stop, straight-line, gate-to-monolith tour:

1. Enter the Park from Kirkeveien: For an illustrated guide and fine souvenir, pick up the 75-kr book in the Visitors Center (Besøkssenter) on your right as you enter. The modern cafeteria has sandwiches (indoor/outdoor seating, daily 9:00–20:30, shorter hours Sun and off-season), plus books, gifts, and WCs. Look at the statue of Gustav Vigeland (hammer and chisel in hand,

Gustav Vigeland
(1869–1943)

As a young man, Vigeland studied sculpture in Oslo, then supplemented his education with trips abroad to Europe's art capitals. Back home, he carved out a successful, critically acclaimed career feeding newly independent Norway's hunger for homegrown art.

During his youthful trips abroad, Vigeland had frequented the studio of Auguste Rodin, admiring Rodin's naked, restless, intertwined statues. Like Rodin, Vigeland explored the yin/yang relationship of men and women. Also like Rodin, Vigeland did not personally carve or cast his statues. Rather, he formed them in clay or plaster, to be executed by a workshop of assistants. Vigeland's sturdy humans capture universal themes of the cycle of life—birth, childhood, romance, struggle, child-rearing, growing old, and death.

---

drenched in pigeon poop) and consider his messed-up life. He lived with his many models. His marriages failed. His children entangled his artistic agenda. He didn't age gracefully. He didn't name his statues, and refused to explain their meanings. While those who know his life story can read it clearly in the granite and bronze, I'd forget Gustav's troubles and see his art as observations on the bittersweet cycle of life in general—from a man who must have had a passion for living.

2. Bridge: The 300-foot-long bridge is bounded by four granite columns: Three show a man fighting a lizard, the fourth shows a woman submitting to the lizard's embrace. Hmmm. (Vigeland was familiar with medieval mythology, where dragons represent man's primal—and sinful—nature.) But enough lizard love; the 58 bronze statues along the bridge are a general study of the human body. Many deal with relationships between people. In the middle, on the right, find the circular statue of a man and woman going round and round—

perhaps the eternal attraction and love between the sexes. But directly opposite, another circle feels like a prison—man against the world, with no refuge. From the man escaping, look down at the children's playground: eight bronze infants circling a head-down fetus.

On your left, see the famous *Sinnataggen*, the hot-headed little boy. It's said Vigeland gave him chocolate and then took it away to get this reaction. The statues capture the joys of life (and, on a sunny day, so do the Norwegians filling the park around you).

3. Fountain: Continue through a rose garden to the earliest sculpture unit in the park. Six giants hold a fountain, symbolically toiling with the burden of life, as water—the source of life—cascades steadily around them. Twenty tree-of-life groups surround the fountain. Four clumps of trees (on each corner) show humanity's relationship to nature and the seasons of life: childhood, young love, adulthood, and winter.

Take a quick swing through life, starting on the right with youth. In the branches you'll see a swarm of children (Vigeland called them "geniuses"): A

boy sits in a tree, boys actively climb while most girls stand by quietly, and a girl glides through the branches wide-eyed and ready for life...and love. Circle clockwise to the next stage: love scenes. In the third corner, life becomes more complicated: a sad woman in an animal-like tree, a lonely child, a couple plummeting downward (perhaps falling out of love), and finally an angry man driving away babies. The fourth corner completes the cycle, as death melts into the branches of the tree of life and you realize new geniuses will bloom.

The 60 bronze reliefs circling the basin develop the theme further, showing man mixing with nature and geniuses giving the carousel of life yet another spin. Speaking of another spin, circle again and follow these reliefs.

The sidewalk surrounding the basin is a maze—life's long and winding road with twists, dead ends, frustrations, and, ultimately, a way out. If you have about an hour to spare, enter the labyrinth (on the side nearest the park's entrance gate, there's a single break in the black border) and follow the white granite path until (on the monolith side) you finally get out. (Tracing this path occupies older kids, affording parents a peaceful break in the park.) Or you

can go straight up the steps to the monolith.

4. Monolith: The centerpiece of the park—a teeming monolith of life surrounded by 36 granite groups—continues Vigeland's cycle-of-life motif. The figures are hunched and clearly earthbound, while Vigeland explores a lifetime of human relationships. At the center, 121 figures carved out of a single block of stone rocket skyward. Three stone carvers worked daily for 14 years, cutting Vigeland's full-size plaster model into the final 180-ton, 50-foot-tall erection.

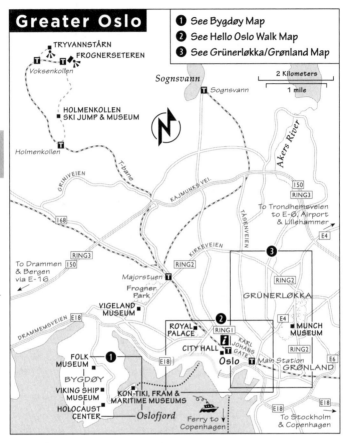

Greater Oslo

❶ See Bygdøy Map
❷ See Hello Oslo Walk Map
❸ See Grünerløkka/Grønland Map

TRYVANNSTÅRN
FROGNERSETEREN
Voksenkollen

Sognsvann

2 Kilometers
1 mile

HOLMENKOLLEN
SKI JUMP & MUSEUM

Holmenkollen

Akers River

150
RING3

To Trondhemsveien
to E-6, Airport
& Lillehammer

E4

KIRKEVEIEN

GRINIVEIEN

T-bane

KAJMUNKS VEI

TÅSENVEIEN

To Drammen
& Bergen
via E-16

168

RING3 150

RING2

Majorstuen

RING2

Frogner
Park

GRÜNERLØKKA

VIGELAND
MUSEUM

DRAMMEMSVEIEN E18

ROYAL
PALACE

❷

RING1

E4

MUNCH
MUSEUM

KARL
JOHANS
GATE

CITY HALL

Oslo

RING2 E6

Main Station
GRØNLAND

FOLK
MUSEUM

❶

E18

BYGDØY

VIKING SHIP
MUSEUM

KON-TIKI, FRAM &
MARITIME MUSEUMS

HOLOCAUST
CENTER

Oslofjord

Ferry to
Copenhagen

E18 E18

To Stockholm
& Copenhagen

Circle the plaza, once to trace the stages of life in the 36 statue groups, and a second time to enjoy how Norwegian kids relate to the art. The statues—both young and old—seem to speak to children.

Vigeland lived barely long enough to see his monolith raised. Covered with bodies, it seems to pick up speed as it spirals skyward. Some people seem to naturally rise. Others struggle not to fall. Some help others. Although the granite groups around the monolith are easy to understand, Vigeland left the meaning of the monolith itself open. Like life, it can be interpreted many different ways.

From this summit of the park, look a hundred yards farther, where four children and three adults are intertwined and spinning in the Wheel of Life. Now, look back at the entrance. If the main gate is at 12 o'clock, the studio where Vigeland lived and worked—now the Vigeland Museum—is at 2 o'clock (see the green copper tower poking above the trees). His ashes sit in the top of the tower in clear view of the monolith. If you liked the park, visit the museum—it's a delightful five-minute walk—for an intimate look at the art and how it was made.

▲▲**Vigeland Museum**—Filled with original plaster casts and well-described exhibits on his work, this palatial city-provided studio was Vigeland's home and workplace. The high south-facing windows provided just the right light.

Vigeland, who had a deeply religious upbringing, saw his art as an expression of his soul. He once said, "The road between feeling and execution should be as short as possible." Here, immersed in his work, Vigeland supervised his craftsmen like a father, from 1924 until his death in 1943 (50 kr; June–Aug Tue–Sun 10:00–17:00, closed Mon; Sept–May Tue–Sun 12:00–16:00, closed Mon; bus #20 or #45 or tram #12 to Frogner Plass, Nobels Gate 32, tel. 23 49 37 00, www.vigeland.museum.no).

Oslo City Museum (Oslo Bymuseum)—This hard-to-be-thrilled-about little museum tells the story of Oslo (50 kr, free on Sat, open Tue–Sun 11:00–16:00, closed Mon, shorter hours off-season, borrow English description sheet, located in Frogner Park at Frogner Manor Farm across street from Vigeland Museum, tel. 23 28 41 70, www.oslobymuseum.no).

▲▲Oslo's Bygdøy Neighborhood

This thought-provoking and exciting cluster of sights is on a park-like peninsula just across the harbor from downtown. It provides a busy and rewarding half-day (at a minimum) of sightseeing. Here, within a short walk, are six important sights (listed in order of importance):

• **Norwegian Folk Museum,** an open-air park with traditional log buildings from all corners of the country.

• **Viking Ship Museum,** showing off the best-preserved Viking longboats in existence.

• *Fram* **Museum,** showcasing the modern Viking spirit with the ship of arctic-exploration fame.

• *Kon-Tiki* **Museum,** starring the *Kon-Tiki* and the *Ra II,* in which Norwegian explorer Thor Heyerdahl proved that early civilizations—with their existing technologies—could have crossed the oceans.

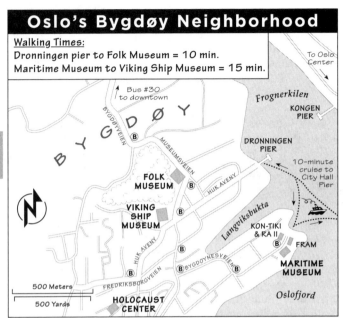

Oslo's Bygdøy Neighborhood

Walking Times:
Dronningen pier to Folk Museum = 10 min.
Maritime Museum to Viking Ship Museum = 15 min.

To Oslo Center

Bus #30 to downtown

BYGDØY

BYGDØYVEIEN

MUSEUMSVEIEN

Frognerkilen

KONGEN PIER

DRONNINGEN PIER

10-minute cruise to City Hall Pier

FOLK MUSEUM

VIKING SHIP MUSEUM

HUK AVENY

Langviksbukta

KON-TIKI & RA II

FRAM

MARITIME MUSEUM

HUK AVENY

BYGDØYNESVEIEN

FREDRIKSBORGVEIEN

Oslofjord

500 Meters
500 Yards

HOLOCAUST CENTER

OSLO

• **Norwegian Maritime Museum,** interesting mostly to old salts, has a wonderfully scenic movie of Norway.

• **Norwegian Holocaust Center,** a high-tech look at the Holocaust in Norway and contemporary racism.

Getting There: Sailing from downtown to Bygdøy is fun, and it gets you in a seafaring mood. Ride the Bygdøy ferry—marked *Public Ferry Bygdøy Museums*—from pier 3 in front of City Hall (36 kr one-way, covered by city transit ticket or Oslo Pass, May–Sept daily 8:45–21:00, usually 3/hr; doesn't run Oct–April). Avoid the nearby, and much more expensive, tour boats. Boats generally leave from downtown and from the museum dock at :05, :25, and :45 past each hour. For a less memorable approach, you can take bus #30 (from train station or National Theater).

Getting Around Bygdøy: The Norwegian Folk and Viking Ship museums are a 10-minute walk from the ferry's first stop (Dronningen). The other boating museums (*Fram, Kon-Tiki,* and Maritime) are at the second ferry stop (Bygdøynes). The Holocaust Center is off Fredriksborgveien, about halfway between these two museum clusters. All Bygdøy sights are within a pleasant (when sunny) 15-minute walk of each other. The walk gives you a picturesque taste of small-town Norway. A city bus (#30) connects the sights four times hourly, making the following stops in this order: the Norwegian Folk Museum, Viking Ship Museum, *Kon-Tiki* Museum, Norwegian Holocaust Center (the stop is a long block away), then passing the ships and folk museum again on its way back to the city center. If you take the bus within an hour of having taken the public ferry, your ticket is still good on the bus. Note that after 17:00, bus and boat departures are sparse. Get there a little early—otherwise the boat is likely to be filled, and you'll have to wait for the next sailing.

Eating at Bygdøy: Lunch options near the *Kon-Tiki* are a sandwich bar (relaxing picnic spots along the grassy shoreline) and a cafeteria (with tables overlooking the harbor). The Norwegian Folk Museum has a decent cafeteria inside and a fun little farmers' market stall across the street from the entrance. The Holocaust Center has a small café on its second floor (daily 11:00–22:00).

▲▲▲Norwegian Folk Museum (Norsk Folkemuseum)— Brought from all corners of Norway, 150 buildings have been reassembled on these 35 acres. While Stockholm's Skansen was the first to open to the public, this museum is a bit older, started in 1882 as the king's private collection (and the inspiration for Skansen).

Think of the visit in three parts: the park sprinkled with old buildings, the re-created old town, and the folk-art museum. In peak season, the park is lively, with craftspeople doing their traditional things and costumed guides all around. (They're paid to happily answer your questions—so ask many.) The evocative Gol stave church, at the top of a hill at the park's edge, is a must-see (built in 1212 in Hallingdal and painstakingly reconstructed here; for more on stave churches). Across the park, the old town comes complete with apartments from various generations (including some reconstructions of actual people's homes) and offers an intimate look at lifestyles here in 1905, 1930, 1950, 1979, and even a modern-day Norwegian-Pakistani apartment.

The museum beautifully presents woody, colorfully painted folk art (ground floor), exquisite-in-a-peasant-kind-of-way folk costumes (upstairs), and temporary exhibits. Everything is thoughtfully explained in English. Don't miss the best Sami culture exhibit I've seen in Scandinavia (across the courtyard in the green building, behind the toy exhibit).

Upon arrival, pick up the site map and review the list of activities, concerts, and guided tours on that day. In summer, guided tours go daily at 12:00 and 14:00; the Telemark Farm hosts a small daily fiddle-and-dance show on the hour; and a folk music-and-dance show is held each Sunday at 14:00. The folk museum is lively only June through mid-August, when buildings are open and staffed. Otherwise, the indoor museum is fine, but the park is just a walk past lots of locked-up log cabins. If you don't take a tour, glean information from the 10-kr guidebook and the informative attendants stationed in buildings throughout the park.

Cost, Hours, Location: 95 kr, 70 kr off-season, daily mid-May–mid-Sept 10:00–18:00, off-season daily 11:00–15:00 but most historical buildings closed, free lockers, Museumsveien 10. Bus #30 stops immediately in front.

▲▲Viking Ship Museum (Vikingskiphuset) —In this impressive museum you'll gaze with admiration at two finely crafted, majestic oak Viking ships dating from the 9th and 10th centuries.

Along with the well-preserved ships, you'll see remarkable artifacts that may cause you to consider these notorious raiders in a different light. Over a thousand years ago, three things drove Vikings on their far-flung raids: hard economic times in their bleak homeland, the lure of prosperous and vulnerable communities to the south, and a mastery of the sea. There was a time when most frightened Europeans closed every prayer with, "And deliver us from the Vikings, Amen." Gazing up at the prow of one of these sleek, time-stained vessels, you can almost hear the screams and smell the armpits of those redheads on the rampage.

The *Oseberg* ship, from A.D. 834, is the first ship you see. With its ornate carving and impressive rudder, it was likely a royal pleasure craft. It seems designed for sailing on calm inland waters during festivals, but not in the open sea.

The *Gokstad* ship, from A.D. 950, is a practical working boat, capable of sailing the high seas. A boat like this brought settlers to the west of France (Normandy was named for the Norsemen). And in a boat like this, explorers such as Eric the Red hopscotched from Norway to Iceland to Greenland and on to what they called Vinland—today's Newfoundland in Canada. Imagine 30 men hauling on long oars out at sea for weeks and months. In 1892, a replica of this ship sailed from Norway to America in 44 days to celebrate the 400th anniversary of Columbus *not* discovering America.

The ships tend to steal the show, but don't miss the hall displaying **jewelry and personal items** excavated along with the ships. The ships and related artifacts survived so well because they were buried in clay as part of a gravesite. Many of the finest items were not actually Viking art, but goodies they brought home after raiding more advanced (but less tough) people. Still, there are lots of actual Viking items, such as metal and leather goods, that give an insight into their culture. Highlights are the cart and sleighs, ornately carved with scenes from Viking sagas.

The museum doesn't offer tours, but it's easy to eavesdrop on the many guides leading big groups through the museum. Everything is well-described in English. You probably don't need the little museum guidebook—it repeats exactly what's already posted on the exhibits.

Cost, Hours, Location: 50 kr, daily May–Sept 9:00–18:00, Oct–April 11:00–16:00, Huk Aveny 35, tel. 22 13 52 80, www.khm .uio.no.

▲Norwegian Holocaust Center (HL-Senteret)—Located in the former home of Nazi collaborator Vidkun Quisling, this museum and study center offers a high-tech look at the racist ideologies that fueled the Holocaust. To show the Holocaust in a Norwegian context, the first floor displays historical documents about the rise of anti-Semitism and personal effects from Holocaust victims. Downstairs, the names of 760 Norwegian Jews killed by the Nazis are listed in a bright, white room. The *Innocent Questions* glass-and-neon sculpture shows an old-fashioned punch card, reminding viewers of how the Norwegian puppet government collected seemingly innocuous information before deporting its Jews. The *Contemporary Reflections* video is a reminder that racism and genocide continue today.

Cost, Hours, Location: 50 kr, ask for free English audioguide, daily in summer 10:00–18:00, off-season 11:00–16:00, Huk Aveny 56—follow signs to *HL-Senteret*, tel. 22 84 21 00, www .hlsenteret.no.

▲▲*Fram* Museum (Frammuseet) —This museum holds the 125-foot, steam- and sail-powered ship that took modern-day Vikings Roald Amundsen and Fridtjof Nansen deep into the

Arctic and Antarctic, farther north and south than any ship had gone before. For three years, the *Fram*—specially designed to survive the pressure of a frozen-over sea—drifted as part of the Arctic ice. The exhibit is engrossing. Read the ground-floor displays, check out the videos below the bow of the ship, then climb the steps to the third-floor gangway to explore the *Fram*'s claustrophobic but fascinating interior. The building also tells the chilling tales of other Arctic and Antarctic adventures undertaken beneath the Norwegian flag. The polar sloop *Gjøa,* dry-docked outside next to the ferry dock, is the boat Amundsen and a crew of six used from 1903 to 1906 to "discover"

the Northwest Passage.

Cost, Hours, Location: 40 kr, daily June–Aug 9:00–18:00, May and Sept 10:00–17:00, Oct–April 10:00–16:00, Bygdøynesveien 36, tel. 23 28 29 50, www.fram.museum.no.

▲▲***Kon-Tiki* Museum (*Kon-Tiki* Museet)**—Next to the *Fram* is a museum housing the *Kon-Tiki* and the *Ra II*, the boats built by Thor Heyerdahl (1914–2002). In 1947, Heyerdahl and five crewmates constructed the *Kon-Tiki* raft out of balsa wood, using only pre-modern tools and techniques. They set sail from Peru on the tiny craft, surviving for 101 days on fish, coconuts, and sweet potatoes. About 4,300 miles later, they arrived in Polynesia. The point was to show that early South Americans could have settled Polynesia. (While Heyerdahl proved they could have, anthropologists doubt they did.) The *Kon-Tiki* story became a best-selling book and award-winning documentary (and helped spawn the "Tiki" culture craze in the USA). In 1970, Heyerdahl's *Ra II* made a similar 3,000-mile journey from Morocco to Barbados to prove that Africans could have populated America. Both boats are well-displayed and described in English. Various 10-minute clips from the *Kon-Tiki* movie (winner of 1951 Oscar for best documentary) play constantly in a small theater at the end of the exhibit

Cost, Hours, Location: 50 kr, daily June–Aug 9:30–17:30, April–May and Sept 10:00–17:00, Oct–March 10:30–16:00, Bygdøynesveien 36, tel. 23 08 67 67, www.kon-tiki.no.

▲**Norwegian Maritime Museum (Norsk Sjøfartsmuseum)**—If you like the sea, this museum is a salt lick, providing a wide-ranging look at Norway's maritime heritage. Its dusty collection includes the charred remains of Norway's oldest boat (2,200 years old), artifacts from the immigration days, and a case devoted to World War II. Don't miss the movie *The Ocean: A Way of Life*, included with your admission. It is a breathtaking widescreen film swooping you scenically over Norway's dramatic sea and fishing townscapes from here all the way to North Cape in a comfy theater (20 min, shown at the top and bottom of the hour, follow signs to Supervideografen).

Cost, Hours, Location: 40 kr, kids under 16 free; mid-May–Aug daily 10:00–18:00; Sept–mid-May daily 10:30–16:00, Thu until 18:00; Bygdøynesveien 37, tel. 24 11 41 50, www.norsk-sjofartsmuseum.no.

Outer Oslo

▲▲**Holmenkollen Ski Jump and Ski Museum**—The site of one of the world's oldest ski jumps (from 1892), Holmenkollen has hosted many championships, including the 1952 Winter Olympics. In order to win the privilege of hosting the 2011 World Ski Jump Championship, Oslo agreed to build a bigger jump to match modern ones. In 2008, they tore down the old Olympic ski jump and started construction of a futuristic, cantilevered, Olympic-standard new **ski jump** with a tilted elevator. The jump empties into a 50,000-seat amphitheater, and spectators can witness ski-jumpers' launches into flight from a glass-enclosed viewing platform. The jump also offers some of the best possible views of Oslo.

While due to open in the spring of 2010, escalating costs have threatened the timetable and project design. Check with the TI or call before you visit to be sure it's open. For the latest updates on construction and the world championships, visit www.oslo2011.no.

The **ski museum,** a must for skiers, traces the evolution of the sport, from 4,000-year-old rock paintings to crude 1,500-year-old wooden sticks to the slick and quickly evolving skis of modern times, including a fun exhibit showing the royal family on skis. The museum should reopen with the ski jump, but if it's still closed, stop by the free visitors center in Kollenstua, at the gateway to the jump arena, to see some temporary exhibits.

Cost and Hours: Remember to confirm at the TI that everything's open; 90-kr ticket includes museum and jump; museum open daily June–Aug 9:00–20:00, May and Sept 10:00–17:00, Oct–April 10:00–14:00; ramp open same hours except Oct–April 10:00–16:00; tel. 22 92 32 64, www.holmenkollen.com or www .skiforeningen.no.

Simulator: To cap your Holmenkollen experience, step into the simulator and fly down the Olympic slopes of Lillehammer in a virtual downhill ski race. My legs were exhausted after the five-minute terror. This simulator (or should I say stimulator?), parked in front of the ski museum, costs 50 kr (if you pay for four tickets, try getting a fifth one free).

Getting There: The T-bane gets you out of the city, through the hills, forests, and mansions that surround Oslo, and to the jump (take any westbound train—that's *tog mot vest*—to Majorstuen, then line #1 to Holmenkollen, and hike up the road 10 min). For an easy downhill jaunt through the Norwegian forest, with a woodsy coffee or meal break in the middle, stay on the T-bane past Holmenkollen to the end of the line (Frognerseteren) and walk 10 minutes downhill to the recommended **Frognerseteren Hovedrestaurant,** a fine traditional eatery with sod roof, reindeer meat on the griddle, and a city view. Continue on the same road another 20 minutes downhill to the ski jump, and then to the Holmenkollen T-bane stop.

▲**Edvard Munch Museum (Munch Museet)**—The only Norwegian painter to have had a serious impact on European art, Munch (pronounced "moonk") is a surprise to many who visit this fine museum, located one mile east of Oslo's center. The emotional, disturbing, and powerfully Expressionistic work of this strange and perplexing man is arranged chronologically. You'll see an extensive collection of paintings, drawings, lithographs, and photographs. Note that Oslo's centrally located—and free—National Gallery, which also displays many Munch works, can be a good alternative if you find the Munch Museum too expensive or time-consuming to reach (75 kr; June–Aug daily 10:00–18:00; Sept–May Tue–Fri 10:00–16:00, Sat–Sun 11:00–17:00, closed Mon; 25-kr audioguide, guided tours daily July–Aug at 13:00, T-bane or bus #20 to Tøyen, Tøyengata 53, tel. 23 49 35 00, www.munch.museum.no). For more on Munch.

The Munch Museum was in the news in August 2004, when two Munch paintings, *Madonna* and a version of his famous *Scream*, were brazenly stolen right off the walls in broad daylight. Two men in black hoods simply entered through the museum café, waved guns at the stunned guards and tourists, ripped the paintings off the wall, and sped off in a black Audi station wagon. Happily, in 2006, the thieves were caught and the stolen paintings recovered. Today they are on display behind glass with heightened security.

Forests, Lakes, and Beaches—Oslo is surrounded by a vast forest dotted with idyllic little lakes, huts, joggers, bikers, and sun-worshippers. Mountain-biking possibilities are endless (as you'll discover if you go exploring without a good map). Consider taking your bike on the T-bane (for the cost of a child's ticket) to the end of line #1 (Frognerseteren, 30 min from National Theater) to gain the most altitude possible. Then follow the gravelly roads (mostly downhill but with some climbing) past several dreamy lakes to Sognsvann at the end of T-bane line #3. Farther east, from Maridalsvannet, a bike path follows the Akers River all the way back into town. (The TI has details.) While Oslo isn't much on bike rentals, you can rent them in summer at Skiservice, located at the Voksenkollen stop on T-bane line #1, at the high end of the woods. Keep in mind that you'll need to bring your bike back here—via T-bane if you like (tel. 22 13 95 00, www.skiservice.no).

For plenty of trees and none of the exercise, ride T-bane line #3 to its last stop, Sognsvann (with a beach towel rather than a bike), and join the lakeside scene. A pleasant trail leads around the lake.

Other popular beaches are located on islands in the harbor (such as Bygdøy Huk—direct boat from pier 3 in front of City Hall). The various island getaways are described in Use It's *Streetwise* magazine.

Tusenfryd—This giant amusement complex just out of town offers a world of family fun. It's sort of a combination Norwegian Disneyland/Viking Knott's Berry Farm, with more than 50 rides, plenty of entertainment, and restaurants.

Cost and Hours: Admission is based on your height: under

95 centimeters (3 feet)—free, under 1.2 meters (4 feet)—240 kr, over 1.2 meters (4 feet)—290 kr (daily June–late Aug 10:30–19:00, closed in winter, tel. 64 97 66 99, www.tusenfryd.no).

Getting There: Bus #541 takes fun-seekers to the park from behind Oslo's train station (30 kr, 2/hr, 20-min ride, departs Oslo 10:00–16:00, departs Tusenfryd 14:30–17:30).

Wet Fun—Oslo offers a variety of water play. In Frogner Park, the **Frognerbadet** has three outdoor pools, a waterslide, high dives, a cafeteria, and lots of young families (69 kr, students-50 kr, mid-May–late Aug Mon–Fri 7:00–19:00, Sat–Sun 10:00–18:00, last entry one hour before closing, closed late Aug–mid-May, Middelthunsgate 28, tel. 23 27 54 50).

Tøyenbadet, a modern indoor/outdoor pool complex with a 330-foot-long waterslide, also has a gym and sauna (73 kr, children-35 kr, Mon–Fri 7:00–19:30, Sat–Sun 10:00–18:00, 10-min walk from Edvard Munch Museum, Helgengate 90, tel. 23 30 44 70). Oslo's free botanical gardens are nearby.

From Akers River to the Grünerløkka District

Connect the dots by following the self-guided "Walk up the Akers River to Grünerløkka" (below).

Akers River—This river, though only about five miles long, powered Oslo's early industry: flour mills in the 1300s, sawmills in the 1500s, and Norway's Industrial Revolution in the 1800s. A walk along the river not only spans Oslo's history, but also shows the contrast the city offers. The bottom of the river (where this walk doesn't go)—bordered by the high-rise Oslo Radisson/SAS Plaza Hotel and the "Little Pakistan" neighborhood of Grønland—has its share of drunks and drugs, reflecting a new urban reality in Oslo. Farther up, the river valley becomes a park as it winds past decent-size waterfalls and red-brick factories. The source of the river (and Oslo's drinking water) is the pristine Lake Maridal, situated at the edge of the Nordmarka wilderness. The idyllic recreation scenes along Lake Maridal are a world apart from the rougher reality downstream.

▲Grünerløkka—The Grünerløkka district is the largest planned urban area in Oslo. It was built in the latter half of the 1800s to house the legions of workers employed at the factories powered by the Akers River. The first buildings were modeled on similar places built in Berlin. (German visitors observe that there's now more turn-of-the-20th-century Berlin here than in present-day Berlin.) While slummy in the 1980s, today it's trendy. Locals sometimes refer to it as "Oslo's Greenwich Village." Although that's way over the mark, it is a bustling area with lots of cafés, good spots for a fun meal, and few tourists.

Grünerløkka can be reached from the center of town by a

Grünerløkka/Grønland Area

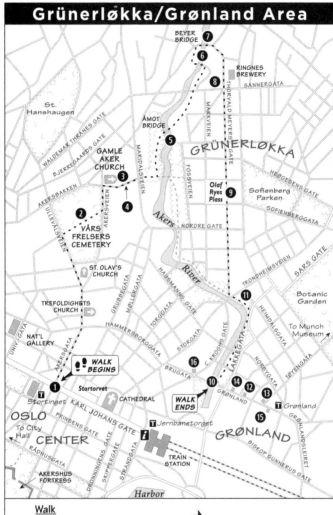

OSLO

BEYER BRIDGE ⑦
⑥
RINGNES BREWERY
⑧
SANNERGATA
THORVALD MEYERS GATE
St. Hanshaugen
ÅMOT BRIDGE
MARKVEIEN
⑤
GRÜNERLØKKA
WALDEMAR THRANES GATE
BJERREGAARDS GATE
GAMLE AKER CHURCH
MARIDALSVEIEN
③
FOSSVEIEN
HØGEENS GATE
AKERSBAKKEN
Olaf Ryes Plass ⑨
Sofienberg Parken
ULLEVÅLSVEIEN
AKERSVEIEN
④
Akers
NORDRE GATE
SOFIENBERGGATA
②
VÅRS FRELSERS CEMETERY
River
SARS GATE
ST. OLAV'S CHURCH
GRUBBEGATA
HAUSMANNS GATE
TRONDHEIMSVEIEN
Botanic Garden
TREFOLDIGHETS CHURCH
MØLLERGATA
TORGGATA
To Munch Museum
HEIMDALSGATA
NAT'L GALLERY
HAMMERSBORGGATA
STORGATA
LÅKKEGATA
NORBYGATA
TØYENGATA
AKERSGATA
WALK BEGINS
BRUGATA
⑯
C. KROGHS GATE
⑪
UNIV. GATA
Stortorvet
① ✝ CATHEDRAL
⑩ **WALK ENDS** ⑭ ⑫ ⑬ GRØNLAND
Grønland
Stortinget KARL JOHANS GATE
Jernbanetorget
⑮
GRØNLAND
OSLO CENTER
PRINSENS GATE
GRØNLANDSLEIRET
To City Hall
RÅDHUSGATA
DRONNINGENS GATE
SKIPPERGATE
STRANDGATA
TRAIN STATION
BISKOP GUNNERUS GATE
AKERSHUS FORTRESS
Harbor

Walk

400 Meters
400 Yards

① Akersgata & Start of Walk
② Vår Frelsers Cemetery
③ Gamle Aker Church
④ Telthusbakken Road
⑤ Åmotbrua (Bridge)
⑥ Big Waterfall
⑦ Fabrikkjentene Statue & Honse-Lovisas Hus
⑧ Thorvald Meyers Gate
⑨ Olaf Ryes Plass
⑩ Vaterlands Bridge & End of Walk

Eateries

⑪ Südøst Restaurant
⑫ Punjab Tandoori & Asylet Restaurant
⑬ Alibaba Restaurant
⑭ Dattera Til Hagen Rest.
⑮ Olympen Brown Pub
⑯ Café Con Bar

short ride on tram #11, #12, or #13, or by taking the short but interesting walk described next.

▲**Walk up the Akers River to Grünerløkka**—While every tourist explores the harborfront and main drag of Oslo, few venture into this neighborhood that evokes the Industrial Revolution. Once housing poor workers, it now attracts hip professionals. A hike up the Akers River, finishing in the stylish Grünerløkka district, shines a truly different light on Oslo. Allow about an hour at a brisk pace, including a fair bit of up and down. Navigate with the TI's free city map and the map in this chapter. This walk is best during daylight hours.

Begin the walk by leaving Karl Johans Gate at the top of the hill, and head right up Akersgata, which becomes Ullevålsveien. Akersgata is Oslo's "Fleet Street" (lined with major newspaper companies) and home to some big government buildings. On the right, notice the red-brick Supreme Court building and then the Department of Finance—an example of Jugendstil, or Art Nouveau, architecture. Then you'll pass the massive brick Trefoldighets Church and St. Olav's Church before reaching the **Vår Frelsers (Our Savior's) Cemetery.** Enter the cemetery across from the Baby Shop store (where Ullevålsveien meets Wessels Gate).

Stop at the big metal map just inside the gate to chart your course through the cemetery: Go through the light-green Æreslunden section—with the biggest plots and highest elevation—and out the opposite end (#13 on the metal map) onto Akersveien. En route, check out some of the tombstones of the illuminati and literati buried in the honorary Æreslunden section. They include Munch, Ibsen, Bjørnson, and many of the painters whose works you can see in the National Gallery (all marked on a map posted at the entrance). Exiting on the far side of the cemetery, walk left 100 yards up Akersveien to the church.

The Romanesque **Gamle Aker Church** (from the 1100s), the oldest building in Oslo, is worth a look inside (free, Mon–Fri 12:00–16:00). The church, which fell into ruins and has been impressively rebuilt, is pretty bare except for a pulpit and baptismal font from the 1700s.

From the church, backtrack 20 yards, head left at the playground, and go downhill on the steep **Telthusbakken Road** toward the huge, gray former grain silos (now student housing). The cute lane is lined with colorful old wooden houses: The people who constructed these homes were too poor to meet the no-wood fire-safety building codes within the city limits, so they built in what used to be suburbs. At the bottom of Telthusbakken, cross the busy Maridalsveien and walk directly through the park to the Akers River. The lively Grünerløkka district is straight across the river from here, but if you have 20 minutes and a little energy, detour upstream first and hook back down. Don't cross the river yet.

Walk along the riverside bike lane upstream through the river gorge park. Just above the first waterfall, cross **Åmotbrua,** the big white springy suspension footbridge from 1852 (moved here in 1958). Keep hiking uphill along the river. At the base of the next big waterfall, cross over again to the large brick buildings, hiking up the stairs to the Beyer bridge (above the falls) with *Fabrikkjentene,* a statue of four women laborers. They're pondering the textile factory where they and 700 like them toiled long and hard. This gorge was once lined with the water mills that powered Oslo through its 19th-century Industrial Age boom. The tiny red house next to the bridge—the **Honse-Lovisas Hus** cultural center—makes a good rest-stop (Tue-Sun 11:00–18:00, closed Mon, coffee and cake). Cross over to the red-brick Ringnes Brewery and follow **Thorvald Meyers Gate** downhill directly into the heart of Grünerløkka. The main square, called **Olaf Ryes Plass,** is a happening place to grab a meal or drink. Trams take you from here back to the center.

• *To continue exploring, you could keep walking (always going straight) until you reach a T-intersection with a busy road (Trondheimsveien). From there (passing the recommended Südøst Restaurant), you can catch a tram back to the center, or drop down to the riverside path and follow it downstream to Vaterlands bridge in the Grønland district. From here the train station is a five-minute walk down Stenersgata. (The last section, around Grønland, is a bit seedy and best done in daylight.)*

Near Oslo

▲**Eidsvoll Manor**—During the Napoleonic period, control of Norway went from Denmark to Sweden. This ruffled the patriotic feathers of Norway's Thomas Jeffersons and Ben Franklins, and on May 17, 1814, Norway's constitution was written and signed in this stately mansion (in the town of Eidsvoll Verk, north of Oslo). While Sweden still ruled, Norway had more autonomy than ever. The mansion is full of elegant furnishings and stirring history.

Cost and Hours: 75 kr; May–Aug daily 10:00–17:00; April and Sept Tue–Fri 10:00–15:00, Sat-Sun 12:00–17:00, closed Mon; Oct–March Wed–Fri 10:00–15:00, Sat-Sun 12:00–17:00, closed Mon–Tue; tel. 63 92 22 10, www.eidsvoll1814.no.

Getting There: Eidsvoll is 45 minutes from Oslo by car (take road E6 toward Trondheim, turn right at *Eidsvolls Bygningen* sign, free parking) or bus (direct bus #854 runs hourly from Oslo Airport). You can also take the train to Eidsvoll (hourly, 45 min plus 15-min walk). If you're driving from Oslo to Lillehammer and the Gudbrandsdal Valley, it's right on the way and worth a stop.

Drøbak—This delightful fjord town is just an hour from Oslo by bus (70 kr one-way, 2/hr, bus #541 or #542 from behind the train station) or ferry (70 kr one-way, sporadic departures, check at pier 1 or ask at Oslo TI). Consider taking the 75-minute boat trip down, exploring the town, having dinner, and taking the bus back.

For holiday cheer year-round, stop into **Tregaarden's Julehuset** Christmas shop, right off Drøbak's main square (generally Mon–Fri 10:00–17:00, Sat 10:00–15:00, variable hours on Sun, longer hours in Dec, closed Jan–Feb, tel. 64 93 41 78, www.julehus .no). Then wander out past the church and cemetery on the north side of town to a pleasant park. Looking out into the fjord, you can see the old **Oscarsborg Fortress,** where Norwegian troops fired their cannons to sink Hitler's battleship, *Blücher.* The attack bought enough time for Norway's king and Parliament to escape capture and eventually set up a government-in-exile in London during the Nazi occupation of Norway (1940–1945). Nearby, a monument is dedicated to the commander of the fortress, and the *Blücher*'s anchor rests aground. (A 70-kr round-trip summer ferry shuttles visitors from the town harbor.)

If you want to spend the night, the **TI** can recommend accommodations (June–Aug Mon–Fri 8:00–18:00, Sat–Sun 10:00–16:00; Sept–May Mon–Fri 8:00–16:00, closed Sat–Sun; tel. 64 93 50 87, www.visitdrobak.no). **Restaurant Skipperstuen** is a good option for dinner, with outdoor seating that overlooks the fjord and all the Oslo-bound boat traffic (entrées from 200 kr, Mon–Sat 11:00–21:00, closed Sun, tel. 64 93 07 03).

Shopping in Oslo

Shops in Oslo are generally open 10:00–18:00. Many stay open until 20:00 on Thursday and close early on Saturday and all day Sunday. Shopping centers are open Monday through Friday 10:00–21:00, Saturday 10:00–18:00, and are closed Sunday. Remember, when you make a purchase of 310 kr or more, you can get the 25 percent tax refunded when you leave the country if you hang on to the paperwork.

Oslo's fanciest department store is **GlasMagasinet** (top end, near the cathedral on Stortorvet, good souvenir shop). The big, splashy **Byporten** mall, adjoining the central train station, is more youthful and hip (Mon–Fri 10:00–21:00, Sat 10:00–18:00, closed Sun). The trendiest boutiques and chic, high-quality shops lie along the street named **Bogstadveien** (running from behind the Royal Palace to Frogner Park). And on Saturday mornings, you can browse the **flea market** at Vestkanttorvet.

Sweaters and colorful Norwegian folk crafts are on many visitors' shopping lists. The **Husfliden shop,** in the basement of the GlasMagasinet department store, is much appreciated for its traditional yarn and Norsk folk items (Mon–Fri 10:00–18:00, Thu until 19:00, Sat 10:00–16:00, closed Sun, tel. 22 42 10 75). For a

superb selection of sweaters and other Norwegian crafts (top quality at high prices), visit **Heimen Husfliden** (Mon–Fri 10:00–17:00,
Thu until 18:00, Sat 10:00–15:00, closed Sun, Rosenkrantz Gate
8, tel. 22 41 40 50). The **Oslo Sweater Shop** has good prices for
sweaters (Mon–Fri 10:00–18:00, Sat 10:00–15:00, closed Sun, off
Skippergata at Biskop Gunnerusgata 3, tel. 22 42 42 25). For flags
(a long, skinny *vimple* dresses up a boat or cabin wonderfully), pop
into **Oslo Flaggfabrikk** (Mon–Fri 9:00–17:00, Sat 10:00–16:00,
closed Sun, near City Hall, across the street from Heimen
Husfliden shop, at Rosenkrantz Gate 18).

Vinmonopolet stores are the only place where you can buy
wine and spirits in Norway. The most convenient location is at the
central train station (Mon–Thu 10:00–18:00, Fri 9:00–18:00, Sat
9:00–15:00, closed Sun). The bottles used to be kept behind the
counter, but now you can actually touch the merchandise. Locals
say it went from being a "jewelry store" to "grocery store."

Sleeping in Oslo

In Oslo, the season and type of hotel dictate the best deals. The
basic formula: In midsummer and on weekends, discounted business-class hotels offer the best value; otherwise, consider a cheap
hotel, a room in a private home, or a hostel.

Like those in its sister Scandinavian capitals, Oslo's hotels
are mostly designed for business travelers; they're expensive during the tourists' off-season (autumn through spring), full in May
and June for conventions, and wide open otherwise. From July
through mid-August—and weekends (Fri–Sat but not Sun) year-
round—fancy business-class hotels deeply discount their rooms.
At half-price (about 800–900 kr for a double), you get a huge
breakfast and a lot of extra comfort for little more than the cost of
a cheap hotel or hostel.

During business days (Sun–Thu) outside of summer, business
hotels hold out for their inflated "rack rates," and budget travelers
opt for Oslo's dumpy-for-Scandinavia (but still nice by European
standards) cheapie options: doubles for about 800 kr in central
"cheap" hotels, or 350 kr in private homes on the outskirts of the
city. For experience and economy—but not convenience—go for
a private home. For convenience and modern comfort, I like the
Thon Budget Hotels (described later).

Only the TI can sort through all of the confusing hotel specials and get you the best deal going on fancy hotel rooms on the
push list. If it's late in the day, the TI's prices get even better.
With the uncertain economy these days, it's tough to get a hotel
to give a straight price in advance. If booking on your own and on
a budget, email several places and see who's willing to offer the

Sleep Code

(6 kr = about $1, country code: 47)

S = Single, **D** = Double/Twin, **T** = Triple, **Q** = Quad, **b** = bathroom, **s** = shower. You can assume credit cards are accepted and breakfast is included unless otherwise noted. Everyone speaks English.

To help you sort through these listings easily, I've divided the rooms into three categories, based on the price for a standard double room with bath:

$$$ Higher Priced—Most rooms 1,000 kr or more.

$$ Moderately Priced—Most rooms between 600–1,000 kr.

$ Lower Priced—Most rooms 600 kr or less.

most aggressive discount.

The most predictable special is the TI's **Oslo Package,** which offers business-class rooms plus an Oslo Pass for 500–800 kr per person (based on double occupancy); prices vary depending on the hotel you choose. The Oslo Package is offered daily year-round. It's a good deal for couples and ideal for families with young children. Two kids under 16 sleep free, breakfast is included, and up to four family members get free Oslo Passes, covering admission to sights and all public transportation (worth as much as 135 kr per person per day). These passes are valid for four days, even if you only stay one night at the hotel (allowing you to squeeze two days of sight-seeing out of a one-night stay—for example, if you take an over-night train or boat out of town on your second evening). Buy the Oslo Package through your travel agent at home, ScanAm World Tours in the US (US tel. 800-545-2204), or—easiest—upon arrival in Oslo at the TI. Even if you show up late in the day when prices are most deeply discounted, you still get the Oslo Pass along with your room. For details on the Oslo Package, see www.visitoslo. com.

Near the Train Station and Karl Johans Gate

These accommodations are within a 15-minute walk of the station. While evidence of an earlier shady time survives in some places, the hotels feel secure and comfortable. Parking in a central garage will run you about 170 kr per day.

Thon Hotels

This chain of business-class hotels (found in big cities throughout Norway) knows which comforts are worth paying for and which are not. They offer little character, but provide maximum comfort per krone in big, modern, conveniently located buildings. Each hotel

OSLO

Oslo Hotels and Restaurants

1. Thon City Hotel Stefan
2. Thon City Hotel Terminus
3. Thon City Hotel Cecil
4. Thon Budget Hotel Spectrum
5. Thon Budget Hotel Astoria
6. To Thon Budget Hotel Munch
7. Thon Budget Hotel Oslo Panorama
8. Hotell Bondeheimen & Kaffistova Cafeteria
9. Oslo Budget Hotel
10. Perminalen Hotel
11. P-Hotel
12. Cochs Pensjonat
13. To Ellingsen's Pensjonat
14. Anker Hostel
15. Deli de Luca
16. Grand Café
17. Brasserie 45 Restaurant
18. City Hall Workers' Cafeteria

has a cheery staff and lobby, tight but well-designed rooms, non-smoking floors, free Internet access, and a big buffet breakfast.

Thon Hotels come in categories: Their "City Hotels" are a cut above their "Budget Hotels." While City Hotels are much more expensive during business times (weekdays outside of summer), Budget Hotels have nearly the same rack rates all year. That means City Hotels can be a better value in low season. City Hotels generally offer free juice and coffee all day. In Budget Hotels (which have no phones or mini-fridges in the rooms), rooms with double beds are a bit bigger than twin-bedded rooms for the same price.

Thon Hotels share a similar price structure: **Thon City Hotels**—Sb-1,525, Db-1,825 kr; discounted rates: Fri–Sat year around and daily mid-June–mid-Aug Sb-900 kr, Db-1,100; **Thon Budget Hotels**—Sb-750 kr, Db-1,075 kr, no weekend deals; summer rates: Sb-650 kr, Db-875 kr. These rates include breakfast (you have the option of saving 50 kr per day per person by not taking breakfast). Extra beds are 300 kr for an adult and 150 kr for a child under 17 (kids under 6 stow away for free). Book by phone or online (central booking tel. 23 08 02 00, www.thonhotels.no).

Thon Hotels generally offer a 10 percent discount for those

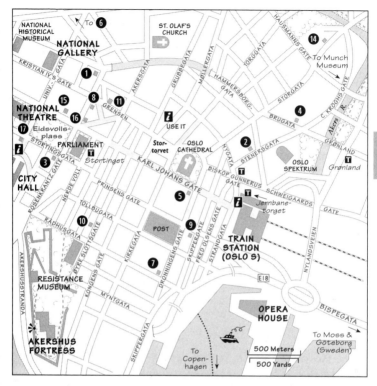

who prepay via their website with no option to change or cancel their booking. If you stay five nights in one year, the free Thon Membership Card offers a 10 percent discount (off-season/week-days only). My price ratings for Thon Hotels are based on their summer/weekend rates. Of the 14 Thon Hotels in Oslo, I find the following most convenient:

$$$ Thon City Hotel Stefan, in a classy and central location two blocks off Karl Johans Gate, is a cut above its sisters in comfort and charm (Rosenkrantz Gate 1, entrance on Kristian Augusts Gate side, tel. 23 31 55 00, fax 23 31 55 55, www.thonhotels.no /stefan, stefan@thonhotels.no).

$$$ Thon City Hotel Terminus is similar but closer to the station (Steners Gate 10, tel. 22 05 60 00, fax 22 17 08 98, www .thonhotels.no/terminus, terminus@thonhotels.no).

$$$ Thon City Hotel Cecil is near the Parliament building a block below Karl Johans Gate (Stortingsgata 8, tel. 23 31 48 00, fax 23 31 48 50, www.thonhotels.no/cecil, cecil@thonhotels.no).

$$ Thon Budget Hotel Spectrum is four blocks from the station near the Grønland Torg shopping street. A quarter of its rooms are plagued by disco noise on weekends (leave station out north entrance toward bus terminal, go across footbridge toward tall glass Radisson/SAS Plaza Hotel, and pass through Grønland Torg, Brugata 7; tel. 23 36 27 00, fax 23 36 27 50, www.thonhotels .no/spectrum, spectrum@thonhotels.no).

$$ Thon Budget Hotel Astoria has the least charm of my recommended Thon Hotels, but it's well-located and perfectly serviceable (3 blocks in front of station, 50 yards off Karl Johans Gate, Dronningens Gate 21, tel. 24 14 55 50, fax 22 42 57 65, www .thonhotels.no/astoria, astoria@thonhotels.no).

$$ Thon Budget Hotel Munch, a few blocks from the National Gallery, is like its sisters (Munchs Gate 5, tel. 23 21 96 00, fax 23 21 96 01, www.thonhotels.no/munch, munch@thon hotels.no).

$$ Thon Budget Hotel Oslo Panorama is a 15-story attempt at a downtown condominium building. The condos didn't work and now it's a budget hotel. While higher rooms are more expensive, even those reserving a cheap room often get bumped up. If you request anything higher than the fourth floor, you'll likely enjoy a bigger room, perhaps with a balcony (just off Dronningens Gate at Rådhusgata 7, about 6 blocks from station, tel. 23 31 08 00, fax 23 31 08 10, www.thonhotels.no/oslopanorama, oslopanorama @thonhotels.no).

More Hotels near the Train Station

$$$ Hotell Bondeheimen ("Farmer's Home") is a historic hotel run by the farmers' youth league, *Bondeungdomslaget.* It once housed the children of rural farmers attending school in Oslo. Now a Best Western, its 127 rooms have all the comforts of a modern hotel (weekday rates too high, Fri–Sat all year and July Db-900 kr, Aug Db-1,100 kr; you generally save money by booking on their website; non-smoking rooms, elevator, Rosenkrantz Gate 8, tel. 23 21 41 00, www.bondeheimen.com, booking@bondeheimen.com). This almost-100-year-old building is also home to the Kaffistova cafeteria (see "Eating in Oslo") and the Heimen Husfliden shop (see "Shopping in Oslo").

$$ Oslo Budget Hotel has clean, basic, and well-worn but homey rooms (many with bunks), in a somewhat seedy fourth-floor location handy to the train station. The hotel originated 100 years ago as a cheap place for Norwegians to sleep while they waited to sail to their new homes in America. It now serves the opposite purpose. With prices the same throughout the year, this hotel is a good value on off-season weekdays (Sun–Thu), when other hotels are at their most expensive (S-490 kr, Sb-590 kr, D-590 kr, Db-790 kr, T-690 kr, Tb-890 kr, Q-790 kr, Qb-990 kr, 10 percent discount with this book—mention when you reserve, breakfast-65 kr, free waffles in afternoon, non-smoking rooms, Prinsens Gate

6, tel. 22 41 36 10, fax 22 42 24 29, www.budgethotel.no, oslo @budgethotel.no).

$$ Perminalen Hotel, a place for military personnel on leave, is perfectly central, spartan, inexpensive, and welcoming to civvies. They have the same fair prices all year. Spliced invisibly into a giant office block on a quiet street, it has sleek woody furniture and a no-nonsense reception desk (Sb-620 kr, twin Db-820 kr, some seventh-floor rooms have balconies, entirely non-smoking, elevator, tram #12 from station to Øvre Slotts Gate 2, tel. 23 09 30 81, fax 23 41 18 58, www.perminalen.com, post .perminalen@iss.no). Single beds in shared quads segregated by sexes (with lockers and breakfast) rent for 360 kr each. Its cheap mess hall is open all day.

$$ P-Hotel, the latest thing in economic hotels in Oslo, rents 92 comfortable rooms—some with hardwood-slick floors—for the same great price every day of the year. You get a boxed breakfast delivered each morning, as well as free Internet access and Wi-Fi. Avoid late-night street noise by requesting a room high up or in the back (Sb-795 kr, Db-895 kr, bigger rooms add 150 kr per person up to five, some sixth-floor rooms have balconies, pay by credit card— no cash accepted, Grensen 19, T-bane: Storting, tel. 23 31 80 00, www.p-hotels.com, oslo@p-hotels.no).

The West End

$$ Cochs Pensjonat has 88 characteristic rooms (20 remodeled doubles), many with kitchenettes. It's right behind the Royal Palace (S-460 kr, Sb-610 kr, D-660 kr, Db-760 kr, newly refurnished Db-820 kr, Q-1,020 kr, Qb-1,180 kr, breakfast-65 kr at nearby café, non-smoking rooms, elevator; T-bane to National Theater, exit to Parkveien, and walk through park; or ride tram #11, #17, or #18 to Høgskolen/Dalsbergsstien; Parkveien 25; tel. 23 33 24 00, fax 23 33 24 10, www.cochspensjonat.no, booking@cochs.no, three generations of the Skram family).

$$ Ellingsen's Pensjonat rents 18 clean, bright rooms with fluffy down comforters. It's in a residential neighborhood four blocks behind the Royal Palace (S-330 kr, Sb-460 kr, D-540 kr, Db-650 kr, extra bed-150 kr, no breakfast, cash only, non-smoking, back rooms have less street noise, tram #19 from central station to Uranienborgveien, near Uranienborg church at Holtegata 25, tel. 22 60 03 59, fax 22 60 99 21, www.ellingsenspensjonat.no, post @ellingsenspensjonat.no).

Private Homes

The central station TI can find you a 350-kr double for a 45-kr fee (minimum two-night stay, likely a tram ride out of the center).

Hostels

$ Anker Hostel, a huge student dorm open to travelers of any age, offers 250 of Oslo's best cheap doubles. Though it comes with the ambience of a bomb shelter, each of its rooms is spacious, simple, and clean. There are kitchens, free parking, and elevators (bed in 6-bed room-210 kr, bed in quad-230 kr, Db-550 kr, sheets-50 kr, towel-20 kr, breakfast-75 kr at adjacent Best Western hotel, self-serve laundry; tram #12, #13, or #15, or bus #30, #31, or #32 from central station, bus and tram stop: Hausmanns Gate; or 10-min walk from station; Storgata 55, tel. 22 99 72 00, fax 22 99 72 20, www.ankerhostel.no, hostel@anker.oslo.no).

$ Haraldsheim Youth Hostel (IYHF), a huge, modern hostel open all year, comes with a grand view, laundry, self-service kitchen, 270 beds...and a long commute (2.5 miles out of town). Beds in the fancy quads with private showers and toilets are 250 kr per person (bed in simple quad with bathroom down the hall-220 kr). They also offer private rooms (S-415 kr, Sb-470 kr, bunk-bed D-540 kr, Db-625 kr; all include breakfast, members get 15 percent off, sheets-50 kr, catch bus #31 or tram #17 or T-bane lines #4 or #6 from Oslo's central train station to Sinsenkrysset, then 5-min uphill hike to Haraldsheimveien 4, tel. 22 22 29 65, fax 22 22 10 25, www.haraldsheim.oslo.no, post@haraldsheim.oslo.no). Eurailers can train to the hostel with their railpass (2/hr, to Grefsen and walk 10 min).

Sleeping on the Train or Boat

Norway's trains and ferries offer ways to travel while sleeping. The eight-hour night train between Bergen and Oslo leaves at about 23:00 in each direction (nightly except Sat). Eurail hobos sleep cheap, if not well, for the cost of a 50-kr train reservation (sleep on a train ride out, cross platform, and sleep back)—for example, Oslo–Vinstra (direction: Trondheim) 23:05–2:55, Vinstra–Oslo 3:14–6:43. Overnight trains connect Oslo with Copenhagen June–August only (leaves nightly at 20:30, arrives at Malmö Central Station at 6:42 the next morning, easy transfers to Copenhagen). The overnight cruise between these Nordic capitals is a clever way to avoid a night in a hotel and to travel while you sleep, saving a day in your itinerary (see "Oslo Connections," later).

Eating in Oslo

Eating Cheaply

How do the Norwegians afford their high-priced restaurants? They don't eat out much. This is one city in which you might just settle for simple or ethnic meals—you'll save a lot and miss little. Many menus list small and large plates. Because portions tend to be large,

Oslo's One-Time Grills

Norwegians are experts at completely avoiding costly restaurants. "One-time grills," or *engangsgrill,* are the rage for locals on a budget. For about 20 kr, you get a disposable outdoor cooker consisting of an aluminum tray, easy-to-light charcoal, and a flimsy metal grill. All that's required is a sunny evening, a grassy park, and a group of friends. During balmy summer evenings, the air in Oslo's city parks is thick with the smell of disposable (and not terribly eco-friendly) grills. It's fun to see how prices for this kind of "dining" aren't that bad in the supermarket: Norwegian beer-12 kr/bottle, potato salad-20 kr/tub, cooked shrimp-75 kr/half kilo, "ready for grill" steak-two for 110 kr, *grill polse* hot dogs-60 kr per dozen, *lomper* (Norwegian tortillas for wrapping hot dogs)-15 kr per stack, and the actual grill itself.

Bars are also too expensive for the average Norwegian. Young night owls drink at home before *(forspiel)* and after *(nachspiel)* an evening on the town, with a couple of hours, generally around midnight, when they go out for a single drink in a public setting. A beer in a bar costs about $8–10 (compared to $6 in Ireland and $2 in the Czech Republic), while they can get an entire six-pack for that price in a grocery store.

choosing a small plate or splitting a large one makes some otherwise pricey options reasonable. You'll notice many locals just drink free tap water, even in fine restaurants. For a description of Oslo's classic (and expensive) restaurants, see the TI's *Oslo Guide* booklet.

Splurge for a hotel that includes breakfast, or pay for it if it's optional. At 75 kr, a Norwegian breakfast fit for a Viking is a good deal. Picnic for lunch or dinner. Basements of big department stores have huge, first-class supermarkets with lots of alternatives to sandwiches for picnic dinners. The little yogurt tubs with cereal come with collapsible spoons. Wasa crackers and meat, shrimp, or cheese spread in a tube are cheap and pack well. The central station has an ICA supermarket with long hours (Mon–Fri 7:00–22:00, Sat–Sun 9:00–18:00).

You'll save 12 percent by getting take-away food from a restaurant rather than eating inside. (The VAT on take-away food is 12 percent; restaurant food is 24 percent.) Fast-food restaurants ask if you want to take away or not before they ring up your order on the cash register. Even McDonald's has a two-tiered price list.

Oslo is awash with little budget eateries (modern, ethnic, fast food, pizza, department-store cafeterias, and so on). **Deli de Luca,** a cheery convenience store chain, notorious for having a store on every key corner in Oslo, is a step up from the similarly ubiquitous 7-Elevens. Most are open 24/7, selling sandwiches, pastries, sushi, and to-go boxes of warm pasta or Asian noodle dishes. You can fill your belly here for about 60 kr. Some outlets (such as the one at the corner of Karl Johans Gate and Rosenkrantz Gate) have seating on the street or upstairs. Beware: Because this is still a *convenience* store, not everything is well-priced. Convenience stores—while convenient—charge double what supermarkets do.

Eating on or near Karl Johans Gate

Consider the restaurants and eateries listed below. They're grouped by those that are from Karl Johans Gate and slightly to the north (between this main boulevard and the National Gallery) and to the south (between Karl Johans Gate and City Hall).

Strangely, **Karl Johans Gate** itself—the most Norwegian of boulevards—is lined with a strip of good-time American chain eateries where you can get ribs, burgers, and pizza, including T.G.I. Fridays and the Hard Rock Cafe. Egon Pizza offers a daily 100-kr all-you-can-eat pizza deal (11:00–18:00). Each place comes with great sidewalk seating and essentially the same prices.

Grand Café is perhaps the most venerable place in town. At lunchtime, they set up a sandwich buffet (100-kr single sandwich, 300-kr all-you-like). Lunch plates are 150 kr, and dinner plates run about 250 kr. Reserve a window, and if you hit a time when there's no tour group, you're suddenly a posh Norwegian (Karl Johans Gate 31, tel. 23 21 20 18).

Deli de Luca, just across from the Grand Café, offers good-value food and handy seats on Karl Johans Gate. For a fast meal with the best people-watching view in town, you may find yourself dropping by here repeatedly (Karl Johans Gate 33, tel. 22 33 35 22).

Kaffistova is where my thrifty Norwegian grandparents always took me. After remaining unchanged for 30 years, it got a facelift in 2007. This alcohol-free cafeteria still serves simple, hearty, and typically Norwegian (read: bland) meals for a good price (Mon–Fri 6:30–21:00, Sat–Sun 7:00–19:00; Rosenkrantz Gate 8, tel. 23 21 42 10).

Brasserie 45, overlooking Stortingsgata and the National Theater from its second-floor perch, is a modern eatery offering decent and affordable Continental cuisine with energetic service. While larger entrées go for about 180 kr, their "light plates" (about 100 kr) are plenty for me. It's worth calling ahead to reserve a window seat with a view of Karl Johans Gate (Mon–Thu 15:00–23:00,

Fri–Sat 14:00–24:00, Sun 14:00–22:00, always a veggie option, Stortingsgata 20, tel. 22 41 34 00).

City Hall workers' cafeteria, just steps off the harborfront, welcomes the public with the cheapest lunch I've found in Oslo.

It has soup, an inexpensive salad bar measured by weight (35 kr for a meal-sized bowl), and a daily hot dish for 30–45 kr (12:30–13:30 Mon–Fri only). While City Hall workers get access to the place before 12:30 and the food can be pretty picked over, it's still a fine, handy value. From the grand harbor entrance, it's up one flight of stairs above the city info desk and WC. From the tour entrance on its inland courtyard, it's just downstairs.

Harborside Dining in Aker Brygge

The **Aker Brygge** harborfront mall is popular with businesspeople and tourists. While it isn't cheap, its inviting cafés and restaurants with outdoor, harborview tables make for a memorable waterfront meal. Before deciding where to eat, you might want to walk the entire lane (including the back side), considering both the regular places (some with second-floor view seating) and the various floating options. Nearly all are open for lunch and dinner.

Druen, the first restaurant on the strip—while not a particularly good food value—is best for people-watching. I like the balcony seats upstairs, under outside heaters and with a harbor view. They serve international dishes—spicy Asian, French, and seafood—in small plates for 150 kr, hearty salads for 130 kr, and big meals for 220–260 kr (daily from 11:00, Stranden 1, Aker Brygge, tel. 23 11 54 60).

Two restaurants are right on the water with a view of the harbor rather than the river of strolling people. **Lekter'n,** a trendy bar with a floating dining area open only when the weather is warm, has the best harbor view. It serves hamburgers, pizza, and shrimp buckets. Budget eaters can split a 160-kr pizza (all outdoors, Stranden 3, tel. 22 83 76 46). Farther out, **Herbern Marina** is *the* place for shrimp on a balmy evening. In the midst of lots of pleasure boats, couples enjoy the fun, laid-back, dockside ambience, and fill up by splitting a 200-kr liter bucket of shrimp with bread. Request a free peeling lesson; rinse in the finger bowl (pizzas, burgers, and salads from 130 kr; daily 11:00–22:00, Stranden 30, tel. 22 83 19 90).

Rorbua, the "Fisherman's Cabin," is a lively yet cozy eatery tucked into this mostly modern stretch of restaurants. Inside, it's extremely woody with a rustic charm and candlelit picnic tables surrounded by harpoons and old B&W photos. Grab a stool at one of the wooden tables, and choose from a menu of meat-and-potato dishes (100–200 kr) and seafood offerings (150–200 kr). There's a hearty daily special with coffee for 125 kr (daily 12:30–23:00, Stranden 71, tel. 22 83 53 86).

Lofoten Fiskerestaurant serves fish amid a dressy yacht-club atmosphere at the end of the strip. While it's beyond the people-watching action, it's comfortable even in cold and blustery weather because of its heated atrium, which makes a meal here practically outdoor dining. Reservations are a must, especially if you want a harborside window table (lunch-150–225 kr, dinner from 275 kr, open daily, Stranden 75, tel. 22 83 08 08).

Budget Tips: If you're on a budget, get a take-out meal from the fast-food stands and grab a bench along the boardwalk. The **ICA "Gourmet"** grocery store—in the middle of the mall a few steps behind all the fancy restaurants—has salads, warm take-away dishes, and more (turn in about midway down the boardwalk, Mon–Fri 9:00–22:00, Sat 9:00–20:00, closed Sun).

Dining near Frogner Park

Lofotstua Restaurant feels transplanted from the far northern islands it's named for. Kjell Jenssen and his son, Jan Hugo, proudly serve up fish Lofoten-style. Evangelical about fish, they will patiently explain to you the fine differences between all the local varieties, with the help of a photo-filled chart. They serve only the freshest catch, perfectly—if simply—prepared. If you want meat, they've got it—whale or seal (180–250-kr plates, Mon–Fri 15:00–22:00, generally closed in July, 5-min walk from gate of Vigeland statue garden, tram #12, in Majorstuen at Kirkeveien 40, tel. 22 46 93 96). This place is packed daily in winter for their famous lutefisk.

Curry and Ketchup Indian Restaurant is filled with in-the-know locals enjoying tasty and hearty meals for 90 kr. This happening place requires no reservations and feels like an Indian market. If you want a reasonable Indian meal in Oslo, this is hard to beat (daily 14:00–23:00, cash only, a 5-min walk from gate of Vigeland statue garden, tram #12, in Majorstuen at Kirkeveien 51, tel. 22 69 05 22).

Trendy Dining at the Bottom of Grünerløkka

Südøst Restaurant, once a big bank, now fills its vault with wine (which makes sense, given Norwegian alcohol prices). Today it's popular with young Norwegian professionals as a place to see and be seen. It's a fine mix of Norwegian-chic woody ambience inside with a formal and expensive menu, and a big riverside terrace outdoors with a more casual menu. Diners enjoy its open-fire grill, smart service, and modern Continental cuisine (Mon–Sat 11:00–22:00, Sun 12:00–18:00, at bottom of Grünerløkka, tram #17 to Trondheimsveien 5, tel. 23 35 30 70).

Eating Cheap and Spicy in Grønland

The street called Grønland leads through this colorful immigrant neighborhood (a short walk behind the train station or T-bane: Grønland). After the cleanliness and orderliness of the rest of the city, the rough edges and diversity of people here can feel like a breath of fresh air. Whether you eat here or not, the street is fun to explore. In Grønland, backpackers and immigrants munch street food for dinner. Cheap and tasty *börek* (feta, spinach, mushroom) is sold hot and greasy to go for 20 kr.

Punjab Tandoori is friendly and serves hearty meals (lamb and chicken curry, tandoori specials) for 70 kr. They're open late when other places aren't. I like eating outside here with a view of the street scene (daily 11:00–23:00, Grønland 24).

Alibaba Restaurant is clean, inviting, filled with smart locals, and cheap for Turkish food. They have good indoor or outdoor seating (99-kr fixed-price meal Mon-Thu only, open daily 12:30–22:30, corner of Grønlandsleiret and Tøyengata at Tøyengata 2, tel. 22 17 22 22). The 99-kr special is much cheaper than the menu items, but isn't advertised very clearly; you may need to request it.

Asylet is more expensive and feels like it was here long before Norway ever saw a Pakistani. This big, traditional eatery—like a Norwegian beer garden—has a rustic, cozy interior and a gravelly backyard filled with picnic tables (150–170-kr plates and hearty dinner salads, daily 11:00–24:00, Grønland 28, tel. 22 17 09 39).

Dattera Til Hagen feels like a college party. It's a lively scene filling a courtyard with picnic tables and benches under strings of colored lights. Locals like it for the tapas, burgers, and salads (140-kr plates, pricey beers, Grønland 10, tel. 22 17 18 61). After 22:00 it becomes a disco.

Olympen Brown Pub is a dressy dining hall that's a blast from the past. You'll eat in a spacious woody saloon with big dark furniture, faded paintings of circa-1920 Oslo lining the walls, and huge chandeliers. They serve hearty 180-kr plates and offer a huge selection of beers. The grill restaurant upstairs comes with music and can be more fun (daily 11:00–2:00 in the morning, Grønlandsleiret 15, tel. 22 17 28 08).

Café Con Bar is a trendy yuppie eatery on the downtown edge of Grønland. Locals consider it to have the best burgers in town (150 kr). While the tight interior seating is very noisy, the sidewalk tables are great for people-watching (open daily, but only drinks served after 20:00; where Grønland hits Brugata).

Roasted Rudolph
Under a Thatched Roof High on the Mountain

Frognerseteren Hovedrestaurant, nestled high above Oslo (and 1,400 feet above sea level), is a classy, sod-roofed old restaurant. Its terrace, offering a commanding view of the city, is a popular stop for famous apple cake and coffee. The café is casual and less expensive, with indoor and outdoor seating (75-kr sandwiches and cold dishes, 125-kr entrées, daily 11:00–22:00, reservations unnecessary). The elegant view restaurant is pricier (250–300-kr plates, 555-kr three-course meal, Mon–Sat 12:00–22:00, Sun 13:00–21:00, reindeer specials, reserve for evening dining, tel. 22 92 40 40).

You can combine a trip into the forested hills surrounding the city with lunch or dinner and get a chance to see the famous Holmenkollen Ski Jump up close.

Oslo Connections

For train information, call 81 50 08 88 and press 4 for English. For international trains, dial 81 56 81 00. Even if you have a rail-pass, reservations are required for long rides (e.g., a reservation to Stockholm in first class costs 140 kr, second class for 60 kr). First class often comes with a hot meal, fruit bowl, and unlimited juice and coffee.

Be warned that international connections from Oslo are often in flux. Schedules can vary depending on the day of the week, so carefully confirm the specific train you need and purchase any required reservations in advance. Aside from the occasional direct train to Stockholm, most trips from Oslo to Copenhagen or Stockholm require a change in Sweden. From June through August only, direct night trains run from Oslo to Stockholm and to Malmö, Sweden (which is very close to Copenhagen).

From Oslo by Train to Bergen: Oslo and Bergen are linked by a spectacularly scenic train ride (3–5/day, 7 hrs, overnight possible daily except Sat). Many travelers take it as part of the **Norway in a Nutshell** route, which combines train, ferry, and bus travel in an unforgettably beautiful trip. For information on times and prices, see the next chapter.

By Train to: Lillehammer (hourly, 2.5 hrs), **Kristiansand** (4/day, 4.5 hrs), **Copenhagen** (4/day, 8 hrs, transfer at Göteborg and likely Malmö; for night train—which runs June–Aug only—sleep on the direct train to Malmö, Sweden, arrive Malmö Central Station around 6:40, easy transfer to Copenhagen, www.sj.se), **Stockholm** (2/day direct InterCity trains, 6 hrs; 2/day with changes in Karlestad or Katrineholm, 7 hrs; plus a direct 9-hour night train June–Aug only).

By Bus to Stockholm: Taking the bus to Stockholm is cheaper but slower than the train (2/day, 8 hrs, www.swebusexpress.se).

By Car to the Jotunheimen Mountains: See "Route Tips for Drivers".

Overnight Cruise to Copenhagen

Consider connecting Oslo and Copenhagen by cruise ship. The boat leaves daily from Oslo at 17:00 (arrives in Copenhagen at 9:30 the following morning; going the other way, it departs Copenhagen at 17:00 and arrives in Oslo at 9:30; about 16 hours sailing each way). The boat leaves Oslo from the far (non-City Hall) side of the Akershus Fortress peninsula (get there via bus #60 from the train station, 2–3/hr, get off at Vippetangen stop and follow signs to DFDS ticket office). Boarding is from 15:30 to 16:00. From Oslo, you'll sail through the Oslofjord—not as dramatic as Norway's western fjords, but impressive if you're not going to Bergen. On board are three gourmet restaurants, dinner and breakfast buffets, cafés, nightclubs, shops, a sauna, hot tub, and swimming pool. This is fun and convenient, but more expensive and not as swanky as the Stockholm–Helsinki cruise.

You can take this cruise one-way or do a round-trip from either city. Book online or call DFDS Seaways' Norwegian office at 22 41 90 90 (Mon–Fri 8:00–17:00, closed Sat–Sun, www.dfds seaways.com), or in the US, call 800-533-3755 (www.seaeurope .com). Book in advance for the best prices.

NORWAY IN A NUTSHELL

A Scenic Journey to the Sognefjord

While Oslo and Bergen are the big draws for tourists, Norway is first and foremost a place of unforgettable natural beauty. There's a certain mystique about the "land of the midnight sun," but you'll get the most scenic travel thrills per mile, minute, and dollar by going west from Oslo rather than north.

Norway's greatest claims to scenic fame are her deep, lush fjords. Three million years ago, an ice age made this land as inhabitable as the center of Greenland. As the glaciers advanced and cut their way to the sea, they gouged out long grooves—today's fjords.

The entire west coast is slashed by stunning fjords, and the Sognefjord—Norway's longest (120 miles) and deepest (1 mile)—is tops. Anything but the Sognefjord is, at best, foreplay. The seductive Sognefjord has tiny but tough ferries, towering canyons, and isolated farms and villages marinated in the mist of countless waterfalls.

A series of well-organized and spectacular bus, train, and ferry connections—appropriately nicknamed "Norway in a Nutshell"—lays Norway's beautiful fjord country before you on a scenic platter. With the Nutshell, you'll delve into two offshoots of the Sognefjord, which make an upside-down "U" route: the Aurlandsfjord and the Nærøyfjord. You'll link the ferry ride to the rest of Norway with two trains and a bus: The main train is an express route that takes you through stark polar scenery above the tree line. To get from the express train down to the ferry, you'll catch an old-fashioned slow train one way (passing waterfalls and forests) and a bus the other way (offering fjord views and more waterfalls). All connections are designed for tourists, explained in

English, convenient, and easy. At the fjord you'll go through the town of Flåm (a transit hub), stop briefly at the workaday town of Aurland, and pass the hamlet of Undredal (by taking the Nutshell trip segments at your own pace, you can visit the latter two fjord towns on your own; all are described in this chapter).

This region enjoys mild weather for its latitude, thanks to the warm Gulf Stream. (When it rains in Bergen, it just drizzles here.) Recently the popularity of the Nutshell route has skyrocketed. And the 2005 completion of the longest tunnel in the world (15 miles between Flåm and Lærdal) rerouted the main E16 road between Bergen and Oslo through this idyllic fjord corner. All of this means that July and August come with a crush of crowds, dampening some of the area's magic. Unfortunately, many tourists are overcome by Nutshell tunnel-vision, and spend so much energy scurrying between boats, trains, and buses that they forget to simply enjoy the fjords. Relax—you're on vacation.

Planning Your Time

Even the blitz tourist needs a day for the Norway in a Nutshell trip. With more time, sleep in a town along the fjord, and customize your fjord experience to include sights outside the Nutshell.

Day 1: The Nutshell works well as a single day (one-way between Oslo and Bergen in either direction, or as a long day trip from either city). Those with a car and only one day should leave the car in Oslo and do the Nutshell by train, bus, and boat. If you're using public transportation and want to make efficient use of your time, organize your trip so that it ends in Bergen, or return to Oslo on a night train (sleeping through all the scenery you saw westbound).

Day 2: If you have enough time, spend the night somewhere on the Sognefjord—either along the Nutshell route itself (in Flåm or Aurland; accommodations listed later), or in another, even more appealing fjordside town (such as Balestrand or Solvorn, both described in the next chapter).

With More Time: The Sognefjord deserves more than a day. If you can spare the time, venture off the Nutshell route. You can easily connect to some non-Nutshell towns (such as Balestrand) via the handy express boat. Drivers can improve on the Nutshell by taking a northern route: From Oslo, drive through the Gudbrandsdal Valley, go over the Jotunheimen Mountains, then along Lustrafjord to Balestrand; from there, you can cross the Sognefjord on a car ferry (such as Kaupanger–Gudvangen) and drive the Nutshell route on to Bergen. (Most of these sights, and the car ferry connection, are covered in the next two chapters.) For more tips, see the "Beyond the Nutshell" sidebar.

Beyond the Nutshell

The Sognefjord is the ultimate natural thrill Norway has to offer, and there's no doubt that the Nutshell route outlined in this chapter is the most efficient way to see it quickly. Unfortunately, its trains, buses, and boats are thronged with other visitors who have the same idea. Those who stick with the Nutshell crowd enjoy it, but—as they spend the day jostling with a United Nations of tourists for the best photo—can't shake that lemming feeling.

Travelers with a bit more time, and the willingness to chart their own course, often have a more rewarding Sognefjord experience. It's surprisingly easy to break out of the Nutshell and hit the northern part of the Sognefjord (for example, using the Bergen-Vik-Balestrand-Aurland-Flåm express boat).

In the next chapter, you'll find some tempting stopovers on the north bank of the Sognefjord, including adorable fjord-side villages (such as Balestrand and Solvorn), evocative stave churches (including Hopperstad and Urnes), and a chance to get up close to a glacier (at the Nigard Glacier).

Read up on your options, then be adventurous about mixing and matching the fjordside attractions that appeal to you most. Use the Nutshell as a springboard for diving into the Back Door fjords of your travel dreams.

Orientation

The most exciting single-day trip you could make from Oslo or Bergen is this circular train/boat/bus/train jaunt through fjord country. Everybody does this famous trip... and if you're looking for a delicious slice of Norway's scenic grandeur, so should you.

Local TIs (listed throughout this chapter) are well-informed about your options, and they sell tickets for various segments of the trip. At TIs, train stations, and hotels, look for souvenir-worthy brochures with photos, descriptions, and exact times (a sidebar later in this chapter has sample schedules).

Route Overview: The route works round-trip from Oslo or Bergen, or one-way between Oslo and Bergen (going in either direction). The basic idea is this: Take a train halfway across the mountainous spine of Norway, make your way down to the Sognefjord for a boat cruise, then climb back up out of the fjord and get back on the main train

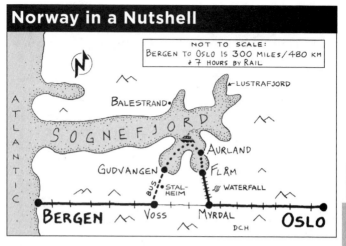

line. Each of these steps is explained in the self-guided tour, below. Transportation along the Nutshell route is carefully coordinated. If any segment of the journey is delayed, your transportation for the next segment will wait (because everyone on board is catching the same connection).

When to Go: The Nutshell trip is possible all year. In the summer (late June–late Aug), the connections are most convenient, the weather is most likely to be good...and the route is at its most crowded. Outside of this time, sights close and schedules become more challenging. Some say the Nutshell is most beautiful in winter, though schedules are severely reduced (and you can't do it as a day trip from Oslo). It's easy to confirm schedules, connections, and prices locally or online (latest info posted each May on www .ruteinfo.net).

Express Boat to Balestrand and Bergen: If you don't want to do the Nutshell Route, take note of this very handy and speedy express boat connecting this area (Aurland and Flåm) with two other worthwhile destinations: Balestrand (on the Sognefjord's northern bank) and Bergen. While this boat misses the best fjord (Nærøyfjord), many travelers use it to craft their own itinerary that escapes the Nutshell rut.

Eating: Options along the route aren't great—on the Nutshell I'd consider food just as a source of nutrition and forget about fine dining. You can buy some food on the fjord cruises (30–60-kr hot dogs, burgers, and pizza) and the Oslo–Bergen train (50–100-kr hot meals, 110-kr daily specials). Depending on the timing of your layovers, Myrdal or Flåm are your best lunch-stop options (both train stations have decent cafeterias, and other eateries surround the Flåm station)—although you won't have a lot of time there if making the journey all in one day. Your best bet is to pack a picnic lunch. While some hotels sell a sack lunch assembled from their breakfast buffet, many will let you snag a sandwich for free if you ask politely. Or you can plan ahead and buy picnic fixings at a grocery store to bring along.

By Yourself or with a Package Deal?

If you have a railpass, or if you're a student or a senior (and therefore eligible for discounts), do the Nutshell on your own. If not, the Fjord Tours packages (described below) will save you time and a bit of money.

On Your Own

To do the Nutshell on your own without a railpass, allow 1,300 kr for a one-way trip between Oslo and Bergen. Doing the Nutshell as a round-trip from Bergen costs only 900 kr, but doesn't include the majestic train ride between Myrdal and Oslo. Likewise, the 2,000-kr round-trip from Oslo doesn't go all the way to Bergen, but does include all the must-sees (the Voss-Bergen stretch is the least-thrilling stretch).

Railpass Discounts: If you have any railpass that includes Norway, the Oslo–Bergen train is covered (except a 50-kr reservation fee for second class; free for first-class passholders) and the Myrdal–Flåm Flåmsbana train is discounted (to 140 kr). You still have to pay full fare for the Gudvangen–Voss bus (86 kr) and the boat cruise (230 kr). Your total one-way cost between Oslo and Bergen: about 450 kr with a first-class pass, 500 kr with a second-class pass.

Buying Tickets: You can get Nutshell train tickets, including the Myrdal–Flåm segment, at the train station in Oslo or Bergen. In summer it's smart to reserve the Oslo–Myrdal segment in advance (see below). Purchase your fjord-cruise ticket on the boat or from the TI in Flåm (or reserve a day ahead in peak season; see below), and buy the tickets for the Gudvangen bus on board from the driver. Always ask about senior and student discounts.

Reservations: At the busiest part of peak season (July–mid-Aug), the Oslo–Bergen train—especially the segment between Oslo and Myrdal—can fill up well in advance: *It's very important to reserve a seat at least a week ahead.* Do it as soon as your itinerary is set: Dial 81 50 08 88 or 23 15 15 15 (from the US: 011-47-81-50-08-88 or 011-47-23-15-15-15), press 4 for English, and book with a credit card. It can be hard to get through—keep trying. Once connected, you can buy a ticket or, if you have a railpass, make a seat reservation. You can also buy tickets—but not make seat reservations—online at www.nsb.no, although some credit cards are only accepted by phone.

It's also wise to reserve ahead for the Flåm–Gudvangen fjord cruise. Although you can't make a reservation for the Myrdal–

Sample Norway in a Nutshell Schedules

Here are several one-day options for doing the Nutshell in the summer (late June–late Aug). Confirm specific times before your trip (www.ruteinfo.net).

Oslo–Bergen: Train departs Oslo-8:11, arrives Myrdal-12:53; Flåmsbana train departs Myrdal-13:02, arrives Flåm-14:00; boat departs Flåm-15:10, arrives Gudvangen-17:00; bus departs Gudvangen upon arrival, arrives Voss-19:05; train departs Voss-19:20, arrives Bergen-20:34. (Several departures allow you to stop over in Voss.)

Bergen-Oslo: Train departs Bergen-8:40, arrives Voss-9:54; bus departs Voss-10:00, arrives Gudvangen-11:10; boat departs Gudvangen-11:30, arrives Flåm-13:40; Flåmsbana train departs Flåm-16:05, arrives Myrdal-17:03; train departs Myrdal-17:52, arrives Oslo-22:32.

Day Trip from Oslo: Train departs Oslo-6:33, arrives Myrdal-11:41; Flåmsbana train departs Myrdal-12:11, arrives Flåm-13:05; boat departs Flåm-13:20, arrives Gudvangen-15:20; bus departs Gudvangen-15:30, arrives Voss-16:50; train departs Voss-17:10, arrives Oslo-22:32.

Day Trip from Bergen: Train departs Bergen-8:40, arrives Voss-9:54; bus departs Voss-10:00, arrives Gudvangen-11:10; boat departs Gudvangen-11:30, arrives Flåm-13:40; Flåmsbana train departs Flåm-14:50, arrives Myrdal-15:47; train departs Myrdal-15:56, arrives Bergen-17:52.

Variations: If you spend a night (or more) on the fjords, you have many options other than the speedy itineraries outlined above. One popular variation is to take the express boat from Bergen to Balestrand for an overnight, then plunge into the Nutshell the next day (or vice versa—do the Nutshell partway, then boat to Bergen).

Flåm train or the Gudvangen–Voss bus, this won't pose a problem for you.

Package Deals

Fjord Tours sells the Nutshell package and other package trips at all Norwegian State Railways stations, including Oslo and Bergen, or through their customer-service line in Norway (tel. 81 56 82 22, www.fjordtours.no). The costs of the Nutshell packages are as follows: one-way from Bergen or Oslo-1,295 kr; round-trip from Oslo via Voss (but not Bergen)-1,800 kr; round-trip from Oslo via Bergen-2,055 kr; round-trip from Bergen via Myrdal (but not Oslo)-935 kr. They also sell a "Sognefjord in a Nutshell" tour, which takes an express boat from Bergen to Flåm, then picks up the Nutshell route from there (round-trip back to Bergen-1,115 kr; one-way to Oslo-1,470 kr). Note that the trip only goes once daily in winter (Oct–April).

Self-Guided Tour

▲▲▲Norway in a Nutshell

If you only have one day for this region, it'll be a thrilling day. The following segments of the Nutshell route are narrated from Oslo to Bergen. If you're going the other way, hold the book upside down.

▲▲Oslo–Bergen Train

This is simply the most spectacular train ride in northern Europe. The scenery crescendos as you climb over Norway's mountainous spine. After a mild three hours of deep woods and lakes, you're into the barren, windswept heaths and glaciers. These tracks were begun in 1894 to link Stockholm and Bergen, but Norway won its independence from Sweden in 1905, so the line served to link the two main cities in the new country—Oslo and Bergen. The entire railway, an amazing engineering feat completed in 1909, is 300 miles long; peaks at 4,266 feet, which, at this Alaskan latitude, is far above the tree line; goes under 18 miles of snow sheds; trundles over 300 bridges; and passes through 200 tunnels in just under seven hours.

Here's what you'll see traveling westward from Oslo: Leaving Oslo, you pass through a six-mile-long tunnel and stop in Drammen, Norway's fifth-largest town. The scenery stays low-key and woodsy up Hallingdal Valley until you reach Geilo, a popular ski resort. Then you enter a land of big views and tough little cabins. Finse, at about 4,000 feet, is the highest stop on the line. From here, you enter the longest high-mountain stretch of railway in Europe. Much of the line is protected by snow tunnels. The scenery gets more dramatic as you approach Myrdal (MEER-doll). Just before Myrdal, look to the right and down into the Flåm Valley (Flåmsdalen), where the branch line winds its way down to the fjord. Nutshell travelers get off at Myrdal.

Cost: Note that the Nutshell route includes only part of this train ride (as a day trip from Oslo, for instance, you take the Oslo–Myrdal and Voss–Oslo segments). Here are the one-way fares for various segments: Oslo–Bergen-788 kr, Oslo–Myrdal-637 kr, Myrdal–Voss-105 kr, Myrdal–Bergen-250 kr, Voss–Bergen-170 kr.

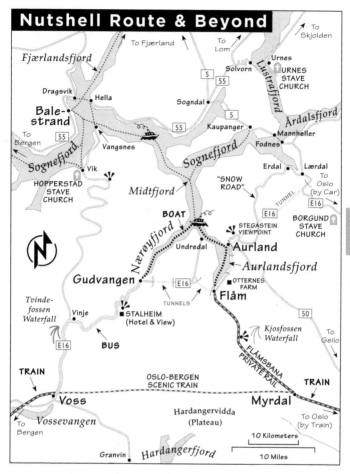

Remember, second-class railpass-holders pay just 50 kr to reserve, and first-class passholders pay nothing. Anyone can pay 90 kr extra to upgrade to "Komfort" class, with more legroom, reclining seats, free coffee and tea, and an electrical socket for your laptop (reserve ahead or ask the conductor when you board).

Schedule: This train runs three to five times per day (overnight possible daily except Sat). The segment from Oslo to Myrdal takes 4.75–5.5 hrs; going all the way to Bergen takes 7–7.5 hours.

Reservations: In peak season, remember to get reservations for this train at least a week in advance.

▲▲Myrdal–Flåm Train (Flåmsbana)

The little 12-mile spur line leaves the Oslo–Bergen line at Myrdal (2,800 feet), which is nothing but a scenic high-altitude train

junction with a decent cafeteria. From Myrdal, the
train winds down to Flåm
(sea level) through 20 tunnels
(more than three miles' worth)
in 55 thrilling minutes. It's
party time on board, and the
engineer even stops the train
for photos at the best waterfall, Kjosfossen. According to
a Norwegian legend, a tempt-

ress lives behind these falls and tries to lure men to the rocks with
her singing...look out for her.

The train line is an even more impressive feat of engineering
when you realize it's not a cogwheel train—it's held to the tracks
only by steel wheels, though it does have five separate braking
systems. Before boarding, pick up the free, multilingual souvenir
pamphlet with lots of info on the trip (or see www.flaamsbana.no).

Cost: 230 kr one-way (or 140-kr supplement for railpass-
holders), 330 kr round-trip (280 kr with a railpass). You can buy
tickets at the ticket desk in the Flåmsbana stations in Myrdal or
Flåm, at local TIs, or—if you're in a rush to make a tight connection—buy them on board.

Schedule: The train departs in each direction nearly hourly.

Reservations: Reservations are not possible—you can buy
your ticket ahead (at any train station in Norway), but that won't
guarantee you a seat on a particular train. (Ticket-sellers assure me
it's exceedingly rare not to get on the train you want.)

▲▲▲Flåm–Gudvangen Fjord Cruise

The Flåmsbana train deposits you at **Flåm,** a scenic, functional

transit hub at the far end of
the Aurlandsfjord. If you're
doing the Nutshell route
nonstop, follow the crowds
and hop on the sightsee-
ing boat that'll take you to
Gudvangen (listen for the
train conductor to announce
which pier number to go

to). With minimal English narration, the boat takes you close to
the goats, sheep, waterfalls, and awesome cliffs.

You'll cruise up the lovely **Aurlandsfjord,** stop at the town
of **Aurland** (a good home base), pass **Undredal,** and hang a left at
the stunning **Nærøyfjord** ("Narrow Fjord"). The cruise ends at the
apex of the Nærøyfjord, in **Gudvangen.**

The Facts on Fjords

The process that created the majestic Sognefjord began during an ice age about three million years ago. A glacier up to 6,500 feet thick slid downhill at an inch an hour, following a former river valley on its way to the sea. Rocks embedded in the glacier gouged out a steep, U-shaped valley, displacing enough rock material to form a mountain 13 miles high. When the climate warmed up, the ice age came to an end. The melting glaciers retreated and the sea level rose nearly 300 feet, flooding the valley now known as the Sognefjord. The fjord is more than a mile deep, flanked by 3,000-foot mountains—for a total relief of 9,300 feet. Waterfalls spill down the cliffs, fed by runoff from today's glaciers. Powdery sediment tinges the fjords a cloudy green, the distinct color of glacier melt.

Why are there fjords on the west coast of Norway, but not, for instance, on the east coast of Sweden? The creation

of a fjord requires a setting of coastal mountains, a good source of moisture, and a climate cold enough for glaciers to form and advance. Due to the earth's rotation, the prevailing winds in higher latitudes blow from west to east, so chances of glaciation are ideal where there is an ocean to the west of land with coastal mountains. When the winds blow east over the water, they pick up a lot of moisture, then bump up against the coastal mountain range, and dump their moisture in the form of snow—which feeds the glaciers that carve valleys down to the sea.

You can find fjords along the northwest coast of Europe—including western Norway and Sweden, Denmark's Faroe Islands, Scotland's Shetland Islands, Iceland, and Greenland; the northwest coast of North America (from Puget Sound in Washington state north to Alaska); the southwest coast of South America (Chile); the west coast of New Zealand's South Island; and on the continent of Antarctica.

As you travel through Scandinavia, bear in mind that, while we English-speakers use the word "fjord" to mean only glacier-cut inlets, Scandinavians often use it in a more general sense to include bays, lakes, and lagoons that weren't formed by glacial action.

The trip is breathtaking in any weather. For the last hour, as you sail down the Nærøyfjord, camera-clicking tourists scurry around the drool-stained deck like nervous roosters, scratching fitfully for a photo that will catch the magic. Waterfalls turn the black cliffs into bridal veils, and you can nearly reach out and touch the cliffs of the Nærøyfjord. It's the world's narrowest fjord: six miles long and as little as 820 feet wide and 40 feet deep. On a sunny day, the ride is one of those fine times—like when you're high on the tip of an Alp—when a warm camaraderie spontaneously combusts between the strangers who've come together for the experience.

Cost: For the whole route (Flåm–Gudvangen), you'll pay 245 kr one-way (123 kr for students with ISIC cards, 340 kr round-trip). Taking the boat for just the 20-min hop between Flåm and Aurland costs 78 kr (more than twice as expensive and twice as slow as the bus). There are no railpass discounts.

Schedule: From late June through late August, boats leave Flåm daily at 9:00, 11:00, 13:20, and 15:10; and leave Gudvangen daily at 10:30, 11:30, 13:20, and 16:00. But note that frequency drops off-season (3/day early June and late Aug–mid-Sept; 2/day May and late Sept; only 1/day Oct–April).

Reservations: It's possible to reserve, but only necessary in the very peak of the season (July–mid-Aug), when the boats can occasionally fill up. To reserve, email fylkesbaatane@fjord1.no or call 55 90 70 70 by 14:00 one business day before.

Other Ways to Cruise Nærøyfjord: While most visitors thunder onto the state-run ferry described above, consider taking a round-trip on a Sognefjorden Cruise ship, or a thrilling ride on little inflatable FjordSafari speedboats (both described later, under "Sights near Flåm"; see page 83).

▲Gudvangen–Voss Bus

Gudvangen is little more than a boat dock and giant tourist kiosk. Nutshellers get off the boat at Gudvangen and take the one-hour bus to Voss (buses meet each ferry—but confirm this in advance if you plan to take the last boat of the day, which arrives in Gudvangen at about 20:00—the ferry crew can call ahead to be sure the bus waits for you). Most buses take the extra-scenic route via Stalheim (described below).

First the bus takes you up the **Nærøydal.** After crossing a river, the bus climbs up a corkscrew series of switchbacks flanked by a pair of dramatic waterfalls. At the top of this road, most buses

NORWAY IN A NUTSHELL

stop at the landmark **Stalheim Hotel** for a last grand view back into fjord country. Though this hotel dates from 1885, there's been an inn here since about 1700, where the royal mailmen would change horses. The hotel is geared for tour groups (genuine trolls sew the pewter buttons on the sweaters), but the priceless view from the backyard is free. Stop in the living room to survey the art showing this perch in the 19th century.

The bus rejoins the main road and heads through pastoral countryside to Voss. Just before Voss, look to the right for the wide and tumbling **Tvindefossen waterfall.** Drivers will find the grassy meadow and flat rocks at its base ideal for letting the mist fog their glasses and enjoying a drink or snack (be discreet, as "picnics are forbidden").

Cost: 76 kr, pay on board, no railpass discounts.

Reservations: Not possible or necessary.

Voss

The Nutshell bus from Gudvangen drops you at the Voss train station, which is on the Oslo–Bergen train line. Drivers should zip right through, and Nutshellers should catch the next train out. A plain town in a lovely lake-and-mountain setting, Voss lacks the striking fjordside scenery of Flåm, Aurland, or Undredal, and is basically a home base for summer or winter sports (Norway's Winter Olympics teams often practice here).

Voss has a **TI** (June–Aug Mon–Fri 8:00–19:00, Sat 9:00–19:00, Sun 12:00–19:00; Sept–May Mon–Fri 8:30–15:30, closed Sat–Sun; in the center of town at Uttrågata 9, tel. 56 52 08 00), a 13th-century church, and little else. Fans of American football will want to see the humble monument to player and coach Knute Rockne, who was born in Voss in 1888; look for the metal memorial plaque on a rock near the train station. Two miles outside town, the Mølstertunet Folk Museum has 16 buildings showing off farm life in the 17th and 18th centuries (50 kr; mid-May–mid-Sept daily 10:00–17:00; mid-Sept–mid-May Mon–Fri 10:00–15:00, Sun 12:00–15:00, closed Sat; Mølstervegen 143, tel. 56 51 15 11).

▲Voss-Bergen Train

The least exciting segment of the trip—but still pleasantly scenic—this train chugs along the valley between the midsize town of Voss (described above) and Bergen. For the best scenery, sit on the right side of the train if coming from Oslo/Voss, or the left side if coming from Bergen. Between Voss and Dale, you'll pass several scenic lakes; near Bergen, you'll go along the Veafjord.

Cost: The train costs 170 kr between Voss and Bergen and is fully covered by railpasses that include Norway.

Schedule and Reservations: Unlike the long-distance Oslo–Bergen journey, this line is also served by more frequent commuter trains (about hourly, 1–1.25 hrs), and reservations aren't necessary.

Voss-Oslo Train: Note that if you're doing the Nutshell round-trip from Oslo, you can catch the train from Voss (rather than Bergen) back to Oslo. The trip takes 5.5–6 hours and costs 683 kr; reservations are strongly recommended in peak season.

Flåm

Flåm (sometimes spelled Flaam, pronounced "flome")—where the boat and Flåmsbana train meet, at the head of the Aurlandsfjord—feels more like a transit junction than a village. But its striking setting, easy transportation connections, and touristy bustle make it appealing as a home base for exploring the nearby area.

Orientation to Flåm

Most of Flåm's services are inside the train station, including the TI (see below), train ticket desk, several Internet terminals, post office, public WC, cafeteria, and souvenir shops hawking over-priced reindeer pelts (cheaper in Bergen). Just outside the station, the little red shed at the head of the tracks serves as a left-luggage desk (25 kr, daily 8:00–19:45, on your right as you depart the train, ring bell if nobody's there), and displays a chart of the services you'll find in the station. The boat dock for fjord cruises is just beyond the end of the tracks. Surrounding the station are a grocery store (Mon–Thu 9:00–17:00, Fri 9:00–18:00, Sat 9:00–15:00, closed Sun) and a smattering of hotels, hostels, travel agencies, and touristy restaurants. Aside from a few scattered farmhouses and some homes lining the road, there's not much of a town here. (The old town center—where tourists rarely venture, and which you'll pass on the Flåm–Myrdal train—is a few miles up the river, in the valley.)

Tourist Information

At the TI inside the train station, you can purchase your boat tickets and load up on handy brochures (daily May–Sept 8:30–16:00, June–Aug also 16:30–20:00, closed Oct–April, tel. 57 63 21 06, www.visitflam.com or www.alr.no, very helpful Vladimir).

Answers to most of your questions can be found on the walls and at the counter here. Bus schedules, boat and train timetables, maps, and more are photocopied and available for your convenience (and the staff's).

Sights near Flåm

Flåm's village activities are all on the pier. There's a free historic train museum next to track 1, a fjord "panorama" movie (50 kr, 23 min), and the Aegir Bryggeri, a micro-brewery offering tastes of its five beers (65 kr) in a great woody brew-pub setting. But the main reason people come to Flåm is to leave it. If you want to linger, consider renting a rowboat or kayak to go out on the usually calm, peaceful waters of the fjord. You can paddle near the walls of the fjord and really get a sense of the immensity of these mountains.

Because Aurland and Flåm are close together (10 minutes away by car or bus, or 20 minutes by boat), I've also listed attractions "Near Aurland," below.

▲▲▲Cruising Nærøyfjord

The most scenic fjord I've seen anywhere in Norway is about an hour from Flåm (basically the last half of the 2-hour Flåm–Gudvangen trip). There are several ways to cruise it: You can take the state-run ferry, described above as part of the Norway in a Nutshell trip (4-hour round-trips departing Flåm at 9:00, 11:00, and 13:20, 340 kr; these also stop in Aurland, and the cruise ends in Gudvangen). Two other Flåm-based options follow:

Sognefjorden Cruise—This private company runs round-trip cruises—from Flåm to Gudvangen and back to Flåm—daily from mid-June through August (330 kr, 660 kr for family of four, 10:00–13:00 or 13:15–16:30 with a 45-min stop in Undredal, tel. 57 66 00 55).

▲▲FjordSafari to Nærøyfjord—FjordSafari takes little groups out onto the fjord in small, open Zodiac-type boats with an English-speaking guide. Participants wear full-body weather suits, furry hats, and spacey goggles (making everyone on the boat look like crash-test dummies). As the boat rockets across the water, you'll be thankful for the gear, no matter what the weather. You'll get the same scant information and stops as on the slow ferry, except that Safari boats stop right under a towering rock cliff—a magnificent experience. Their two-hour Flåm–Gudvangen–Flåm tour focuses on the Nærøyfjord, and gets you all the fjord magnificence you can imagine (500 kr). Their three-hour tour (640 kr) is the same as the two-hour tour, except that it includes a stop in Undredal, where you can see goat cheese being made and wander that sleepy village. They run several departures daily from June through August (fewer off-season, kids get discounts, tel. 99 09 08 60, www.fjordsafari.no, Johanna). They also offer a 90-minute "mini" tour that costs 430 kr and misses the Nærøyfjord...so what's the point?

▲Flåm Valley Bike Ride or Hike

For the best single-day, non-fjord activity from Flåm, take the train to Myrdal, then hike or mountain-bike along the road (part gravel but mostly paved) back down to Flåm (2–3 hours by bike, gorgeous waterfalls, great mountain scenery, and a cute church with an evocative graveyard, but no fjord views). The Flåm TI rents mountain bikes (50 kr/hr, 250 kr/day) as does the youth hostel (50 kr/hr, 200 kr/day). It costs 80 kr to take a bike to Myrdal on the train. You can hike just the best two hours from Myrdal to Berekvam, where you can catch the train into the valley. Pick up the helpful map with this and other hiking options (easy to strenuous) at the Flåm TI.

▲▲Otternes Farms

This humble but magical cluster of four centuries-old farms, realistically accessible only to drivers, is perched high on a ridge, up a twisty gravel road midway between Flåm and Aurland. Laila Kvellestad runs this low-key sight, valiantly working to save and share traditional life as it was back when butter was the farmers' gold. (That was before emigration decimated the workforce, coinage replaced barter, and industrialized margarine became more popular than butter, leaving farmers to eke  out a living relying only on their goats and the cheese they produce.) Until 1919 the only road between Aurland and Flåm passed between this huddle of 27 buildings, high above the fjord. First settled in 1522, farmers lived here until the 1990s. Laila gives 45-minute English tours through several time-warp houses and barns at 10:00, 12:00, 14:00, and 16:00 (50 kr, June–Sept daily 10:00–17:00, tel. 57 63 11 32, www.otternes.no). It's wise to call first to confirm tour times and that it's open. For 170 kr, Laila serves a traditional lunch with your tour (sour-cream porridge, dried meat, dessert, and a drink).

Over (or Under) the Mountains, to Lærdal and Borgund

To reach these sights, you'll first head along the fjord to Aurland. Of the sights below, the Lærdal Tunnel, Stegastein viewpoint, and

Aurlandsvegen "Snow Road" are best for drivers. The Borgund Stave Church can be reached by car, or by bus from Flåm or Aurland.

For more specifics on driving through the Lærdal Tunnel or on the Aurlandsvegen "Snow Road," see below.

Lærdal Tunnel

Drivers find that this tunnel makes connecting Flåm and Lærdal a snap. It's the world's longest road-vehicle tunnel, stretching 15 miles between Aurland and Lærdal as part of the E16 highway. It also makes the wonderful Borgund Stave Church (described below) less than an hour's drive from Aurland. The downside to the tunnel is that it goes beneath my favorite scenic drive in Norway (the Aurlandsvegen "Snow Road," described next). But with a little more than an hour, you can drive through the tunnel to Lærdal and then return via the "Snow Road," with the Stegastein viewpoint as a finale, before dropping back into Aurland.

▲▲Stegastein Viewpoint and Aurlandsvegen "Snow Road"

With a car and clear weather, consider twisting up the mountain

behind Aurland on route 243 for about 20 minutes for a fine view over the Aurlandsfjord. A new viewpoint called Stegastein—which looks like a giant, wooden, inverted number "7"—provides a platform from which you can enjoy stunning views across the fjords. Immediately beyond the viewpoint, you leave the fjord views and enter the mountaintop world of the Aurlandsvegen "Snow Road." When you finally hit civilization on the other side, you're a mile from the Lærdal tunnel entrance and about 30 minutes from the fine Borgund Stave Church.

▲▲Borgund Stave Church

About 16 miles east of Lærdal, in the village of Borgund, is Norway's most-visited and one of its best-preserved stave churches. Borgund's church comes with one of Norway's best stave-church history museums, which beautifully explains these icons of medieval Norway. Dating from around 1180, the interior features only a few later

additions, including a 16th-century pulpit, 17th-century stone altar, painted decorations, and crossbeam reinforcements.

The oldest and most authentic item in the church is the stone baptismal font. In medieval times, priests conducting baptisms would go outside to shoo away the evil spirits from an infant before bringing it inside the church for the ritual. (If infants died before being baptized, they couldn't be buried in the churchyard, so parents would put them in little coffins and hide them under the church's floorboards to get them as close as possible to God.)

Explore the dimly lit interior, illuminated only by the original, small, circular windows up high. Notice the X-shaped crosses of St. Andrew (the church's patron), carvings of dragons, and medieval runes.

Cost and Hours: 70 kr, buy tickets in museum across street, daily mid-June–mid-Aug 8:00–20:00, May–mid-June and mid-Aug–Sept 10:00–17:00, closed Oct–April. The museum has a shop and a fine little cafeteria serving filling and tasty lunches (70 kr soup with bread, tel. 57 66 81 09).

Getting There: It's about a 30-minute **drive** east of Lærdal, on E16 (the road to Oslo—if coming from Aurland or Flåm, consider taking the scenic route via the Stegastein viewpoint, described above). There's also a convenient **bus** connection: The bus departs Flåm and Aurland around midday and heads for the church, with a return bus departing Borgund in mid-afternoon (240 kr, get ticket from driver, about 1 hour each way, about 2 hours at the church, bus runs daily May–Sept).

Sleeping and Eating in Flåm

My recommended accommodations are away from the tacky train-station bustle, but a close enough walk to be convenient. The first two places are located along the waterfront a quarter-mile from the station: Walk around the little harbor (with the water on your left) for about 10 minutes. It's more enjoyable to follow the level, gravel waterfront path than to hike up the main road.

Dining options beyond your hotel's dining room or kitchenette are sparse. The cafeteria section of Furukroa Restaurant in the station complex has reasonably priced food.

$$$ Flåm Marina and Apartments, perched right on the fjord, is ideal for families and longer stays. They offer 10 new-feeling, self-catering apartments that sleep 2–4 people each. All units offer views of the fjord with a balcony, kitchenette, and small dining area (Db-1,095 kr June–late Sept, less off-season, 300 kr more for each additional adult, 150 kr more for each additional child, save 150 kr/person by using your own sheets, check online or ask about specials for longer stays, no breakfast, boat rental,

> # Sleep Code
>
> **(6 kr = about $1, country code: 47)**
> **S** = Single, **D** = Double/Twin, **T** = Triple, **Q** = Quad, **b** = bathroom,
> **s** = shower. All of these places accept credit cards.
>   To help you sort easily through these listings, I've divided
> the rooms into three categories, based on the price for a
> standard double room with bath:
>
>   **$$$ Higher Priced**—Most rooms 1,000 kr or more.
>   **$$ Moderately Priced**—Most rooms 600–1,000 kr.
>   **$ Lower Priced**—Most rooms 600 kr or less.
>
> Note that the season is boom or bust here. It can be dead in
> June and packed in July and August.

laundry facilities, next to the guest harbor just below Heimly
Pensjonat—see next, tel. 57 63 35 55, fax 57 63 35 44, www.flam
marina.no, booking@flammarina.no).

$$ Heimly Pensjonat, with 23 straightforward rooms, is
clean, efficient, and the best small hotel in town. Sit on the porch
with new friends and watch the clouds roll down the fjord (Sb-895
kr, Db-995 kr, view Db costs 100 kr more in summer, extra bed-
325 kr for adult or 225 kr for child, includes breakfast, cheaper
Oct–May, Db rooms are mostly twins, try to reserve a room with a
view at the standard price, bike and car rental, tel. 57 63 23 00, fax
57 63 23 40, www.heimly.no, post@heimly.no). The budget annex
out back has more rooms that share bathrooms (D-470 kr, sheets
and towels-90 kr/person, breakfast-95 kr).

$–$$ Flåm Youth Hostel and Camping Bungalows,
voted Scandinavia's most beautiful campground, is run by the
friendly Haland family, who rent the cheapest beds in the area
(hostel: bunk in 4-bed room-190 kr, S-330 kr, D-470–570 kr;
newer, fancier building: bunk in 4-bed room-265 kr, Db-755;
4-bed cabins-600–930 kr; for all beds: sheets-65 kr, towels-15
kr, showers-10 kr, 15 percent discount for members, no meals but
kitchen access, laundry, apple grove, tel. 57 63 21 21, www.flaam
-camping.no, camping@flaam-camping.no). It's a five-minute walk
toward the valley from the train station: Cross the bridge and turn
left up the main road; then look for the hostel on the right.

Aurland

A few miles north of Flåm, Aurland is more of a real town and less of a tourist depot. While it's nothing exciting (Balestrand is more lively and appealing, and Solvorn is cuter—see next chapter), it's a good, easygoing fjordside home base. And thanks to its location—on the main road and boat lines, near Flåm—it's relatively handy for those taking public transportation.

Getting There: Aurland is an easy 10-minute drive or bus trip from Flåm. If you want to stay overnight in Aurland, note that every train (except the late-night one) arriving in Flåm connects with a bus or boat to Aurland. Eleven buses and at least four ferries link the towns daily in summer (bus-30 kr, 10 min; boat-79 kr, 20 min). The Flåm–Gudvangen boat stops at Aurland en route, so it's possible to continue the Nutshell route from Aurland without backtracking to Flåm. Boat tickets bought at the Aurland TI come with a reservation (helpful on the busiest days in July and August, when the boats can fill up in Flåm). The Bergen–Balestrand–Flåm express boat stops in Aurland.

Orientation to Aurland

From Aurland's dingy boat dock area, walk one block up the paved street into the heart of town. On your right is the Spar supermarket (handy for picnic supplies) and Aurlandskafeen, the best restaurant in town (at the bridge). To your left is the Vangsgården Guest House and, behind it, Aurland Fjordhotel. To reach the TI, go straight ahead and bear right, then look behind the white church (800 years old and worth a peek). The bus stop, with buses to Flåm, is in front of the TI.

Tourist Information

The TI stocks English-language brochures about hikes and day trips from the area, offers Internet terminals, and hosts a small history exhibit (mid-June–Aug Mon–Fri 9:00–18:00, Sat 10:00–17:00, closed Sun; Sept–mid-June Mon–Fri 8:30–15:30, closed Sat–Sun; behind the white church—look for green-and-white *i* sign; tel. 57 63 33 13, www.alr.no).

Sleeping in Aurland

$$$ Aurland Fjordhotel is big, modern, and centrally located. While a bit faded, many of its 30 rooms come with gorgeous fjord-view balconies (Sb-945 kr, Db-1,190 kr, Tb-1,290, check website for deals, includes breakfast, free Wi-Fi, tel. 57 63 35 05, fax 57

63 36 22, www.aurland-fjordhotel.com, post@aurland-fjordhotel .com, Steinar and Dorte Kjerstein).

$$ Vangsgården Guest House, closest to the boat landing, is a complex of old buildings dominating the old center of Aurland and run from one reception desk (tel. 57 63 35 80, www.vangs gaarden.no, vangsgaarden@alb.no, open all year, Astrid). The main building is a simple, old guest house offering basic rooms, a large self-serve kitchen, and a fine old-timey living room (Sb-550 kr, Db-875 kr). Their old-fashioned **Aabelheim Pension** is Aurland's best *koselig* (cozy)-like-a-farmhouse place (same prices). And lining the waterfront are their six adorable, woody cabins, each with a kitchen, bathroom, and two bedrooms (2–6 people, 1,075 kr, sheets-60 kr/person). The optional 75-kr breakfast is served in a wonderfully traditional dining room. The owners also run the Duehuset Pub (see "Eating in Aurland," below).

Near Aurland

$$ Skahjem Gard is an active farm run by Aurland's former deputy mayor, Nils Tore, and his wife Dagrun. They've converted their old sheep barn into seven spick-and-span family apartments with private bathrooms and kitchenettes, each sleeping up to four people (600 kr for studio, 700 kr with separate bedroom; rustic, cozy fishing cottage with a separate bathroom-450 kr; sheets and towels-70 kr/person, two miles up the valley—road #50, follow *Hol* signs, tel. 57 63 33 29, mobile 95 17 25 67, www.skahjemgard .com, nskahjem@online.no). It's a 25-minute walk from town, but Nils will pick up and drop off travelers at the ferry. This is best for families and foursomes with cars.

$ Winjum Huts, 500 yards toward the "Snow Road" from Aurland, rents 14 very basic cabins on a peaceful perch overlooking the majestic fjord (300–400 kr for up to 4 people, sheets-50 kr/ person, no food available—just beer, tel. 57 63 34 61).

Eating in Aurland

Aurlandskafeen is a basic little café/diner serving the best-value food in town from its inviting cafeteria line. It's a block from the main square, at the bridge over the river. Sit upstairs or on its river- side terrace (90-kr daily plates, open daily 10:00–19:00—provided there are customers, tel. 57 63 36 66).

Duehuset Pub ("The Dove's House"), run by Vangsgården Guest House, serves up decent food in the center of town (190–240- kr pizzas big enough for four, 155–240-kr main dishes; June–Sept daily 15:00–23:00; Oct–May Fri–Sun 18:00–23:00, closed Mon– Thu). For cheap eats on dockside benches, gather a picnic at **Spar supermarket** (Mon–Fri 9:00–20:00, Sat 9:00–18:00, closed Sun).

Undredal

This almost impossibly remote community is home to about 75 people (and 400 goats). A huge percentage of the town's former population (300 people) emigrated to the US between 1850 and 1925. Undredal was accessible only by boat until 1988, when the road from Flåm opened. There's not much in the town, which is famous for its church and its goat cheese, but I'll never forget the picnic I had on the ferry wharf. While appealing, Undredal is quiet (some say better from the boat) and difficult to reach—you'll have to be patient to connect to other towns. For more information on the town, see www.undredal.no.

Undredal has Norway's smallest still-used **church,** seating 40 people for services every fourth Sunday. The original church was built in 1147 (look for the four original stave pillars inside). It was later expanded, pews added, and the interior painted in the 16th century in a way that resembles the traditional Norwegian *rosemaling* style (which came later). You can get in only with an overpriced 15-minute tour (60 kr, mid-June–mid-Aug daily 9:30–18:30, less in shoulder season, closed Oct–April).

Undredal's farms exist for cheese. The beloved local cheese comes in two versions: brown and white. The brown version is unaged and slightly sweet, while the white cheese has been aged and is mild and a bit salty. For samples, visit the Undredalsbui grocery store at the harbor (Mon–Fri 9:00–17:00, Sat 9:00–15:00, Sun 12:00–16:00).

The 15-minute drive from Flåm is mostly through a new tunnel. By sea, you'll sail past Undredal on the Flåm–Gudvangen boat (you can request a stop). To get the ferry to pick you up in Undredal, turn on the blinking light (though some express boats will not stop).

This sleepy town can accommodate about eight visitors a night. **$$ Undredal Overnatting** rents four modern, woody, comfortable rooms. The reception is at the café on the harbor, while the rooms are at the top of town (Db-700 kr, sheets-50 kr/person, tel. 57 63 30 80 or 57 63 31 00, visit@undredal.no).

MORE ON THE SOGNEFJORD

Balestrand • The Lustrafjord • Scenic Drives

Norway's world of fjords is decorated with medieval stave churches, fishing boats, cascading waterfalls, dramatic glaciers, and brightly painted shiplap villages. Travelers in a hurry zip through the fjords on the Norway in a Nutshell route (see previous chapter). Their heads spin from all the scenery, and most wish they had more time on the Sognefjord. If you can linger in fjord country, this chapter is for you.

Snuggle into the fjordside village of Balestrand, which has a variety of walking and biking options and a fun local arts scene. Balestrand is also a handy jumping-off spot for adventures great and small, including a day trip up the Fjærlandsfjord to gaze at a receding tongue of the Jostedal Glacier, or across the Sognefjord to the truly medieval-feeling Hopperstad Stave Church. Farther east is the Lustrafjord, a tranquil branch of the Sognefjord offering drivers an appealing concentration of visit-worthy sights. On the Lustrafjord, you'll enjoy enchanting hamlets with pristine fjord views (such as Solvorn), historic churches (including Norway's oldest stave church at Urnes and the humble village Dale Church in Luster), an opportunity to touch and even hike on a glacier (the Nigard), and more stunning fjord views.

This region is important to the people of Norway. After four centuries under Danish rule, the soul of the country was nearly lost. With independence and a constitution in the early 1800s, the country experienced a resurgence of national pride. Urban Norwegians headed for the fjord country here in the west. Norway's first Romantic painters and writers were drawn to Balestrand, inspired by the unusual light and dramatic views of mountains plunging

MORE ON THE SOGNEFJORD

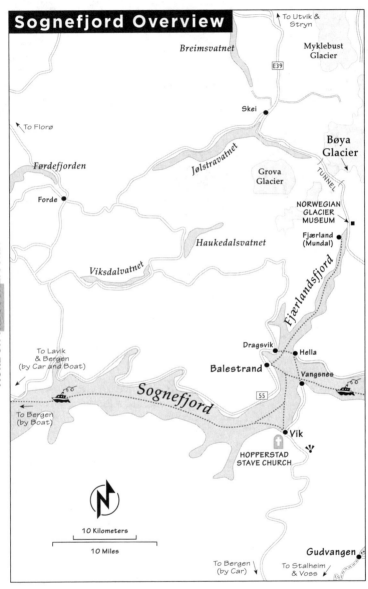

Sognefjord Overview

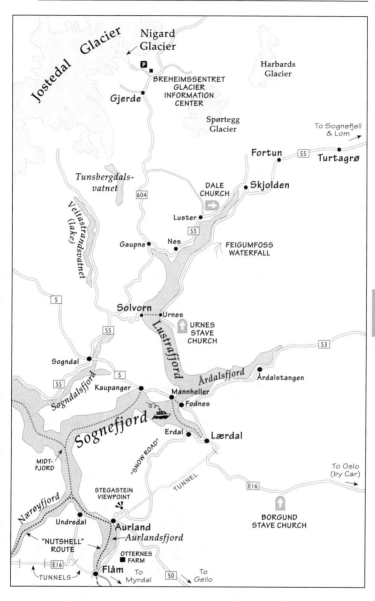

into the fjords. The Sognefjord, with its many branches, is featured in more Romantic paintings than any other fjord.

Planning Your Time

If you can spare a day or two off the Norway in a Nutshell route, spend it here. Balestrand is the best home base, especially if you're

relying on public transportation (it's well-connected by express boat both to the Nutshell scene and to Bergen). If you have a car, consider staying in the heart of the Lustrafjord region in sweet little Solvorn (easy ferry connection to the Urnes Stave Church and a short drive to the Nigard Glacier). As fjord home bases go, Balestrand and Solvorn are both better—but less convenient—than Flåm or Aurland on the Nutshell route (see previous chapter).

With one night in this area, you'll have to blitz the sights on the way between destinations; with two nights, you can slow your pace (and your pulse) to enjoy the fjord scenery and plenty of day-trip possibilities.

Balestrand

The pleasant fjord town of Balestrand (pop. 2,000) has a long history of hosting tourists, thanks to its landmark Kviknes Hotel.

But it also feels real and lived-in, making Balestrand a nice mix of cuteness and convenience. The town is near, but not *too* near, the Nutshell bustle across the fjord— and yet it's an easy express-boat trip away if you'd like to dive into the Nuttiness. In short, consider Balestrand a worthwhile detour

from the typical fjord visit—allowing you to dig deeper into the Sognefjord, just like the glaciers did during the last ice age.

With two nights, you can relax and consider some day trips: Cruise up the nearby Fjærlandsfjord for a peek at a distant tongue of the ever less-mighty Jostedal Glacier, or head across the Sognefjord to the beautiful Hopperstad Stave Church in Vik. Balestrand also has outdoor activities for everyone, from dreamy fjordside strolls and strenuous mountain hikes to wildly scenic bike

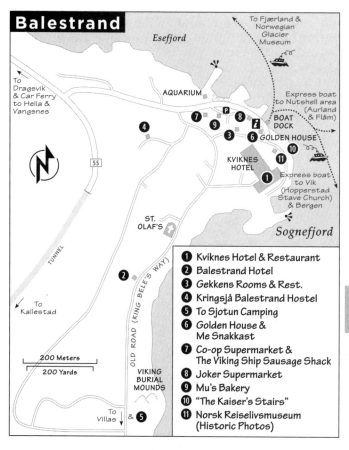

Balestrand

Esefjord

To Fjærland &
Norwegian
Glacier
Museum

To
Dragsvik
& Car Ferry
to Hella &
Vangsnes

AQUARIUM

Express boat
to Nutshell area
(Aurland
& Flåm)

P

BOAT
DOCK

GOLDEN HOUSE

KVIKNES
HOTEL

Express boat
to Vik
(Hopperstad
Stave Church)
& Bergen

Sognefjord

ST.
OLAF'S

TUNNEL

To
Kallestad

OLD ROAD (KING BELE'S WAY)

200 Meters

200 Yards

VIKING
BURIAL
MOUNDS

To
Villas

➊ Kviknes Hotel & Restaurant
➋ Balestrand Hotel
➌ Gekkens Rooms & Rest.
➍ Kringsjå Balestrand Hostel
➎ To Sjøtun Camping
➏ Golden House &
   Me Snakkast
➐ Co-op Supermarket &
   The Viking Ship Sausage Shack
➑ Joker Supermarket
➒ Mu's Bakery
➓ "The Kaiser's Stairs"
⓫ Norsk Reiselivsmuseum
   (Historic Photos)

MORE ON THE SOGNEFJORD

rides. For dinner, splurge on the memorable *smörgåsbord*-style *store koldt bord* dinner in the Kviknes Hotel dining room, then sip coffee from its balcony as you watch the sun set (or not) over the fjord.

Planning Your Time

Balestrand's key advantage is its easy express-boat connection to Bergen, offering an alternative route to the fjord from the typical Nutshell train-bus combo. Consider zipping here on the Bergen boat, then continuing on via the Nutshell route.

One night is enough to get a taste of Balestrand. But two nights buy you some time for day trips. Note that the first flurry of day trips depart early, around 7:30–8:05 (includes the boat to Vik/Hopperstad Stave Church, the full-day Fjærlandsfjord glacier excursion, and the Glacier Bus connection to Nigard Glacier), and the next batch departs around noon (the half-day Fjærlandsfjord glacier excursion and the boat to Flåm). If you wait until after 12:00 to make your choice, you'll miss the boat... literally.

Balestrand pretty much shuts down from September through May—when most of the activities, sights, hotels, and restaurants listed here are likely closed.

Orientation to Balestrand

Most travelers arrive in Balestrand on the express boat from Bergen or Flåm. The tidy harbor area has a TI, two grocery stores, a couple of galleries, a town history museum, and a small aquarium devoted to marine life found in the fjord. The historic wooden Kviknes Hotel and its ugly modern annex dominate Balestrand's waterfront.

Even during tourist season, Balestrand is quiet. How quiet? The police station closes on weekends. And it's tiny—from the harbor to the Balestrand Hotel is a five-minute stroll, and you can walk from the aquarium to the Kviknes Hotel in less than that.

Balestrand became accessible to the wider world in 1858 when an activist minister (from the church you see across the fjord from town) brought in the first steamer service. That put Balestrand on the Grand Tour map of the Romantic Age. Even the German Kaiser chose to summer here. Today, people from around the world come here to feel the grandeur of the fjord country and connect with the essence of Norway.

Tourist Information

At the TI, located next to the Joker supermarket at the harbor, pick up the free, helpful *Outdoor Activities in Balestrand* brochure. If you're planning on a longer hike, consider buying the good 70-kr hiking map. The TI has numerous brochures about the Sognefjord area and detailed information on the more challenging hikes. It offers terminals with Internet access (1 kr/min) and free Wi-Fi, rents bikes (40 kr/hr, 200 kr/day), sells day-trip excursions to the glacier, and more (late June–late Aug Mon–Sat 7:30–18:00, Sun 10:00–17:30, shorter hours in spring and fall, closed Oct–April, tel. 57 69 12 55—answered all year).

Local Guide: Bjørg Bjøberg, who runs the Golden House art gallery, knows the town well and is happy to show visitors around (500 kr/2 hours, tel. 91 56 28 42).

Sights in Balestrand

Balestrand Harborfront Stroll—The tiny harbor stretches from the aquarium to the big, old Kviknes Hotel. Stroll its length, starting at the aquarium (described later) and little marina. Across the street, at The Viking Ship shack, a German woman named Carola sells German sausages with an evangelical zeal (see "Eating in Balestrand," later). Next door, the Spindelvev ("Spider's Web") shop sells handicrafts made by people with physical and mental disabilities. A local home for the disabled was closed in the 1980s, but many of its former residents stayed in Balestrand because the government gave them pensions and houses in town.

Then, in the ugly modern strip mall, you'll find the TI, supermarket, and a community bulletin board with the schedule for the summer cinema (the little theater, 800 yards away, runs films nightly in their original language). On the corner is the Golden House art gallery and museum (described later). Just beyond that is the dock where the big Bergen-Sognefjord express catamaran ties up.

Across the street is a cute white house (at #8), which used to stand at the harborfront until the big Joker supermarket and Kviknes Hotel, with its modern annex, partnered to ruin the town center. This little house was considered historic enough to be airlifted 100 yards to this new spot. It's flanked by two other historic buildings, housing a gallery and an artisans' workshop.

Farther along, find the rust-red building that was the waiting room for the 19th-century steamer that first brought tourism to town. Today it houses the Norsk Reiselivsmuseum (Norwegian Travel Museum). It's filled with historic photos, described in English, that show this part of Norway over the last 150 years (free and open daily).

Walk a few steps farther, and stop at the tall stone monument erected to celebrate the North Bergen Steamship Company. Its boats first connected Balestrand to the rest of the world in 1858. In front of the monument, some nondescript concrete steps lead into the water. These are "The Kaiser's Stairs," built for the German emperor, Kaiser Wilhelm II, who made his first summer visit (complete with navy convoy) in 1899 and kept returning until the outbreak of World War I.

Behind the monument stands one of the largest old wooden buildings in Norway, the Kviknes Hotel. It was built in the 1870s and faces the rare little island in the fjord, which helped give the town its name: "Balestrand" means the strand or promenade in front of an island. (The island is now connected to the hotel's front yard and is part of a playground for its guests.) Hike up the black driveway that leads from the monument to the hotel's modern lobby. Go inside and find (to your left) the plush old lounge, a virtual painting gallery. All the pieces are by artists from this area, celebrating the natural wonder of the fjord country—part of the trend that helped 19th-century Norway reconnect with its heritage. (While you're here, consider making a reservation and choosing a table for a *smörgåsbord* dinner tonight.) Leave the hotel lobby (from the door opposite to the one you entered), and head up to St. Olaf's Church (300 yards, described next). To continue this stroll, take King Bele's Way (described later) up the fjord.

St. Olaf's Church—This distinctive wooden church was built in 1897. Construction was started by Margaret Sophia Kvikne, the wife of Knut Kvikne (of the Kviknes Hotel family; her portrait is in the rear of the nave), but she died in 1894, before the church was finished. This devout Englishwoman wanted a church in Balestrand where English services were held...and to this day, bells ring to announce services by British clergy (free, open daily, services in English every Sun late May–Aug). St. Olaf, who brought Christianity to Norway in the 11th century, was the country's patron saint in Catholic times. The church was built in a "Neo-stave" style, with lots of light from its windows and an altar painting inspired by the famous *Risen Christ* statue in Copenhagen's Cathedral of Our Lady. Here, Christ is flanked by fields of daisies (called "Priests' Collars" in Norwegian) and peace lilies. From the door of the church, enjoy a good view of the island in the fjord.

Golden House (Det Gylne Hus)—This golden-colored house facing the ferry landing was built as a general store in 1928. Today it houses an art gallery and a quirky museum created by local watercolorist and historian Bjørg Bjøberg, and her Scottish husband, Arthur Adamson.

On the ground floor, you'll find Bjørg's gallery, with her watercolors celebrating the beauty of Norway, and Arthur's paintings, celebrating the beauty of women. Upstairs is a free exhibit of historical knickknacks, contributed by locals wanting to preserve treasures from their own families' past. You'll see a medicine cabinet stocked with old-fashioned pills, an antiquated tourist map, lots of skis, and WWII-era mementos. A wheel in the wall once powered a crane that could winch up goods from the fjord below (before today's embankment was built, when this store was right on the waterfront). While there are no written English explanations, Bjørg is happy to explain things (free, May–Aug daily 10:00–22:00, shorter hours late April and Sept, tel. 91 56 28 42).

Unable to contain her creative spirit, Bjørg has put together an eccentric wonderland experience with her private tour of the Golden House's hidden rooms, which includes a 30-minute movie merging her art and local nature (50 kr/person, 100-kr minimum, 200-kr maximum, one hour). Bjørg and Arthur also run the recommended on-site café, Me Snakkast.

Strolling King Bele's Way up the Fjord—For a delightful walk (or bike ride), head west out of town up the "old road"—once the

main road from the harbor—for about a mile. It follows the fjord's edge, passing numerous "villas" from the late 1800s. At the time, this Swiss style was popular with some locals, who hoped to introduce a dose of Romanticism into Norwegian architecture. Look for the dragons' heads (copied from Viking-age stave churches) decorating the gables. Along the walk, you'll pass a swimming area, a campground, and two burial mounds from the Viking age, marked by a ponderous statue of the Viking King Bele. Check out the wooden shelters for the mailboxes; some give the elevation (*m.o.h.* stands for "meters over *havet*"—the sea)—not too high, are they? The walk is described in the *Outdoor Activities in Balestrand* brochure (free at the TI or your hotel).

Aquarium—The tiny aquarium gives you a good look at marine life in the Sognefjord. For descriptions, borrow the English booklet at the front desk. While not thrilling, the well-explained place is a decent rainy-day option. A 15-minute slide show starts at the top and bottom of each hour. The last room is filled with wood carvings depicting traditional everyday life in the fjordside village of Munken (70 kr, June–Aug daily 9:30–17:00, closed Sept–May, tel. 57 69 13 03). The fish-filled tanks on the dock outside are also worth a look.

Biking—You can cycle around town, or go farther by circling the scenic Esefjord (north of town, en route to the ferry landing at Dragsvik—about 6 miles each way). Or pedal scenically west up Sognefjord along King Bele's Way (described above). The roads here are relatively flat. Rental bikes are available at the TI.

Kayaking—A local outfit offers three-hour tours (450 kr, daily at 10:00 and 15:00, see TI for details).

Near Balestrand

These two side-trips are possible only if you've got the better part of a day in Balestrand. With a car, you can see Hopperstad Stave Church on the drive to Bergen.

▲▲Hopperstad Stave Church (Hopperstad Stavkyrkje) in Vik

The most accessible stave church in the area—and perhaps the most scenically situated in all Norway—is located just a 15-minute  express-boat ride across the Sognefjord, in the town of Vik. Hopperstad Stave Church boasts a breathtaking exterior, with several tiers of dragon heads overlooking rolling fields between fjord cliffs. The interior is notable for its emptiness. Instead of being crammed full of later additions, the church is blissfully uncluttered, as it was when built in the mid-12th century.

Cost and Hours: 50 kr, good 30-kr color booklet in English, daily mid-June–mid-Aug 9:00–19:00, May–mid-June and mid-Aug–Sept 10:00–17:00, tel. 57 69 52 70.

Tours: The attendant will give you a free tour at your request, provided she's not too busy. (Ask where the medieval graffiti is, and she'll grab her flashlight and show you.)

Location: The church is a 20-minute walk up the valley from Vik's harbor. From the boat landing, walk up the main street from the harbor about 200 yards (past the TI, a grocery store, and hotel). Take a right at the sign for *Hopperstad Stavkyrkje*, walk 10 minutes, and you'll see the church perched on a small hill in the distance.

Getting There: Pedestrians can ride the express passenger boat between Balestrand and Vik (68 kr each way, 15 min). The only way to get to the church and back in one day (only possible Mon–Sat) is to take the 7:50 departure from Balestrand, then return on the 11:30 departure from Vik, arriving back in Balestrand at 11:50—just in time to join a 12:00 glacier excursion (described below). Since cars can't go on this express boat, **drivers** must go around the small Esefjord to the town of Dragsvik, then catch the ferry across the Sognefjord to Vangsnes (a 20-min drive from Vik and the church).

◑ Self-Guided Tour: Originally built around 1140 and retaining most of its original wood, Hopperstad was thoroughly restored and taken back to basics in the 1880s by renowned architect Peter Blix. Unlike the famous stave church at Urnes (described later), whose interior has been re-jiggered by centuries of engineers and filled with altars and pews, the Hopperstad church looks close to the way it did when it was built. You'll see only a few non-original features, including the beautifully painted canopy that once covered a side altar (probably dating from around 1300), and a tombstone from 1738. There are only a few colorful illustrations and some very scant medieval "graffiti" carvings and runic inscriptions. Notice the intact chancel screen (the only one surviving in Norway), which separates the altar area from the congregation. As with the iconostasis (panel of icons) in today's Orthodox faith, this screen gave priests privacy to do the spiritual heavy lifting. Because Hopperstad's interior lacks the typical adornments, you can really grasp the fundamentally vertical nature of stave church architecture, leading your gaze to the heavens. Follow that impulse and look up to appreciate the Viking-ship rafters. Imagine the comfort this ceiling brought the church's original parishioners, whose seafaring ancestors had sought refuge under overturned boats. For a unique angle on this graceful structure, lay your camera on the floor and shoot the ceiling.

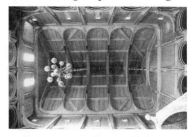

▲Excursion to Fjærland and the Jostedal Glacier

From Balestrand, cruise up the Fjærlandsfjord to visit the Norwegian Glacier Museum in Fjærland and to see a receding tongue of the Jostedal Glacier (Jostedalbreen). Half-day (524 kr) and full-day (570 kr) excursions are sold by Balestrand's TI or on board the boat. Reservations are smart (daily May–Sept only, www.fjord1.no, fylkesbaatane@fjord1.no).

While the museum and the glacier's tongue are underwhelming, it's a pleasant excursion with a dreamy fjord cruise (80 min each way). The full-day trip is essentially the same price as the half-day version. To take the all-day trip, catch the 8:05 ferry; for the shorter trip, hop on the noon boat. They both return on the same boat, getting you back in Balestrand at 16:55 (in time to catch the fast boat back to Bergen). Both tours offer the same fjord ride, museum visit, and trip to the glacier. The all-day version, however, gives you a second glacier viewing point and 2.5 hours to hang out in the town of Fjærland. (This sleepy village, famous for its secondhand book shops, is about as exciting as Walter Mondale, the vice president whose ancestors came from here.)

The ferry ride (no stops, no narration) is just a scenic 80-minute glide with the gulls. Bring a picnic, as there's almost no food sold on board, and some bread to toss to the gulls (they do acrobatics to catch whatever you loft into the air). You'll be met at the ferry dock (labeled *Mundal*) by a bus—and your guide, who reads a script about the glacier as you drive up the valley for about 15 minutes. You'll stop for an hour at the **Norwegian Glacier Museum** (Norsk Bremuseum). After watching an 18-minute aerial tour of the dramatic Jostedal Glacier in the theater, you'll learn how glaciers were formed, experiment with your own hunk of glacier, weigh evidence of the woolly mammoth's existence in Norway, and learn about the effect of global climate change on the fjords (way overpriced at 110 kr, included in excursion price, daily June–Aug 9:00–19:00, April–May and Sept–Oct 10:00–16:00, tel. 57 69 32 88, www.bre.museum.no). From the museum, the bus runs you up to a café near a lake, at a spot that gives you a good look at the Boyabreen, a tongue of the Jostedal Glacier. Marvel at how far the glacier has retreated—10 years ago, the visit was more dramatic. With global warming, glacier excursions like this become more sad than majestic. I wonder how long they'll even be able to bill this as a "glacier visit."

Considering that the fjord trip is the highlight of this journey, you could save time and money by just riding the ferry up and back (8:05–11:30). At 310 kr for the round-trip boat ride, it's much cheaper than the 524-kr tour.

Note that if you're into glaciers, a nearby arm of the Jostedal, called the **Nigard Glacier,** is a more dramatic and boots-on experience. It's easy for drivers. Non-drivers can catch the Glacier Bus in Sogndal for an all-day visit by public transportation. From Balestrand, the bus to Sogndal (to meet up with the Glacier Bus) departs Mon–Fri in July–Aug at 7:30, and returns at 20:00 (no bus connection Sat–Sun or Sept–June).

Sleeping in Balestrand

$$$ **Kviknes Hotel** is the classy grande dame of Balestrand, dominating the town and packed with tour groups. The picturesque wooden hotel—and five generations of the Kvikne family—have welcomed tourists to Balestrand since the late 19th century. The hotel has two parts: a new wing, and the historic wooden section, with 17 older, classic rooms, and no elevator. All rooms come  with balconies. The elegant Old World public spaces in the old section make you want to just sit there and sip tea all afternoon (Db-1,700 kr in new building or 2,040 kr in old building, about 400 kr more with view; includes breakfast, mostly non-smoking, free Wi-Fi, family rooms available, closed Oct–April, tel. 57 69 42 00, fax 57 69 42 01, www.kviknes.no, booking@kviknes.no). Part of the Kviknes ritual is gorging on the *store koldt bord* buffet

Sleep Code

(6 kr = about $1, country code: 47)

S = Single, **D** = Double/Twin, **T** = Triple, **Q** = Quad, **b** = bathroom, **s** = shower. Unless otherwise noted, these accommodations accept credit cards.

To help you sort easily through these listings, I've divided the rooms into three categories, based on the price for a standard double room with bath:

$$$ Higher Priced—Most rooms 1,000 kr or more.
$$ Moderately Priced—Most rooms between 500–1,000 kr.
$ Lower Priced—Most rooms 500 kr or less.

dinner—open to non-guests, and a nice way to soak in the hotel's old-time elegance without splurging on an overnight (see "Eating in Balestrand," below; cheaper if you stay at the hotel for 2 or more nights).

$$ Balestrand Hotel, family-run by Unni-Marie Kvikne, her California-born husband Eric Palmer, and their three children, is your best fjordside home. Open late May through early September, this cozy, welcoming place has 30 well-appointed, comfortable, quiet rooms; a large, modern common area with lots of English paperbacks; laundry service, free Wi-Fi, balconies (in some rooms), and outdoor benches for soaking in the scenery. They also have a waterfront yard with inviting lounge chairs and a mesmerizing view. When reserving, let them know your arrival time, and they'll pick you up at the harborfront (non-view Sb-670 kr, view Sb-770 kr, non-view Db-990 kr, view Db-1,190 kr, includes breakfast, 5-min walk from dock, past St. Olaf's Church—or free pick-up, tel. 57 69 11 38, www.balestrand.com, info@balestrand.com).

$$ At Gekken's Rooms, Geir rents four homey rooms above his restaurant in the town center (D-550 kr, small D-450 kr, extra bed-150 kr, shared kitchen and WC, open June–Aug only, tel. 57 69 14 14, mobile 97 51 29 26, baleson2004@yahoo.com).

$–$$ Kringsjå Balestrand Hostel, a camp school for sixth-graders, rents beds and rooms to budget travelers from mid-June to mid-August. Half of their 58 beds are in doubles. All the four-bed rooms have private bathrooms and view balconies (bunk in 4-bed dorm-260 kr, Sb-510 kr, Db-790 kr, extra bed-120 kr, includes breakfast, discount for hostel members, sheets/towels-50 kr/person, free Wi-Fi, tel. 57 69 13 03, www.kringsja.no, kringsja @kringsja.no).

$ Sjotun Camping rents the cheapest beds around, in rustic huts (4-person hut-250 kr, no linen, a mile west of town, tel. 57 69 12 23, www.sjotun.com).

Eating in Balestrand

Balestrand's dining options are limited, but good.

Kviknes Hotel offers a splendid, spendy *store koldt bord* buffet dinner in a massive yet stately old dining room. For a memorable fjordside *smörgåsbord* experience, it doesn't get any better than this. Don't rush. Consider taking a preview tour—surveying the reindeer meat, lingonberries, and fjord-caught seafood—before you dive in, so you can budget your stomach space. Get a new plate with each course and save room for dessert. Each dish is labeled in English (500 kr/person, May–Sept daily 19:00–21:00, closed Oct–April). After dinner, head into the rich lounge to pick up your cup of coffee or tea (included), which you'll sip sitting on classy old-fashioned furniture and basking in fjord views.

Me Snakkast ("Let's Talk"), inside the Golden House at the harbor, dishes up Norwegian home cooking and a variety of salads. Sit outside—or indoors, in a dining area built to resemble a traditional Norwegian kitchen. The restaurant upstairs shows off part of owner Bjørg's antique collection. They serve 30–100-kr light meals—sandwiches, soups, cakes, and more—throughout the day, and pricier meals after 15:00, such as 120–220-kr meat and fish dishes (May–Sept daily 9:30–21:30, closed off-season, tel. 91 56 28 42).

Gekkens is an informal summer restaurant serving good-value meat, fish, and vegetarian dishes, along with burgers, fish-and-chips, and other fried fare. Sit in the simply decorated interior, or out on the shaded little terrace. Geir Arne "Gekken" Bale can trace his family's roots back 400 years in Balestrand. He has filled his walls with fascinating historic photos and paintings, making his dining hall an art gallery of sorts (light dishes-60–100 kr, daily dinner plates-100–140 kr, June–Aug daily 12:00–22:00, closed Sept–May, above and behind the TI from the harbor, tel. 57 69 14 14).

The Viking Ship, the hot-dog stand facing the harbor, is proudly run by Carola. A bratwurst missionary from Germany, she claims it took her years to get Norwegians to accept the tastier

Express Boat Between
Bergen and the Sognefjord

The made-for-tourists express boat, called Fylkesbaatane, makes it a snap to connect Bergen with Balestrand and other Sognefjord towns (for foot passengers only—no cars). In summer, the boat goes twice each day in both directions, linking up Bergen, Vik, Balestrand, Aurland, and Flåm. You can also use this boat to connect towns on the Sognefjord, such as zipping from quiet Balestrand to busy Flåm, in the heart of the Nutshell action (reservations are smart—email fylkesbaatane@fjord1.no or call 55 90 70 70, discounts for students and seniors, tickets also sold on boat and at TI, www.fjord1.no).

Between Bergen and the Sognefjord: The boat trip between Bergen and **Balestrand** takes four hours (470 kr,

departs Bergen May–Sept daily at 8:00, also Mon–Fri at 16:30, Sat at 14:15, some Sun at 16:30—but not mid-June-late Aug; Oct–April Mon–Fri at 8:00, Sun–Fri at 16:30, Sat at 14:15; departs Balestrand May–Sept daily at 16:55, Mon–Sat also at 7:50, some Sun at 11:30—but not mid-June-late Aug; Oct–April Mon–Sat at 7:50, Sun at 15:55). In summer, the 8:00 boat from Bergen continues to **Flåm** (645 kr). If you're traveling with two or more people, you'll save about 25 percent.

Between Flåm and Balestrand: Going by boat between Flåm and Balestrand takes about 1.5 hours (220 kr, departs Flåm May–Sept daily at 15:30, stops at Aurland, arrives in Balestrand at 16:55; second boat sometimes runs from Flåm Mon–Fri at 6:00, arrives Balestrand at 8:00; departs Balestrand daily at 11:50 arriving Flåm at 13:25; a different boat departs Balestrand Mon–Fri at 8:30 in July–early Aug; no express boats between Flåm and Balestrand Oct–April).

From Oslo to Balestrand via the Nutshell: This variation on the standard Norway in a Nutshell route is called "Sognefjord in a Nutshell" (Oslo-Myrdal-Flåm-Balestrand-Bergen). From **Oslo,** you can take an early train to Flåm (no later than the 8:11 train as part of the Norway in a Nutshell route—see previous chapter), then catch the 15:30 express boat to Balestrand. After your visit, you can continue on the express boat to Bergen, or return to the Nutshell route by taking the express boat to Midtfjord, and transferring to the next boat to Gudvangen (June–Aug only, otherwise transfer in Flåm).

bratwurst over their beloved *pølser* weenies. Eat at her picnic tables or across the street on the harbor park (fine sausages, fish-and-chips, May–Sept daily 11:00–20:00, closed Oct–April).

Picnic: The delightful waterfront park next to the aquarium has benches and million-dollar fjord views. The Co-op and Joker **supermarkets** at the harbor have basic grocery supplies, including bread, meats, cheeses, and drinks. Co-op is bigger and has a wider selection (both open Mon–Fri 9:00–18:00, Sat 9:00–15:00, closed Sun). **Mu's Bakery** heats up baked goodies trucked here all the way from Germany (Mon–Sat 9:30–18:00, Sun 9:30–15:00, closed mid-Sept–early May, between Co-op and Joker supermarkets).

Balestrand Connections

Because Balestrand is separated from the Lustrafjord by the long Fjærlandsfjord, most Balestrand connections involve a boat trip.

From Balestrand by Express Passenger Boat

The easiest way to reach Balestrand is on the handy express boat, which connects to **Bergen, Vik** (near Hopperstad Stave Church), **Aurland,** and **Flåm** (see sidebar on previous page for schedules). Note that you can also use this boat to join the Nutshell trip mid-fjord (transferring at Midtfjord—literally from boat to boat, in the middle of the fjord—to the Kaupanger–Gudvangen ferry; possible only June–Aug). From here, continue on the Nutshell boat down the Nærøyfjord to Gudvangen, where you'll join the crowd onward to Voss, then Bergen or Oslo. As you're making schedule and sightseeing decisions, consider that the Balestrand–Flåm boat skips the Nærøyfjord, the most dramatic arm of the Sognefjord.

From Balestrand by Car Ferry

Balestrand's main car-ferry dock is at the village of **Dragsvik,** a six-mile, 15-minute drive around the adorable little Eselfjord. From Dragsvik, a car ferry makes the short crossing east to **Hella** (a 30-min drive from Sogndal and the Lustrafjord), then crosses the Sognefjord south to **Vangsnes** (a 20-min drive to Hopperstad Stave Church and onward to Bergen). The ferry goes at least once per hour (2/hr in peak times, fewer boats Sun, 74 kr for car and driver).

Note that you can also drive through Sogndal to catch the **Kaupanger–Gudvangen** or **Mannheller–Fodnes** ferries (described under "Lustrafjord Connections," near the end of this chapter).

The Lustrafjord

This arm of the Sognefjord is rugged country—only 2 percent of the land is fit to build or farm on. The Lustrafjord is ringed with

tiny villages where farmers sell cherries and giant raspberries. A few interesting attractions lie along the Lustrafjord: the village Dale Church at Luster; the impressive Nigard Glacier (a 45-minute drive up a valley); the postcard-pretty village of Solvorn; and, across the fjord, Norway's oldest stave church at Urnes. While a bit trickier to explore by public transportation, this beautiful region is easy by car, but still feels remote. There are no ATMs between Lom and Gaupne—that's how remote this region is.

Suggested Route for Drivers

The Lustrafjord can be seen either coming from the north (over the Sognefjell pass from the Jotunheimen region—see next chapter) or from the south (from Balestrand or the Norway in a Nutshell route—see previous chapter). Note that public buses between Lom and Sogndal follow this same route (see "Lustrafjord Connections," later).

Here's what you'll see if you're driving from the north (if you're coming from the south, read this section backwards): Descending from Sognefjell, you'll hit the fjord at the village of Skjolden (decent TI in big community center, tel. 97 60 04 43). Follow Route 55 along the west bank of the fjord. In the town of Luster, consider visiting the beautifully decorated Dale Church (described next). Farther along, near the hamlet of Nes, you'll have views across the fjord of the towering Feigumfoss waterfall. Drops and dribbles come from miles around for this 650-foot tumble. Soon Route 55 veers along an inlet to the town of Gaupne, where you can choose to detour about an hour to the Nigard Glacier (up Route 604; described under "Sights on the Lustrafjord," next). After Gaupne, Route 55 enters a tunnel and cuts inland, emerging at a long, fjord-like lake at the town of Hafslo. Just beyond is the turnoff for Solvorn, a fine home-base town with the ferry across to Urnes and its stave church (Solvorn and Urnes Stave Church both described under "Sights on the Lustrafjord," next). Route 55 continues to Sogndal, where you can choose to turn off for the Kaupanger and Mannheller ferries across the Sognefjord, or continue on Route 55 to Hella and the boat across to either

Dragsvik (near Balestrand) or Vangsnes (across the Sognefjord, near Vik and Hopperstad Stave Church).

Route Timings: If you're approaching from Lom in the Gudbrandsdal Valley, figure about 1.5 hours over Sognefjell to the start of the Lustrafjord at Skjolden, then another 30 minutes to Gaupne (with the optional glacier detour: 2 hours to see it, 4 hours to hike on it). From Gaupne, figure 30 minutes to Solvorn or 40 minutes to Sogndal. Solvorn to Sogndal is about 30 minutes. Sogndal to Hella, and its boat to Balestrand, takes about 40 minutes. These estimated times are conservative, but they don't include photo stops.

Sights on the Lustrafjord

These attractions are listed as you'll reach them driving from north to south along the fjordside Route 55. If you're sleeping in this area, you could visit all four sights in a single day (but it'd be a busy, somewhat rushed day). If you're passing through, Dale Church and Solvorn are easy, but the other two involve major detours—choose one or skip them both.

▲Dale Church (Dale Kyrkje) in Luster

The namesake town of Luster, on the west bank of the Lustrafjord, boasts a unique 13th-century Gothic church. In a land of wooden stave churches, this stone church, with its richly decorated interior, is worth a quick stop as you pass through town (free entry but donation requested, good posted English info inside, 5-kr English brochure, open daily 10:00–20:00 but often closed for services and off-season, just off the main road—look for red steeple, WC in

graveyard, fresh goodies at bakery across the street).

The soapstone core of the church dates from about 1250, but the wooden bell tower and entry porch were likely built around 1600. As you enter, on the left you'll see a tall, elevated platform with seating, surrounded by a wooden grill. Nicknamed a "birdcage" for the feathery fashions worn by the ladies of the time, this high-profile pew—three steps higher than the pulpit—was built in the late-17th century by a wealthy parishioner. The beautifully painted pulpit, decorated with faded images of the four evangelists, dates from the 13th century. In the chancel (altar area), restorers have uncovered frescoes from three different time periods: the 14th, 16th, and 17th centuries. Most of the ones you see here were likely created around the year 1500. The crucifix high over the pews, carved around 1200, predates the church, as does the old bench (with lots of runic carvings)—making them more than eight centuries old.

▲▲Jostedal's Nigard Glacier

The Nigard Glacier (Nigardsbreen) is the most accessible branch of mainland Europe's largest glacier (the Jostedalsbreen, 185 square

miles). Hiking to or on this glacier offers Norway's best easy opportunity for a hands-on glacier experience. It's a 45-minute detour from the Lustrafjord up Jostedal Valley. Visiting a glacier is a quintessential Norwegian experience, bringing you face-to-face with the majesty of nature. If you can spare the time, it's worth the detour (even if you don't do a guided hike). But if glaciers don't give you tingles and you're feeling pressed, skip it.

Getting There: It's straightforward for **drivers.** When the main Route 55 along the Lustrafjord reaches Gaupne, turn onto Route 604, which you'll follow for 25 miles up the Jostedal Valley to the Breheimsenteret glacier information center. Access to the glacier itself is down the toll road past the information center (all described below).

In July and August, a **Glacier Bus** connects the Nigard Glacier to various home-base towns around the region (leaves Sogndal at 8:45, passes through Solvorn en route, arrives at the glacier around 10:30; departs glacier at 17:00, arrives back in Sogndal around 18:40; buses or boats from other towns—including Balestrand, Flåm, and Aurland—coordinate to meet this bus in Sogndal; combo-tickets include various glacier visits and hikes; no bus Sept–June; for complete timetable, see www.jostedal.com). While handy, the bus is designed for those spending the entire day at the glacier.

Breheimsenteret Glacier Information Center—This national park center, in a starkly modern building, stands at the entrance to the Nigard Glacier valley. The center has WCs, a gift shop, a cafeteria, free Wi-Fi, and a modest but pricey museum (50 kr). You'll watch a relaxing 20-minute film showing highlights of the glacier and region, then tour a gallery of glacier-related exhibits that use models and illustrations to explain these giant, slow-moving walls of ice. Even if you're not interested in the museum, drop by here to confirm your glacier plans—likely with Peter, who runs the place (daily mid-June–mid-Aug 9:00–19:00, May–mid-June and mid-Aug–Sept 10:00–17:00, closed Oct–April, tel. 57 68 32 50, www .jostedal.com).

Visiting the Glacier—The best quick visit is to walk to, but not on, the glacier. (If you want to walk *on* it, see "Hikes on the Glacier," next.) From the information center, a 25-kr toll road continues two miles to a lake facing the actual tongue of the glacier. About 75 years ago, the glacier reached all the way to today's parking lot. (It's named for the ninth farm—*ni gard*—where it finally stopped, after crushing eight farms higher up the valley.) From the lot, you can hike all the way to the edge of today's glacier (about 45 min each way); or, to save about 20 minutes of walking, take a special boat to a spot that's a 20-minute hike from the glacier (15 kr each way, 10-min boat trip, 4/hr, mid-June–mid-Sept 10:00–18:00).

The walk is uneven but well-marked—follow the red *T*'s and take your time. You'll hike on stone polished smooth by the glacier, and scramble over and around boulders big and small that were deposited by it. The path takes you right up to the face of the Nigardsbreen. Respect the glacier. It's a powerful river of ice, and fatal accidents do happen. If you want to walk on the glacier, read the next listing first.

Hikes on the Glacier—If you want to actually walk on top of the glacier, don't attempt it by yourself. The Breheimsenteret glacier information center offers guided family-friendly walks that include about one hour on the ice (200 kr, 100 kr for kids, minimum age 5, I'd rate the walks PG-13 myself, about 4/day, generally between 11:30–15:00, no need to reserve— just call glacier center to find out time and show up). Leave the

information center one hour before your tour, then meet the group on the ice, where you'll pay and receive your clamp-on crampons. One hour roped up with your group gives you the essential experience. You'll find yourself marveling at how well your strap-on crampons work on the 5,000-year-old-ice. Even if it's hot, wear long pants, a jacket, and your sturdiest shoes. (Think ahead. It's awkward to empty your bladder after you're roped up.)

Longer, more challenging, and much more expensive hikes get you higher views, more exercise, and real crampons (starting at 410 kr, includes boots, June–Aug daily at 11:45 and 12:45, additional departure in July and Aug at 14:30, 4 hours including 2 hours on the ice, book by phone the day before—tel. 57 68 32 50, arrive at the information center 30 min early to pay for tickets and pick up your gear). If you're adventurous, ask about even longer hikes and glacier kayaking. While it's legal to go on the glacier on your own, it's dangerous and crazy to do so without crampons.

▲▲Solvorn

On the west bank of the Lustrafjord, 10 miles northeast of Sogndal, idyllic Solvorn is a sleepy little Victorian town with colorful wooden sheds lining its waterfront. My favorite town on the
Lustrafjord is tidy and quaint,
well away from the bustle of
the Nutshell action. Its tiny
ferry crosses the fjord regularly
to Urnes and its famous stave
church (see below). While

not worth going far out of your way for, Solvorn is a mellow and surprisingly appealing place to kill some time waiting for the ferry...or just munching a picnic while looking across the fjord. A pensive stroll or photo shoot through the village's back lanes is a joy (look for plaques that explain historic buildings in English). Best of all, Solvorn also has a pair of excellent accommodations: a splurge (Hotel Walaker) and a budget place (Eplet Bed & Apple), described later under "Sleeping on the Lustrafjord."

Getting There: Solvorn is a steep five-minute **drive** down a switchback road from the main Route 55. The main road into town leads right to the Urnes ferry (see below) and dead-ends into a handy parking lot (free, 2-hour posted—but unmonitored—limit). It's a 30-minute drive or bus trip into Sogndal, where you can transfer to other **buses** (2–3 buses/day between Solvorn and Sogndal, including the Glacier Bus to the Nigard Glacier—described earlier).

▲▲Urnes Stave Church

The hamlet of Urnes (sometimes spelled "Ornes") has Norway's

oldest surviving stave church, dating from 1129. While not easy to reach (it's across the Lustrafjord from other attractions), it's worth the scenic ferry ride. The exterior is smaller and simpler than most stave churches, but its interior—modified in fits and starts over the centuries—is uniquely eclectic. If you want to pack along a bike (rentable in Solvorn), see "Bring a Bike?" at the end of this listing.

Cost and Hours: 50 kr, includes 25-minute English tour (departs at :40 past most hours, to coincide with ferry arrival—

described below); June–Sept daily 10:30–17:45; closed Oct–May, tel. 57 68 39 45.

Services: A little café/restaurant is at the farm called Urnes Gard, across from the church (same hours as church, homemade apple cakes, tel. 57 68 39 44).

Getting There: Urnes is perched on the east bank of the Lustrafjord (across the fjord from Route 55 and Solvorn). Ferries running between Solvorn and Urnes depart Solvorn at the top of most hours and Urnes at the bottom of most hours (30 kr one-way passenger fare, 80 kr one-way for car and driver, no round-trip discount, 15-min ride). You can either drive or walk onto the boat—but, since you can't drive all the way up to the church, you might as well leave your car in Solvorn. Once across, it's about a five-minute uphill walk to the main road and parking lot (where drivers must leave their cars; parking lot at the church only for disabled visitors). From here, it's a steep 15-minute walk up a switchback road to the church (follow signs for *Urnes*).

Planning Your Time: Don't dawdle on your way up to the church, as the tour is scheduled to depart at :40 past most hours, about 25 minutes after the ferry arrives (giving most visitors just enough time to make it up the hill to the church). The first boat of the day departs Solvorn at 10:00; the last boat departs Solvorn at 16:00 (last tour at 16:40); and the last boat back to Solvorn departs Urnes at 18:00. Confirm the "last boat" time, and keep an eye on your watch to avoid getting stranded in Urnes.

☉ Self-Guided Tour: Most visitors to the church take the included 25-minute tour (scheduled to begin soon after the ferry arrives—described above). Here are some highlights:

Buy your ticket in the white house across from the church. Visit the little museum here after you see the church, so you don't miss the tour.

Many changes were made to the exterior to modernize the church after the Reformation (the colonnaded gallery was replaced, the bell tower was added, and modern square windows were cut into the walls). Go around the left side of the church, toward the cemetery. This is the third church on this spot, but the carved doorway embedded in the wall here was inherited from the second church. Notice the two mysterious beasts— a warm-blooded predator (standing) and a cold-blooded dragon—weaving and twisting around each other, one entwining the other. Yet, as they bite each other on the neck, it's impossible to tell which one is "winning"... perhaps symbolizing the everlasting struggle

of human existence. The door you see in the middle, however, has a very different message: the harmony of symmetrical figure-eights, an appropriately calming theme for those entering the church.

Now go around to the real entry door (with a wrought-iron lock and handle probably dating from the first church) and head inside. While it feels ancient and creaky, a lot of what you see in here is actually "new" compared to the 12th-century core of the church. The exquisitely carved, voluptuous, column-topping capitals are remarkably well-preserved originals. The interior initially was stark (no pews) and dark—lit not by windows (which were added much later), but by candles laid on the floor in the shape of a cross. Looking straight ahead, you see a cross with Mary on the left (where the women stood) and John the Baptist on the right (with the men). When they finally added seating, they kept things segregated: Notice the pews carved with hearts for women, crowns for men.

When a 17th-century wealthy family wanted to build a special pew for themselves, they simply sawed off some of the pinecone-topped columns to make way for it. When the church began to lean, it was reinforced with the clumsy, off-center X-shaped supports. Churchgoers learned their lesson, and never cut anything again.

The ceiling, added in the late 17th century, prevents visitors from enjoying the Viking-ship roof beams. But all of these additions have stories to tell. Experts can read various cultural influences into the church decorations, including Irish (some of the carvings) and Romanesque (the rounded arches).

Bring a Bike? To give your Lustrafjord excursion more dimension, take a bike on the ferry to Urnes (free passage, rentable for 150 kr/day with helmets from Eplet Bed & Apple hostel in Solvorn, where you can park your car for free). From the stave church, bike the super-scenic fjordside road (4.5 miles—with almost no traffic—to big Feigumfossen waterfall and back).

Sleeping on the Lustrafjord

These accommodations are along the Lustrafjord, listed from north to south.

In Nes
$$ Nes Gard Farmhouse B&B rents 15 homey rooms, offering lots of comfort in a grand 19th-century farmhouse for a good price (D-750 kr, Db-900 kr, rooms in main building more traditional, family apartment, tel. 95 23 26 94 or 61 36 23 45, www.nesgard .no, post@nesgard.no, Manum family). Mari and Asbjorn serve a three-course dinner for 280 kr.

$ **Viki Fjord Camping** has great fjordside huts—many directly on the water, with fjord views and balconies—located directly across from the Feigumfossen waterfall (230–450 kr without a private bathroom, 380–850 kr with bathroom, price depends on size and season, sheets-60 kr, tel. 57 68 64 20, mobile 99 53 97 30, http://home.c2i.net/sanaess, viki.camp@c2i.net, Berit and Svein).

In Solvorn

For more on this delightful little fjordside town—my favorite home base on the Lustrafjord—see the description earlier in this chapter. While it lacks the handy boat connections of Flåm, Aurland, or Balestrand, that's part of Solvorn's charm.

$$$ **Walaker Hotel,** a former inn and coach station, has been run by the Walaker family since 1690 (that's a lot of pressure on eighth-generation owner Ole Henrik, who has just taken over the reins from Oda and Hermod). The hotel, set right on the Lustrafjord (with a garden perfect for relaxing and, if necessary, even convalescing), is open May through September. In the main house, the halls and living rooms are filled with tradition. Notice the patriotic hymns on the piano. The 22 rooms are divided into two types: nicely appointed standard rooms in the modern annex (big Sb-1,400 kr, Db-1,600 kr); or recently renovated "historic" rooms with all the modern conveniences in two different old buildings: rooms with Old World elegance in the main house, and brightly painted rooms with countryside charm in the Tingstova house next door (Db-2,100 kr, 500 kr more for larger #20 and #23; all prices include breakfast, non-smoking, free Wi-Fi, sea kayak rental, tel. 57 68 20 80, fax 57 68 20 81, www.walaker.com, hotel @walaker.com). They serve excellent four-course dinners (525 kr plus drinks, nightly at 19:30, savor your dessert with fjordside setting on the balcony). Their impressive gallery of Norwegian art is in a restored, historic farmhouse out back (free for guests; Ole Henrik leads one-hour tours of the collection, peppered with some family history, nightly after dinner).

$-$$ **Eplet Bed & Apple** is my kind of hostel: innovative and friendly. It's creatively run by Trond, whose entrepreneurial spirit and positive attitude attract enjoyable guests. With welcoming public spaces and 22 beds in seven rooms (all with views, some with decks), this place is worth considering even if you don't normally sleep at hostels (open May–Sept only; camping space-90 kr, bunk in 7-bed dorm-140 kr plus 50 kr for sheets, S-450 kr, D-550 kr, T-750 kr, S/D/T cost 100 kr less for 2 nights or more, laundry-50 kr, kitchen, Wi-Fi, free loaner bikes for guests, tel. 41 64 94 69, www.eplet.net, trondhenrik@eplet.net). It's about 300 yards uphill from the boat dock—look for the white house with a giant red apple painted on it. It's surrounded by a raspberry and apple farm (they make and sell tasty juices from both). The hostel rents bikes and helmets to non-guests for 150 kr/day. If you plan to bike along the fjord from Urnes, consider that if you stay at the hostel, the free bikes will save you 300 kr (for two people).

Eating in Solvorn: Sleepy Solvorn is blessed with the cheery **Linahagen Kafé,** next door to Walaker Hotel, where delightful Signe and her family serve up good meals (120-kr dinner salads, 140-kr dinner plates, June–Aug daily 12:30–19:30, closed Sept–May).

In Sogndal

Sogndal is the only sizeable town in this region. While it lacks the charm of Solvorn and Balestrand, it's big enough to have a busy shopping street and a helpful **TI** (mid-June–mid-Aug Mon–Fri 9:00–18:00, Sat 10:00–16:00, closed Sun; shorter hours in May and Sept, closed in winter; in the Kulturhus at Hovevegen 2, tel. 97 60 04 43).

$$ Loftesnes Pensjonat, with 12 rooms, houses travelers mid-June through mid-August, and mostly students—reserving four rooms for travelers—during the school year (S-400 kr, Sb-420 kr, D-600 kr, Db-650 kr, no breakfast, kitchen, above a Chinese restaurant near the water, tel. & fax 57 67 15 77, mobile 90 93 51 71, loftesnes-pensjonat@hotmail.com).

$-$$ Sogndal Youth Hostel rents good, cheap beds (bunk in 4-bed room-200 kr, S-280 kr, D-480 kr, Db-660 kr, 15 percent less for members, breakfast included, sheets-60 kr, towel-30 kr, members' kitchen—B.Y.O. pots, mid-June–mid-Aug only, closed 10:00–17:00, at fork in the road as you enter town, tel. 57 62 75 75, mobile 90 93 51 71, fax 57 62 75 70, www.vandrerhjem.no, sogndal @hihostels.no).

Lustrafjord Connections

Sogndal is the transit hub for the Lustrafjord region.

From Sogndal by Bus

Buses go to **Lom** over the Sognefjell pass (2/day late June–Aug only, road closed off-season, 3.25 hrs), **Solvorn** (3/day in summer, 2/day in winter, fewer Sat–Sun, 30 min), **Balestrand** (3/day, fewer Sat–Sun, 1.25 hrs, includes ride on Hella–Dragsvik ferry), **Nigard Glacier** via the Glacier Bus (1/day, 1.5 hrs, departs Sogndal daily at 8:45, returns to Sogndal in the afternoon, also stops at Solvorn in each direction, July–Aug only). Most buses run less (or not at all) on weekends—check the latest at www.ruteinfo.net.

By Boat

Car ferries cost roughly $5 per hour for walk-ons and $20 per hour for a car and driver. Reservations are generally not necessary, and on many short rides, aren't even possible (for info and free and easy reservations for longer rides, call 55 90 70 70). Confirm schedules at www.ruteinfo.net. From near Sogndal, various boats fan out to towns around the Sognefjord. Most leave from two towns at the southern end of the Lustrafjord: **Kaupanger** (a 15-min drive from Sogndal) and **Mannheller** (a 5-min drive beyond Kaupanger, 20 min from Sogndal).

From Kaupanger: While Kaupanger is little more than a ferry landing, the small stave-type church at the edge of town merits a look. Boats go from Kaupanger all the way down the gorgeous Nærøyfjord to **Gudvangen,** which is on the Norway in a Nutshell route (where you catch the bus to Voss). Taking this boat allows you to see the best part of the Nutshell fjord scenery (the Nærøyfjord), but misses the other half of that cruise (Aurlandsfjord). The boat leaves Kaupanger daily in summer at 9:30, 12:05, 16:00, and 18:50 for the two-hour trip (these times are for June–Aug, only goes 1/day in May and Aug–mid-Sept departing Kaupanger at 9:30 and Gudvangen at 12:00, none mid-Sept–April; car and driver-565 kr, adult passenger-230 kr; reserve at least one day in advance—or longer in July–Aug, especially for the popular 12:05 departure; tel. 55 90 70 70). Prices are high because this route is mainly taken by tourists, not locals. Boats also connect Kaupanger to **Lærdal,** but the crossing from Mannheller to Fodnes is easier (described next).

From Mannheller: Ferries frequently make the speedy 15-minute crossing to **Fodnes** (63 kr for a car and driver, 3/hr, no reservations possible). From Fodnes, drive through the five-mile-long tunnel to Lærdal and the main E16 highway (near Borgund Stave Church, the long tunnel to Aurland, and the scenic overland road to the Stegastein fjord viewpoint—all described in the previous chapter).

To Balestrand: To reach Balestrand from the Lustrafjord, you'll take a short ferry trip (Hella–Dragsvik). For information on the car ferries to and from Balestrand, see "Balestrand Connections," earlier.

Scenic Drives from the Sognefjord

If you'll be doing a lot of driving, pick up a good local map. The 1:335,000-scale *Sør-Norge nord* map by Cappelens Kart is excellent (about 100 kr, available at local TIs and bookstores).

▲▲From the Lustrafjord to Aurland

The drive to the pleasant fjordside town of Aurland (see previous chapter) takes you either through the world's longest car tunnel,

 or over an incredible mountain pass. If you aren't going as far as Lom and Jotunheimen, consider taking the pass, as the scenery here rivals the famous Sognefjell pass drive.

From Sogndal, drive 20 minutes to the Mannheller–Fodnes ferry (described under "Lustrafjord Connections," earlier), float across the Sognefjord, then drive from Fodnes to Lærdal. From Lærdal, you have two options to Aurland: The speedy route is on E16 through the new 15-mile-long **tunnel** from Lærdal, or the Aurlandsvegen **"Snow Road"** over the pass.

The tunnel is free, and impressively nonchalant—it's signed as if it were just another of Norway's countless tunnels. But driving it is a bizarre experience: A few miles in, as you find yourself trying not to be hypnotized by the monotony, it suddenly dawns on you what it means to be driving under a mountain for 15 miles. To keep people awake, three rest chambers, each illuminated by a differently colored light, break up the drive visually. Stop and get out—if no cars are coming, test the acoustics from the center.

The second, immeasurably more scenic route is a breathtaking one-hour, 30-mile drive that winds over a pass into Aurland, cresting at over 4,000 feet and offering classic aerial fjord views (it's worth the messy pants). From the Mannheller–Fodnes ferry, take the first road to the right (to Erdal), then leave E68 at Erdal (just west of Lærdal) for the Aurlandsvegen. This road, while well-maintained, is open only in summer, and narrow and dangerous during snowstorms (which can hit with a moment's notice, even in warm weather). You'll enjoy vast and terrifying views of lakes, snowfields, and remote mountain huts and farmsteads on what feels like the top of Norway. As you begin the 12-hairpin zigzag descent to Aurland, you'll reach the new "7"-shaped **Stegastein viewpoint**—well worth a stop.

▲From the Lustrafjord to Bergen, via the Nutshell Route (Nærøyfjord and Gudvangen)

Car ferries take tourists between Kaupanger and the Nutshell town of Gudvangen through an arm and elbow of the Sognefjord, including the staggering Nærøyfjord (for details on the ferry, see "Lustrafjord Connections," earlier). From Gudvangen, it's a 90-mile drive to Bergen, via Voss (figure about one hour to Voss, then another two hours into Bergen). This follows essentially the same route as the Norway in a Nutshell (Gudvangen–Voss bus, Voss–Bergen train).

Get off the ferry in Gudvangen and drive up the Nærøy valley past a river. You'll see the two giant falls just before the road marked *Stalheimskleiva*. Follow the sign (exiting left) to the little Stalheimskleiva road. This incredible road doggedly worms its way up into the ozone. My car overheated in a few minutes. Take it easy. (The main road gets you there more easily—through a tunnel and about a mile back up a smaller road—but you miss the twisty road and views.) As you wind up, you can view the falls from several turnouts. At the top, stop for a break at the touristy Stalheim Hotel.

The road rejoins E16 and continues into a mellower beauty, past lakes and farms, toward Voss. Soon before you reach Voss itself, watch the right side of the road for Tvindefossen, a waterfall with a handy campground/WC/kiosk picnic area that's worth a stop. Highway E16 takes you through Voss and into Bergen. If you plan to visit Edvard Grieg's home and the nearby Fantoft Stave Church, now is the ideal time, since you'll be driving near them and they're a headache to reach from downtown. Both are worth a detour if you're not rushed, and open until 18:00 in summer.

▲▲From Balestrand to Bergen, via Vik

If you're based in Balestrand and driving to Bergen, you have two options: Take the Dragsvik–Hella ferry, drive an hour to Kaupanger (via Sogndal), and drive the route described above; or, take the following slower, twistier, more remote, and more scenic route, with a stop at the beautiful Hopperstad Stave Church. This route is slightly longer, with more time on mountain roads and less time on the boat. Figure 20 minutes from Vangsnes to Vik, then about 1.5 hours to Voss, then another 2 hours into Bergen.

From Vagsnes, head into Vik on the main Route 13. In Vik, follow signs from the main road to Hopperstad Stave Church (described earlier in this chapter). Then backtrack to Route 13 and follow it south, to Voss. You'll soon begin a series of switchbacks that wind you up and out of the valley. The best views are from the Storesvingen Fjellstove restaurant (on the left). Soon after, you'll crest the ridge, go through a tunnel, and find yourself on

 top of the world, in a desolate and harshly scenic landscape of scrubby mountaintops, snow banks, lakes, and no trees, scattered with vacation cabins. After cruising atop the plateau for a while, the road twists its way down (next to a waterfall) into a very steep valley, which it meanders through the rest of the way to Voss. This is an hour-long, middle-of-nowhere journey, with few road signs—you might feel lost, but keep driving toward Voss. When Route 13 dead-ends into E16, turn right (toward Voss and Bergen) and reenter civilization. From here, the route follows the same roads described in the Lustrafjord–Bergen drive described above (including the Tvindefossen waterfall).

GUDBRANDSDAL VALLEY AND JOTUNHEIMEN MOUNTAINS

Norway in a Nutshell is a great day trip, but with more time and a car, consider a scenic meander from Oslo to Bergen. You'll arc up the Gudbrandsdal Valley and over the Jotunheimen Mountains, then travel along the Lustrafjord (see previous chapter).

After an introductory stop in Lillehammer, with its fine folk museum, you might spend the night in a log-and-sod farmstead-turned-hotel, tucked in a quiet valley under Norway's highest peaks. Next, Norway's highest pass takes you on an exhilarating roller-coaster ride through the heart of the myth-inspiring Jotunheimen, bristling with Norway's biggest mountains. Then the road hairpins down into fjord country (see previous chapter).

Planning Your Time

While you could spend five or six days in this area on a three-week Scandinavian rampage, this slice of the region is worth three days. By car, I'd spend them like this:

Day 1: Leave Oslo early, and spend midday at Lillehammer's Maihaugen Open-Air Folk Museum for a tour and picnic. Drive up the Gudbrandsdal Valley, stopping at the stave church in Lom. Stay overnight in the Jotunheimen countryside.

Day 2: Drive the Sognefjell road over the mountains, then down along the Lustrafjord, stopping to visit the Dale Church and the Nigard Glacier (see previous chapter). Sleep in your choice of fjord towns, described in previous chapters (such as Solvorn, Balestrand, or Aurland).

Day 3: Cruise the Aurland and/or Nærøy fjords and try to visit another stave church or two (such as Urnes, Hopperstad, or

Borgund) before carrying on to Bergen.

This plan can be condensed into two days if you skip the Nigard Glacier side-trip.

Lillehammer and the Gudbrandsdal Valley

The Gudbrandsdal Valley is the tradition-steeped country of Peer Gynt, the Norwegian Huck Finn. This romantic valley of time-worn hills, log cabins, and velvet farms has connected northern and southern Norway since ancient times. While not as striking as other parts of the Norwegian countryside, Gudbrandsdal offers a suitable first taste of the natural wonders that crescendo farther north and west (in Jotunheimen and the Sognefjord). Throughout this region, the government subsidizes small farms to keep the countryside populated and healthy. (These subsidies would not be permitted if Norway were a member of the European Union.)

Orientation to Lillehammer

The de facto capital of Gudbrandsdal, Lillehammer, is a pleas-ant winter and summer resort town of 25,000. While famous for its brush with Olympic greatness (as host of the 1994 Winter Olympiad), Lillehammer is a bit disappointing—worthwhile only for its excellent Maihaugen Open-Air Folk Museum, or to break up the long drive between Oslo and the Jotunheimen region. If you do wind up here, Lillehammer has happy, old, woody pedes-trian zones (Gågata and Storgata).

Tourist Information
Lillehammer's TI is inside the train station (mid-June–mid-Aug Mon–Fri 9:00–18:00, Sat–Sun 10:00–17:00; mid-Aug–mid-June Mon–Fri 9:00–16:00, Sat 10:00–14:00, closed Sun; Jernbanetorget 2, tel. 61 28 98 00, www.lillehammerturist.no).

Sights in Lillehammer

Lillehammer's two most worthwhile sights are up the hill behind the center of town. It's a fairly steep 15-minute walk from the train station to either sight and a 10-minute, mostly level walk between the two (follow the busy main road that connects them). Because the walk from the station is uphill (and not very well-signed),

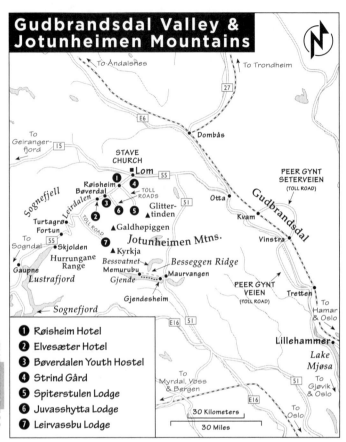

Gudbrandsdal Valley & Jotunheimen Mountains

- ❶ Røisheim Hotel
- ❷ Elvesæter Hotel
- ❸ Bøverdalen Youth Hostel
- ❹ Strind Gård
- ❺ Spiterstulen Lodge
- ❻ Juvasshytta Lodge
- ❼ Leirvassbu Lodge

GUDBRANDSDAL

consider catching the bus from in front of the train station (bus #005 or #003 to Olympics Museum, 2/hr; bus #007 to Maihaugen, 1/hr; 22 kr one-way for either bus).

▲▲**Maihaugen Open-Air Folk Museum (Maihaugen Friluftsmuseet)**—This idyllic park, full of old farmhouses and pickled slices of folk culture, provides a good introduction to what you'll see as you drive through the Gudbrandsdal Valley. Anders Sandvig, a "visionary dentist," started the collection in 1887. You'll divide your time between the fine indoor museum at the entrance and the sprawling exterior exhibits.

Upon arrival, ask about special events, crafts, or musical performances. A TV monitor shows what's going on in the park.

Summer is busy with crafts in action and people reenacting life in the past, à la Colonial Williamsburg. There are no tours, so it's up to you to initiate conversations with the "residents." Off-season it's pretty dead, with no live crafts and most buildings locked up.

The outdoor section, with 200 buildings from the Gudbrandsdal region, is divided into three areas: the "Rural Collection," with old sod-roof log houses and a stave church; the

"Town Collection," with reconstructed bits of old-time Lillehammer; and the "Residential Area," with 20th-century houses that look like most homes in today's Norway. The time trip can be jarring: In the 1980s house, a bubble-gum-chewing girl enthused about her new, "wireless" TV remote and played ABBA tunes from a cassette-tape player.

The museum's excellent "We Won the Land" exhibit (at the entry) sweeps you through Norwegian history from the Ice Age to the Space Age. The Gudbrandsdal art section shows village life at its best. And you can walk through Dr. Sandvig's old dental office and the original shops of various crafts- and tradespeople.

Because English descriptions are scant, the 95-kr English guidebook is worth considering (120 kr in summer, 80 kr off-season; 150-kr combo-ticket with Norwegian Olympics Museum; June–Aug daily 10:00–17:00; Sept–May Tue–Sun 11:00–16:00, closed Mon; paid parking, tel. 61 28 89 00; www.maihaugen.no).

Though the museum welcomes picnickers and has a simple cafeteria, Lillehammer's town center (a 10-min walk below the museum), with lots of fun eateries, is better for lunch (see "Eating in the Gudbrandsdal Valley," later).

Norwegian Olympics Museum (Norges Olympiske Museum)—This cute museum is housed in the huge Olympic ice-hockey arena, Håkon Hall. With brief English explanations, an emphasis on Norwegians and Swedes, and an endearingly gung-ho Olympic spirit, it's worth a visit on a rainy day or for sports fans. The ground-floor exhibit traces the ancient history of the Olympics, then devotes one wall panel to each of the summer and winter Olympiads of the modern era (with special treatment for the 1952 Oslo games). Upstairs, walk the entire concourse, circling the arena seating while reviewing the highlights (and lowlights) of the 1994 games (remember Tonya Harding?). While you're up there, check out the gallery of great Norwegian athletes and the giant egg used in the Lillehammer opening ceremony (75 kr, 150-kr combo-ticket with Maihaugen Open-Air Folk Museum; June–Aug daily 10:00–17:00; Sept–May Tue–Sun 11:00–16:00, closed Mon; tel. 61 25 21 00, www.ol.museum.no). With more time, see the 13-minute film on the 1994 Lillehammer Olympiad (included in museum ticket, 2/hr, usually in English, near ticket desk).

On the hillside above Håkon Hall (a 30-min hike or quick drive) are two ski jumps that host more Olympics sights, including a ski lift, the ski jump tower, and a bobsled ride (www.olympia parken.no). In the summer, ski jumpers practice on the ski jumps, which are sprayed with water.

In the Gudbrandsdal Valley

If you're driving from Oslo to the Gudbrandsdal Valley, you'll go right past the historic Eidsvoll Manor.

Scenic Drives—The main E6 road north of Lillehammer (en route to Otta and Lom) passes through a bucolic valley with fine

but unremarkable scenery. Along this road, a pair of toll-road side-trips (Gynt Veien and Peer Gynt Seterveien) loop off the E6 road. While they sound romantic, they're basically windy, curvy dirt roads over high, desolate heath and scrub-brush plateaus with fine mountain views. They're scenic, but pale in comparison to the Sognefjell road between Lom and the Lustrafjord (described later in this chapter).

Sleeping in the Gudbrandsdal Valley

I prefer sleeping in the more scenic and Norwegian-feeling Jotunheimen area (described later). But if you're sleeping here, Lillehammer and the surrounding valley offer several good options. My choices for Lillehammer are near the train station; the accommodations in Kvam provide a convenient stopping point in the valley.

In Lillehammer

$$$ Mølla Hotell, true to its name, is situated in an old mill along the little stream running through Lillehammer. The 58 rooms blend Old World charm with modern touches. It's more cutesy-cozy and less businesslike than other Lillehammer hotels in this price range (Db-1,200–1,400 kr depending on demand,

---

Sleep Code

(6 kr = about $1, country code: 47)

S = Single, **D** = Double/Twin, **T** = Triple, **Q** = Quad, **b** = bathroom, **s** = shower. You can assume credit cards are accepted unless otherwise noted.

    To help you sort easily through these listings, I've divided the rooms into three categories, based on the price for a standard double room with bath:

  $$$ **Higher Priced**—Most rooms 1,000 kr or more.
   $$ **Moderately Priced**—Most rooms between 500–1,000 kr.
    $ **Lower Priced**—Most rooms 500 kr or less.

---

elevator, free Internet access and Wi-Fi, a block below Gågata at Elvegata 12, tel. 61 05 70 80, fax 61 05 70 81, www.mollahotell.no, post@mollahotell.no).

    $$ First Hotel Breiseth is a business-class hotel with 89 rooms in a handy location directly across from the train station (Db-1,300 kr, discounted to 1,000 kr for most of June–Aug, Sb costs 200 kr less, free parking, Jernbanegaten 1–5, tel. 61 24 77 77, www.firsthotels.no/breiseth, breiseth@firsthotels.no).

    $ Vandrerhjem Stasjonen, Lillehammer's youth hostel, is actually upstairs inside the train station. With 75 beds in 28 institutional but new-feeling rooms—including 18 almost hotel-like doubles—it's a winner (325-kr bunk in a 3- to 4-bed dorm, Sb-700 kr, Db-840 kr, 15 percent cheaper for members, includes sheets and breakfast, elevator, free Wi-Fi, Jernbanetorget 2, tel. 61 26 00 24, www.stasjonen.no, post@stasjonen.no).

In Kvam

This is a popular vacation valley for Norwegians, and you'll find loads of reasonable small hotels and campgrounds with huts for those who aren't quite campers (*hytter* means "bungalows," *rom* is "private room," and *ledig* means "vacancy"). These huts normally cost about 400–600 kr, depending on size and amenities, and can hold from four to six people. Although they are simple, you'll have a kitchenette and access to a good WC and shower. When available, sheets rent for about an extra 60 kr per person. Here are a couple of listings in the town of Kvam, located midway between Lillehammer and Lom.

    $$ Sinclair Vertshuset Motel has a quirky Scottish-Norwegian ambience. The 15 fine rooms are in old-fashioned motel wings, while the main building houses an inexpensive cafeteria, described below (Sb-790 kr, Db-990 kr, includes breakfast, family

GUDBRANDSDAL

deals, free Internet access and Wi-Fi, tel. 61 29 54 50, fax 61 29 54 51, www.vertshuset-sinclair.no, post@vertshuset-sinclair.no). The motel was named after a Scotsman who led a band of adventurers into this valley, attempting to set up their own Scottish kingdom. They failed. All were kilt.

$-$$ Kirketeigen Ungdomssenter ("Church Youth Center"), behind the town church, welcomes travelers year-round (camping spots-120 kr/tent; small cabins without water-400 kr; cabins with kitchen and bath-700 kr, sleeps up to 5 people; simple 4-bed rooms in the main building-400 kr for 2–4 people with sheets; sheets and blankets-90 kr, Wi-Fi, tel. 61 21 60 90, www.kirketeigen.no, post@kirketeigen.no).

Eating in the Gudbrandsdal Valley

In Lillehammer: Good restaurants are scattered around the city center, but for the widest selection, head to where the main pedestrian drag (Gågata) crosses the little stream running downhill through town. Poke a block or two up and down **Elvegata,** which stretches along the river and hosts a wide range of tempting eateries—from pubs (both rowdy and upscale) to pizza and cheap sandwich stands.

In the Valley: Sinclair Vertshuset, described above, has a cafeteria handy for a quick and filling bite on the road between Lillehammer and Lom (50–70-kr sandwiches, 100–180-kr meals, daily 7:00–24:00).

Jotunheimen Mountains

Norway's Jotunheimen Mountains ("Giants' Home") feature the country's highest peaks and some of its best hikes and drives. This national park stretches from the fjords to the glaciers. You can play roller-coaster with mountain passes, take rugged hikes, wind up scenic toll roads, get up close to a giant stave church...and sleep in a time-passed rural valley. The gateway to the mountains is the unassuming town of Lom.

Lom

Pleasant Lom—the main town between Lillehammer and Sogndal—feels like a modern ski resort village. It's home to one of Norway's most impressive stave churches. While Lom has little else to offer, the church causes the closest thing to a tour-bus traffic jam this neck of the Norwegian woods will ever see.

Orientation to Lom

Park by the stave church—you'll see its dark spire just over the bridge. The church shares a parking lot with a gift shop/church museum and some public WCs. Across the street is the TI. If you're heading over the mountains, Lom's bank (at the Kommune building) has the last ATM until Gaupne.

Tourist Information

Lom's TI is an excellent source of information for hikes and drives in the Jotunheimen Mountains (mid-June–mid-Aug Mon–Fri 9:00–19:00, Sat–Sun 10:00–19:00; May–mid-June and mid-Aug–Sept Mon–Fri 9:00–16:00, Sat–Sun 10:00–17:00; Oct–April Mon–Fri 10:00–15:00, closed Sat–Sun; in the sod-roofed building across the busy road from the stave church parking lot, tel. 61 21 29 90, www.visitlom.com and www.visitjotunheimen.com).

The TI also serves as a national park office and hosts a worthwhile **Mountain Museum** (Norsk Fjellmuseum), tracing the history of the people who have lived off the land in Jotunheimen from the Stone Age to today. This is one of the better exhibits in fjord country. Its theater shows a 10-minute montage of images backed by Kenny G-type music, and the displays are well-presented with plenty of actual historic artifacts (50 kr, same hours as TI). The museum also has a computer with free Internet access for travelers.

Sights in Lom

▲▲Lom Stave Church (Lom Stavkyrkje)

Despite extensive renovations, Lom's church (from 1158) remains a striking example of a Nordic stave church.

Cost and Hours: 45 kr, daily mid-June–mid-Aug 9:00–20:00, mid-May–mid-June and mid-Aug–mid-Sept 10:00–16:00, closed in winter and during funerals, fine 10-kr leaflet.

Tours: Try to tag along with a guided tour—or, if it's not too busy, a docent can give you a quick private tour (included in ticket). Even outside of opening times—including winter—small groups can arrange a tour (40 kr/person, 300-kr minimum, call 97 07 53 97 in summer or 61 21 73 00 in winter).

❷ Self-Guided Tour: Buy your ticket and go inside to take in the humble **interior** (still used by locals for services—notice the posted hymnal numbers). Men sat on the right, women on the left, and prisoners sat with the sheriff in the caged area in the rear. Standing in the middle of the nave, look overhead to see the earliest surviving parts of the church, such as the circle of X-shaped St. Andrew crosses and the Romanesque arches above them. High above the door (impossible to see without a flashlight—ask a docent to show you) is an old painting of a dragon- or lion-like creature—likely an old Viking symbol, possibly drawn here to smooth the forced conversion local pagans made to Christianity. When King Olav II (later to become St. Olav) swept through this valley in 1021, he gave locals an option: convert or be burned out of house and home.

On the white town flag, notice the spoon—a symbol of Lom. Because of its position nestled in the mountains, Lom gets less rainfall than other towns, so large spoons were traditionally used to spread water over the fields. The apse (behind the altar) was added in 1240, when trendy new Gothic cathedrals made an apse a must-have accessory for churches across Europe. Lepers came to the grilled window in the apse for a blessing. When the Reformation hit in 1536, the old paintings were whitewashed over. The church has changed over the years: Transepts, pews, and windows were added in the 17th century. And the circa-1720 paintings were done by a local priest's son.

Drop into the **gift shop/church museum** in the big black building in the parking lot. Its one-room exhibit celebrates 1,000 years of the stave church—interesting if you follow the loaner English descriptions (10 kr, mid-July–mid-Aug daily 9:00–20:00, progressively shorter hours in shoulder season, in winter Mon–Sat 10:00–15:00, closed Sun, tel. 61 21 19 05). Inside you'll find a pair of beautiful model churches, headstones and other artifacts, and the only surviving stave-church dragon-head "steeple." In the display case near the early-1900s organ, find the little pencil-size stick carved with runes, dating from around 1350. It's actually a love letter from a would-be suitor. The woman rejected him, but she saved them both from embarrassment by hiding the stick under the church floorboards beneath a pew...where it was found in 1973. (Docents inside the church like to show off a replica of this stick.)

Before or after your church visit, explore the tidy, thought-provoking **graveyard** surrounding the church. Also, check out the precarious-looking little footbridge over the waterfall (the best view is from the modern road bridge into town).

Sleeping near Lom

(6 kr = about $1, country code: 47)
Lom itself has a handful of hotels, but the most appealing way to overnight in this area is at a rural rest stop in the countryside. All of these are on Route 55 south of Lom, toward Sognefjord—Strind

Gård first, then Bøverdalen, Røisheim, and finally Elvesæter (all within 20 minutes of Lom).

$$$ Røisheim, in a marvelously remote mountain setting, is an extremely expensive storybook hotel composed of a cluster of centuries-old, sod-roofed log farmhouses. Its posh and generous living rooms are filled with antiques. Each of the 20 rooms (in eight different buildings) is rustic but elegant, with fun "barrel bathtubs" and four-poster or canopy beds. Some rooms are in old, wooden farm buildings—*stabburs*—with low ceilings and heavy beams. The deluxe rooms are larger, with king beds and fireplaces. Call ahead so they'll be prepared for your arrival (open mid-May–Sept; standard Db-3,600 kr, deluxe Db-3,950 kr; includes breakfast, packed lunch, and an over-the-top four-course traditional dinner served at 19:30; non-smoking, Wi-Fi, 10 miles south of Lom on Route 55, tel. 61 21 20 31, fax 61 21 21 51, www.roisheim .no, booking@roisheim.dvgl.no, Haavard Lunde).

$$$ Elvesæter Hotel has its own share of Old World romance, but is bigger, cheaper, and more modest. Delightful public spaces bunny-hop through its traditional shell, while its 200 beds sprawl through nine buildings. The Elvesæter family has done a great job of retaining the historic character of their medieval farm, even though the place is big enough to handle large tour groups. The renovated "superior" rooms are new-feeling, but have sterile modern furniture; the older, cheaper "standard" rooms are well-worn but more characteristic (open May–Sept, standard Db-1,050 kr, superior Db-1,550 kr, extra bed-450 kr, family deals, includes breakfast, good 300-kr three-course dinners, strictly non-smoking, Wi-Fi, swimming pool, farther up Route 55, just past Bøverdal, tel. 61 21 99 00, fax 61 21 99 01, www.elveseter.no, post @elveseter.no). Even if you're not staying here, stop by to wander through the public spaces and pick up a flier explaining the towering Sagasøyla (Saga Column). It was started in 1926 to celebrate the Norwegian constitution, and was to stand in front of Oslo's Parliament Building—but the project stalled after World War II (thanks to the artist's affinity for things German and membership in Norway's fascist party). It was eventually finished and erected here in 1992.

$ Bøverdalen Youth Hostel offers 32 cheap-but-comfortable beds and a far more rugged clientele—real hikers rather than car hikers. While a bit institutional, it's well-priced and well-run (open late May–Sept, bunk in 4- to 6-bed room-175 kr, D-400 kr; 4-person cabins-600 kr with shower and toilet, 500 kr with toilet but no shower; 15 percent discount for members, sheets-65 kr, breakfast-70 kr, free Wi-Fi, kitchen, hot meals, self-serve café, tel. & fax 61 21 20 64, boverdalen@hihostels.no, Anna Berit). It's in the center of the little community of Bøverdal (store, campground,

GUDBRANDSDAL

and toll road up to Galdhøpiggen area).

$ Strind Gård is your very rustic option if you can't spring for Røisheim or Elvesæter, but still want the countryside-farm experience. This 150-year-old farmhouse, situated by a soothing waterfall, rents two rooms and one apartment, plus four sod-roofed log huts. The catch: Many of the buildings have no running water, so you'll use the shared facilities at the main building. While not everyone's cup of tea, this place will appeal to romantics who always wanted to sleep in a humble log cabin in the Norwegian mountains—it's downright idyllic for those who like to rough it (2-person huts: without bathroom-220–450 kr depending on size, beautiful private hut with bathroom-700 kr; rooms in main house: D-300–450 kr depending on size, apartment for 4–6 with private bath-700 kr; no breakfast, free Wi-Fi, low ceilings, farm smells, valley views, 2 miles south of Lom on Route 55, tel. 61 21 12 37, www.strind-gard .no, Anne Jorunn and Trond Dalsegg).

Drives and Hikes in the Jotunheimen Mountains

Route 55, which runs between Lom and the Sognefjord to the south, is the sightseeing spine of this region. From this main (and already scenic) drag, other roads spin upwards into the mountains—offering even better views and exciting drives and hikes. Many of these get you up close to Norway's highest mountain, Galdhøpiggen (8,100 feet). I've listed these attractions from north to south, as you'll reach them driving from Lom to the Sognefjord; except for the first, they all branch off from Route 55. The hike to the Nigard Glacier near Lustrafjord is another great high-mountain experience nearby.

Remember that the TI in Lom acts as a national park office, offering excellent maps and advice for drivers and hikers—a stop here is obligatory if you're planning a jaunt into the mountains (see "Orientation to Lom," earlier).

Besseggen

This trail offers an incredible opportunity to walk between two lakes separated by a narrow ridge and a 1,000-foot cliff. It's one of Norway's most beloved hikes, which can make it crowded in the summer. To get to the trailhead, drivers detour down Route 51 after Otta south to Maurvangen. Turn right to Gjendesheim to park your car. From Gjendesheim, catch the boat to Memurubu, where the path starts at the boat dock. Hike along the ridge—with a blue lake (Bessvatnet) on one side and a green lake (Gjende) on the other—and keep your balance. The six-hour trail loops back to Gjendesheim. Because the boat runs sporadically, time your visit to catch one (100 kr for 20-min ride, 3 morning departures daily, latest schedules at www.gjende.no, tel. 61 23 85 09). This is a thrilling but potentially hazardous hike, and it's a major detour: Gjendesheim is about 90 minutes and 50 miles from Lom.

Spiterstulen

From Røisheim, this 11-mile toll road (50 kr) takes you from Route 55 to the Spiterstulen mountain hotel/lodge in about 30 minutes (3,600 feet). This is the best destination for serious all-day hikes to Norway's two mightiest mountains, Glittertinden and Galdhøpiggen (a 5-hour hike up and a 3-hour hike down, doable without a guide). Or consider a guided, two-hour glacier walk (tel. 61 21 94 00, www.spiterstulen.no).

Juvasshytta

This toll road, starting from Bøverdal, takes you in about 40 minutes to the highest you can drive and the closest you can get to Galdhøpiggen by car (6,050 feet). At the end of the 85-kr toll road, daily, guided, six-hour hikes go across the glacier to the summit and back (150 kr, late June–late Sept daily at 10:00, July–mid-Aug also daily at 11:30, check in 30 min before, strict age limit—no kids under age 7, 4 miles each way, easy ascent but very dangerous without a guide, hiking boots required—possible to rent from nearby ski resort). You can sleep in the **$$ Juvasshytta lodge** (Db-660 kr with sheets, D without sheets-500 kr, sheets-100 kr, breakfast-100 kr, dinner-300 kr, tel. 61 21 15 50, www.juvasshytta.no).

Leirvassbu

This 11-mile, 40-kr toll road (about 30 min one-way from Bøverkinnhalsen, south of Elvesæter) is most scenic for car hikers. It takes you to a lodge at 4,600 feet with great views and easy walks. A serious (5-hr round-trip) hike goes to the lone peak, Kyrkja—"The Cathedral," which looms like a sanded-down mini-Matterhorn on the horizon (6,660 feet).

▲▲Sognefjell Drive to the Sognefjord

Norway's highest pass (at 4,600 feet, the highest road in northern Europe) is a thrilling drive through a cancan line of mountains, from Jotunheimen's Bøverdal Valley to the Lustrafjord (an arm of the Sognefjord—see previous chapter). Centuries ago, the farmers of Gudbrandsdal took their horse caravans over this difficult mountain pass on treks to Bergen. Today, the road (Route 55) is still narrow, windy, and otherworldly (and usually closed mid-Oct–May).

As you begin to ascend just beyond Elvesæter, notice the

viewpoint on the left for the
Leirdalen Valley—capped at
the end with the Kyrkja peak
(described earlier). Then you'll
twist up into a lake-filled valley,
then through a mild canyon with
grand waterfalls. Before long, as
you corkscrew up more switchbacks, you're above the tree line,

enjoying a "top of the world" feeling. The best views (to the south)
are of the cut-glass range called Hurrungane ("Noisy Children").
The 10 hairpin turns between Turtagrø and Fortun are exciting. Be
sure to stop, get out, look around, and enjoy the lavish views. Treat
each turn as if it were your last.

Just before you descend to the fjord, the terrain changes, and
you reach a pullout on the right, next to a hilltop viewpoint—
offering your first glimpse of the fjord. The Lustrafjord village of
Skjolden is just around the bend (and down several more switchbacks). Entering Skjolden, continue following Route 55, which
now traces the west bank of the Lustrafjord.

Connections

Cars are better, but if you're without wheels: **Oslo to Lillehammer**
(trains almost hourly, 2.5 hrs, just 2 hrs from Oslo airport),
Lillehammer to Otta (6 trains/day, 1.5 hrs); a bus meets some
trains (confirm schedule at the train station in Oslo) for travelers
heading on to **Lom** (2 buses/day, 1 hr) and onward from **Lom to
Sogndal** (2 buses/day late June–Aug only, road closed off-season,
3.25 hrs).

Route Tips for Drivers

Use low gears and lots of patience both up (to keep the engine
cool) and down (to save your brakes). Uphill traffic gets the right-
of-way, but drivers, up or down, dive for the nearest fat part of the
road whenever they meet. Ask backseat drivers not to scream until
you've actually been hit or have left the road.

From Oslo to Jotunheimen: It's 2.5 hours from Oslo to
Lillehammer and 3 hours after that to Lom. Wind out of Oslo
following signs for *E6* (not to *Drammen*, but for *Stockholm* and
then to *Trondheim*). In a few minutes, you're in the wide-open
pastoral countryside of eastern Norway. Norway's Constitution
Hall—Eidsvoll Manor—is a five-minute detour off E6, several
miles south of Eidsvoll in Eidsvoll Verk (follow the signs to
Eidsvoll Bygningen). Then E6 takes you along Norway's largest
lake (Mjøsa), through the town of Hamar, and past more lake

scenery into Lillehammer. Signs direct you uphill from downtown Lillehammer to the Maihaugen Open-Air Folk Museum. From Lillehammer, signs to *E6/Trondheim* take you up the valley of Gudbrandsdal. At Otta, exit for Lom. Halfway to Lom, on the left, look for the long suspension bridge spanning the milky-blue river—a good opportunity to stretch your legs, and a scenic spot to enjoy a picnic.

BERGEN

Bergen is permanently salted with robust cobbles and a rich sea-trading heritage. Norway's capital in the 12th and 13th centuries, Bergen's wealth and importance came thanks to its membership in the heavyweight medieval trading club of merchant cities called the Hanseatic League. Bergen still wears her rich maritime heritage proudly.

Bergen gets an average of 80 inches of rain annually (compared to 30 inches in Oslo). A good year has 60 days of sunshine. The natives aren't apologetic about their famously lousy weather. In fact, they seem to wear it as a badge of local pride. "Well, that's Bergen," they'll say matter-of-factly as they wring out their raincoats. When I complained about an all-day downpour, a local cheerfully informed me, "There's no such thing as bad weather—just inappropriate clothing"...a local mantra that rhymes in Norwegian.

With 250,000 people, Bergen has big-city parking problems and high prices, but visitors sticking to the old center find it charming. Enjoy Bergen's salty market, then stroll the easy-on-foot old quarter, with cute lanes of delicate old wooden houses. From downtown Bergen, a funicular zips you up a little mountain for a bird's-eye view of this sailors' town.

Planning Your Time

Bergen can be enjoyed even on the tail end of a day's scenic train ride from Oslo before returning on the overnight train. But that teasing taste will make you wish you had more time. On a three-week tour of Scandinavia, Bergen is worth a whole day.

While Bergen's sights are visually underwhelming and pricey, nearly all come with thoughtful tours in English. If you dedicate the time to take advantage of these tours, otherwise barren attractions (such as Håkon's Hall and Rosenkrantz Tower, the Bryggen quarter, the Leprosy Museum, and Gamle Bergen) become surprisingly interesting. For a busy day, you could do this (enjoying tours at all but the last): 9:00—Stroll through the fish market; 10:00—Visit Håkon's Hall and Rosenkrantz Tower; 12:00—Take the Bryggen Walking Tour; 14:00—Take a harbor cruise or check out the Leprosy Museum; 16:00—Enjoy some free time in town (consider returning to the Bryggens Museum using your tour ticket), or catch the bus out to Gamle Bergen; 18:00—Ride up the Fløibanen funicular.

Although Bergen has plenty of attractions and charms of its own, it's most famous as the "Gateway to the Fjords." If you plan to use Bergen as a springboard for the fjord country, you have three options: Pick up a rental car here (fjord wonder is a three-hour drive away); take the express boat down the Sognefjord (about four hours to Balestrand and Flåm/Aurland); or do the "Norway in a Nutshell" as a scenic loop from Bergen. The "Nutshell" option also works well as a detour midway between Bergen and Oslo (hop the train from either city to Voss or Myrdal, then take a bus or spur train into the best of the Sognefjord; scenic ferry rides depart from there). While there are a million ways to enjoy the fjords, first-timers should start with this region (covered thoroughly in the Norway in a Nutshell and More on the Sognefjord chapters).

Also note that Bergen, a geographic dead-end, is actually an efficient place to begin or end your Scandinavian tour. Consider flying "open jaw"—for example, into Bergen and out of Helsinki (or vice versa).

Orientation to Bergen

Bergen clusters around its harbor—nearly everything listed in this chapter is within a few minutes' walk. The busy Torget (market

square and fish market) is at the head of the harbor. As you face the sea from here, Bergen's TI is across the street behind you. The town's historic Hanseatic Quarter (Bryggen) lines the harbor on the right. Express boats to the Sognefjord (Balestrand and Flåm) and Stavanger dock at the harbor on the left.

Protected from the open sea by a lone sheltering island, Bergen is a place of refuge from heavy winds for the giant working boats that serve the North Sea oil rigs. (Much of Norway's current affluence is funded by the oil it drills just offshore.) Bergen is also one of the most popular cruise-ship ports in northern Europe, hosting 260 ships a year and up to 7 ships a day in peak season. Each morning is rush hour, as cruisers hike past the fortress and into town.

Charming cobbled streets surround the harbor and climb the encircling hills. Bergen's popular Fløibanen funicular climbs high above the city to the top of Mount Fløyen for the best view of the town. Surveying the surrounding islands and inlets, it's clear why this city is known as the "Gateway to the Fjords."

Tourist Information

The TI, filling the historic old Bergen Exchange building, is frescoed with old murals showing local and traditional life (June–Aug daily 8:30–22:00; May and Sept daily 9:00–20:00; Oct–April Mon–Sat 9:00–16:00, closed Sun; across from fish market at Vågsallmenningen 1, tel. 55 55 20 00, www.visitbergen.com). The TI covers Bergen and western Norway, provides information and tickets for tours, has a fjord information desk, books rooms, and maintains a very handy events board listing today's and tomorrow's slate of tours, concerts, and other events. Pick up this year's edition of the free *Bergen Guide* (also likely at your hotel), which has a fine map and lists all sights, hours, and special events. This booklet can answer most of your questions. If you need assistance and there's a line, take a number.

Bergen Card: This greedy little card gets cut back each year. You have to really work to make it pay. It gives you free use of the city buses, half off the Mount Fløyen funicular, free admission to most museums (but not the Hanseatic Museum), and discounts on some tours, events, and sights—such as a measly 10 percent discount on the Bryggen Walking Tour, and a 50 percent discount on Edvard Grieg's Home. It also covers the aquarium—if you're here in the winter (190 kr/24 hrs, 250 kr/48 hrs, sold at TI, train station, and most hotels).

Arrival in Bergen

By Train or Bus: Bergen's train and bus stations are on Strømgaten, facing a park-rimmed lake. The small, manageable train station has an office open long hours for booking all your travel in Norway—get your Nutshell reservations here if you haven't already (Mon–Fri 6:45–19:30, Sat 7:30–16:10, Sun 7:30–19:30). There are luggage lockers (30 kr/day, daily 6:30–23:30), pay toilets, a newsstand, sandwich shop, and coffee shop. (To get to the bus station, follow the covered walkway behind the Narvesen newsstand via the Storcenter shopping mall.) Taxis wait to the right (with the tracks at your back). From the train station, it's a 10-minute walk to the TI: Cross the street (Strømgaten) in front of the station and take Marken, a cobbled street (see map).

By Plane: Bergen's cute little Flesland Airport is 12 miles south of the city center. The airport bus runs between the airport and downtown Bergen, stopping at the SAS Radisson Hotel in Bryggen, the harborfront area near the TI (if you ask), the SAS Hotel Norge (in the modern part of town at Ole Bulls Plass), and the bus station (85 kr, pay driver, 4/hr at peak times, less in slow times, 30-min ride). Taxis take up to four people and cost about 400 kr for the 20-minute ride (depending on the time of day). Airport info: tel. 55 99 80 00; SAS info: tel. 81 52 04 00.

By Car: Driving is a headache in Bergen—avoid it if you can. Approaching town on E16 (from Voss and the Sognefjord area), follow signs for *Sentrum*, which spits you out near the big, modern bus station and parking garage. Parking is difficult and costly—ask at your hotel for tips. Note that all drivers entering Bergen must pay a 15-kr toll, but there are no toll-collection gates (since the system is entirely automated for locals). It's Norway's new way of collecting tolls: Assuming they bill you, it'll just show up on your credit card (which they access through your rental car company). For details, ask your rental company or see www.autopass.no.

Helpful Hints

Museum Tours: Many of Bergen's sights are hard to appreciate without a guide. Fortunately, many include a wonderful and intimate guided tour with admission. Make the most of the following sights by taking full advantage of their included tours: Håkon's Hall and Rosenkrantz Tower, Bryggens Museum, Hanseatic Museum, Leprosy Museum, Gamle Bergen, and Edvard Grieg's Home.

Laundry: Jarlens Vaskoteque is at Lille Øvregate 17, one block uphill from the church called Korskirken (2-hr drop-off service for 110 kr, self-service for 80 kr, Mon–Fri 10:00–18:00, Wed–Thu until 20:00, Sat 10:00–15:00, closed Sun, tel. 55 32 55 04).

Getting Around Bergen

Most in-town sights can easily be reached by foot; only the aquarium and Gamle Bergen (and the outlying sights of Fantoft Stave Church, Edvard Grieg's Home at Troldhaugen, and the Ulriken643 cable car) are more than a 10-minute walk from the TI.

By Bus: The free "Sentrum-VilVite bus" runs every 10 minutes from the big parking garage near the bus station, past the TI and fish market, and around Bryggen. It's designed to encourage people to park and ride. Hop on for a free circular joyride through town (Mon–Fri 7:30–21:00, no bus Sat–Sun).

City buses cost 24 kr per ride (pay driver). The best city buses for a city joyride are #20 (north along the coast) and #11 (into the hills).

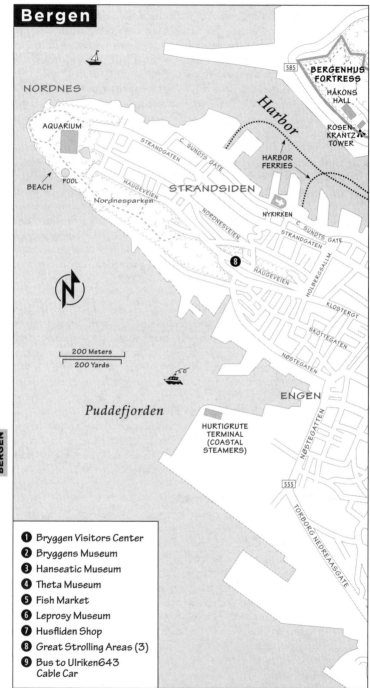

Bergen

BERGENHUS FORTRESS
585
HÅKONS HALL
ROSEN-KRANTZ TOWER

NORDNES

Harbor

AQUARIUM

STRANDGATEN

C. SUNDTS GATE

HARBOR FERRIES

BEACH

POOL

HAUGEVEIEN

STRANDSIDEN

NYKIRKEN

Nordnesparken

NORDNESVEIEN

C. SUNDTS GATE

STRANDGATEN

8

HAUGEVEIEN

HOLBERGSALM.

KLOSTERGT.

200 Meters
200 Yards

SKOTTEGATEN

NØSTEGATEN

ENGEN

Puddefjorden

HURTIGRUTE TERMINAL (COASTAL STEAMERS)

NØSTEGATTEN

555

TORBORG NEDREAASGATE

BERGEN

❶ Bryggen Visitors Center
❷ Bryggens Museum
❸ Hanseatic Museum
❹ Theta Museum
❺ Fish Market
❻ Leprosy Museum
❼ Husfliden Shop
❽ Great Strolling Areas (3)
❾ Bus to Ulriken643 Cable Car

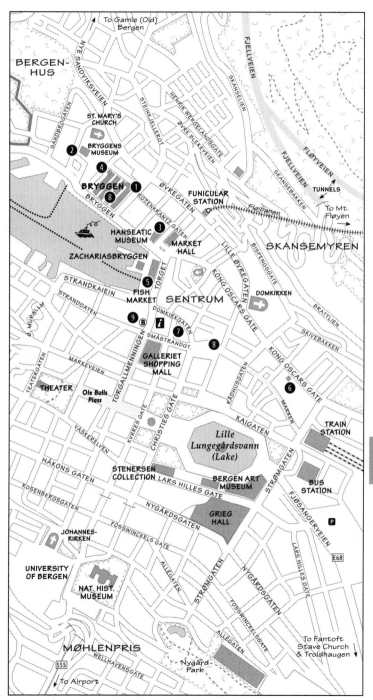

By Ferry: The *Beffen*, a little orange ferry, chugs across the harbor every half-hour (20 kr, Mon–Fri 7:30–16:30, no weekend runs). This three-minute "poor man's cruise" has good harbor views. The Vågen "Akvariet" ferry departs from in front of the fish market for the aquarium (40 kr one-way, 60 kr round-trip, 2/hr, daily May–Aug 10:00–18:00).

By Taxi: For a taxi, call 07000 or 08000 (not as expensive as you might expect).

Tours in Bergen

▲▲▲**Bryggen Walking Tour**—This tour of the historic Hanseatic district is one of Bergen's best activities. Local guides take visitors on an excellent 90-minute walk through 900 years of Bergen history via the old Hanseatic town (20 min in Bryggens Museum, 20-min visit to the medieval Hanseatic Assembly Rooms, 20-min walk through Bryggen, and 20 min in Hanseatic Museum). Tours leave from the Bryggens Museum (next to the big, modern SAS Radisson Hotel). When you consider that the tour price includes entry tickets to the Hanseatic and Bryggens museums and the Hanseatic Assembly Rooms, the tour more than pays for itself (100 kr, June–Aug daily

at 11:00 and 12:00, none Sept–May, tel. 55 58 80 10). While the museum visits are a bit rushed, your tour ticket allows you to re-enter the museums for the rest of the day.

Other Walking Tours—Bergen Guide Service offers 1.5-hour bilingual walking tours of the city center daily in peak season (in Norwegian and English, 95 kr, mid-June–mid-Aug daily at 15:00, departs from TI, tel. 55 30 10 60, www.bergenguideservice.com). You can also contact Bergen Guide Service to hire your own local guide.

▲**Bus Tours**—The TI sells tickets for various bus tours. The 1.5-hour bus tour of the city center isn't very appealing, since you can enjoy everything better by foot (150 kr, June–Aug daily at 9:30 and 16:30). But the three-hour version that adds Edvard Grieg's Home at Troldhaugen is a handy way to reach that outlying sight. The bus is comfy, with big views and a fine recorded commentary (300 kr, May–Sept daily at 12:00, departs from curb across from fish market outside TI). There are also several full-day tour options from Bergen, including bus/boat tours to nearby Hardanger and Sogne fjords. The TI is packed with brochures describing all the excursions.

▲**Harbor Tours**—The *White Lady* leaves from the fish market daily in summer at 14:30 for a 50-minute cruise. The ride is both scenic and informative, with a relaxing sun deck and good—if scant—recorded narration (130 kr, June–late Aug). A four-hour fjord trip is also available (400 kr, May–Aug daily at 10:00, July–late Aug also daily at 15:30, sporadic departures in Sept, tel. 55 25 90 00).

Tourist Train—The tacky little "Bergen Express" train departs from in front of the Hanseatic Museum for a 55-minute loop around town (120 kr, May daily 10:00–16:00, June–Aug daily 10:00–19:00, Sept daily 11:00–15:00, 2/hr in peak season, otherwise hourly, headphone English commentary).

Sights in Bergen

▲▲**Bergen Town Walk**—For a quick and historic orientation walk through Bergen, start at the fortress and tower, head up to St. Mary's Church, peruse the old wooden Hanseatic Quarter, and loiter through the fish market. Then head into the modern center of town, the Torgallmenningen square, and finish with a stroll around the little lake. (These sights are all described below, in the order of this walk.) Ideally, you'll get side-tracked in the museums, and will take advantage of the excellent on-site tours (included with admission). As you explore, remember two points that shape the city you'll see:

While the city dates from 1070, little survives from before the last big fire in 1702. In its earlier heyday, Bergen was one of the largest wooden cities in Europe. Congested wooden buildings, combined with lots of small fires (to provide heat and light in this cold and dark corner of Europe), spelled disaster for Bergen. Over the centuries, the city suffered countless fires, including 10 devastating blazes. Each time the city burned, the destroyed material was tossed into the harbor, creating a haphazard landfill upon which much of the old town you see today was eventually built. After 1702, the city rebuilt using more stone and brick, and suffered fewer fires.

One of the biggest explosions of World War II, which occurred in the harbor on April 20, 1944, also shaped the city. An ammunition ship loaded with 120 tons of dynamite blew up just in front of the fortress. The blast leveled entire neighborhoods on either side of the harbor (notice the ugly 1950s construction opposite the fortress) and did serious damage to Håkon's Hall and Rosenkrantz Tower. How big was the blast? There's a hut called "the anchor cabin" a couple of miles away in the mountains. That's where the ship's anchor landed. While April 20 happened to be Hitler's birthday and the ship blew up about 100 yards away from the Nazi commander's headquarters (in the fortress), the blast is considered to be accidental.

BERGEN

▲Bergen's Fortress: Håkon's Hall and Rosenkrantz Tower
—Back in the 13th century, Bergen was the Kingdom of Norway's first capital. (Prior to the 13th century, kings would circulate, staying on royal farms.) This fortress was a garrison, with a tower for the king's residence and a large hall for his banquets. Today the fortress grounds are used for big events (Bruce Springsteen filled it in 2009).

The tower and hall, sitting boldly out of place on the harbor just beyond Bryggen, are reminders of Bergen's medieval importance. Both sights feel vacant and don't really speak for themselves; the included guided tours, which provide a serious introduction to Bergen's history, are essential for grasping their significance. While each sight is covered by a separate ticket and tour, it's best to consider them as one and start at Håkon's Hall (tours leave at the top of the hour). Stick with your guide, as the Rosenkrantz Tower is part two of his tour.

Håkon's Hall, dating from the 13th century, is the largest secular medieval building in Norway. It's essentially a giant, grand reception hall (used today  for banquets) under a ceiling that feels like an upturned Viking boat. While recently rebuilt, the ceiling's design is modeled after grand wooden roofs of that era. Beneath the hall is a whitewashed cellar. Banquets were a men-only affair. The raised seats gave royal, church, and military dignitaries the appropriate elevation.

Rosenkrantz Tower, the keep of a 13th-century castle, has a jumbled design, thanks to a Renaissance addition. The tour brings  it to life. There's a good history exhibit on the top floors and a fine view from the rooftop.

Cost and Hours: The tower and hall cost 40 kr each and include a guided tour (leaves from Håkon's Hall at the top of each hour, last tour departs at 15:00). Both are open mid-May–Aug daily 10:00–16:00. The hall is also open Sept–mid-May daily 12:00–15:00, when the tower is closed (tel. 55 31 60 67).

St. Mary's Church (Mariakirken)—Dating from the 12th century, and still used for services today, this is Bergen's oldest building. This was the stately church of the Hanseatic merchants.

Its dour stone interior, enlivened by a colorful, highly decorated pulpit, is closed through 2014 while a 100-million-kroner renovation is under way. Behind the church is the back wall of the Hanseatic Quarter and the entrance to the communal Hanseatic Assembly Rooms (Schøtstuene).

Bergen's Hanseatic Quarter (Bryggen)—A horrific plague decimated the population and economy of Norway in 1350, killing about half of its people. A decade later, German merchants arrived and established a Hanseatic trading post (see sidebar), bringing order to that rustic society. For the next four centuries, the port of Bergen was German territory.

Bergen's old German trading center was called "the German wharf" until World War II, and is now just called "the wharf," or "Bryggen" (BREW-gun). From 1370 to 1754, German merchants controlled Bergen's trade. In 1550, it was a Germanic city of 1,000 workaholic merchants—surrounded and supported by some 5,000 Norwegians.

The German merchants were very strict and lived in a harsh, all-male world (except for Norwegian prostitutes). This wasn't a military occupation, but a mutually beneficial economic partnership. The Norwegian cod fishermen of the far north shipped their dried cod to Bergen, where the Hanseatic merchants marketed it to Europe. Norwegian cod provided much of Europe with food (a source of easy-to-preserve protein) and cod oil (which lit the lamps until about 1850).

The wharf area is mostly reclaimed from the sea. Each time the warehouses burned, the merchants would toss the refuse into the bay and rebuild. Gradually, the land crept out, and so did the buildings. (Looking at the Hanseatic Quarter from the harborfront, you can see how the buildings have settled. The foundations, composed of debris from the many fires, settle as they rot.) The long "tenements" (rows of warehouses) we see today date from the early 1700s—built after that last great fire in 1702. To prevent future fires, the Germans forbade all fires and candles for light or warmth except in isolated and carefully guarded communal houses behind each tenement. It was in these communal houses that apprentices studied, people dried out their soggy clothes, hot food was cooked, and the men drank and partied. One of these

The Hanseatic League and Cod

Middlemen in trade, the clever German merchants of the Hanseatic League ruled the waves of northern Europe for 500 years (c. 1250–1750). These sea-traders first banded together in a *Hanse*, or merchant guild, to defend themselves against pirates. As they spread out from Germany, they established trading posts in foreign lands, cut deals with local leaders for trading rights, built boats and wharves, and organized armies to protect ships and ports.

By the 15th century, these merchants had organized more than a hundred cities into the Hanseatic League, a free-trade zone that stretched from London to Russia. The League ran a profitable triangle of trade: Fish from Scandinavia were exchanged for grain from the eastern Baltic and luxury goods from England and Flanders. Everyone benefited, and the German merchants—the middlemen—reaped the profits.

At its peak in the 15th century, the Hanseatic League was the dominant force—economic, military, and political—in northern Europe. This was an age when much of Europe was fragmented into petty kingdoms and dukedoms. Revenue-hungry kings and robber-baron lords levied chaotic and extortionist tolls and duties. Pirates plagued shipments. It was the Hanseatic League, rather than national governments, that brought the stability that allowed trade to flourish.

Bergen's place in this Baltic economy was all about cod—a form of protein that could be dried, preserved, and shipped any-

medieval Hanseatic Assembly Rooms is preserved and open to the public (the Schøtstuene—separate entrance behind St. Mary's Church, included in Bryggen Walking Tour, difficult to appreciate without a guide).

Half of Bryggen (the stretch between the old wooden facades and the Hanseatic Museum—standing apart from the others at the head of the bay) was torn down around 1900. The man who owned the wooden building that now houses the Hanseatic Museum recognized the value of the city's heritage and kept his building as it was. Considered a nutcase back then, today he's celebrated as a visionary, as his decision left today's visitors with a fine example of an old merchant house to tour.

After World War II, Bryggen was again slated for destruction. Most of the locals wanted it gone—it reminded them of the Germans who had occupied Norway for several miserable years. Then excavators discovered rune stones indicating that the area predated the Germans. This boosted Bryggen's approval rating, and the quarter was saved.

From the front of Bryggen, look down at the Rosenkrantz

where. Though cursed by a lack of natural resources, the city was blessed with a good harbor conveniently located between the rich fishing spots of northern Norway and the markets of Europe. Bergen's port shipped dried cod and fish oil southward and imported grain, cloth, beer, wine, and ceramics.

Bryggen was one of four principal Hanseatic trading posts (*Kontors*), along with London, Bruges, and Novgorod. It was the last *Kontor* opened (c. 1360), the least profitable, and the last one closed (1754). Bryggen had warehouses, offices, and living quarters. Ships docked here were unloaded by counterpoise cranes. At its peak, as many as a thousand merchants, journeymen, and apprentices lived and worked here.

Bryggen was a self-contained German enclave within the city. The merchants came from Germany, worked a few years here, and retired back in the home country. They spoke German, wore German clothes, and attended their own churches. By law, they were forbidden to intermarry or fraternize with the Bergeners, except on business.

The Hanseatic League peaked around 1500, then slowly declined. Rising nation-states were jealous of the Germans' power and wealth. The Reformation tore apart old alliances. Dutch and English traders broke the Hanseatic monopoly. Cities withdrew from the League and *Kontors* closed. In 1754, Bergen's *Kontor* was taken over by the Norwegians. When it closed its doors on December 31, 1899, a sea-trading era was over, but the city of Bergen had become rich...by the grace of cod.

Tower. The little red holes at its top mark where cannons were once pointed at the German quarter by the Norwegian royalty. The threat was never taken seriously, however, because everyone knew that without German grain, the Norwegians would starve.

Bryggen is now touristy and boutiquey, but still lots of fun. Strolling through it, you feel swallowed up by history. Explore its wooden core, with medieval-style double-tenements—long rows of planky buildings leaning haphazardly across narrow alleys. Wander. You'll find plenty of art and artisan shops, sweater shops, atmospheric restaurants, and two worthwhile museums within a five-minute walk of each other (the Bryggens and Hanseatic museums, explained later). The little **visitors' center** plans to add exhibits about maintenance and restoration of the tenement houses (good 98-kr Bryggen guidebook, mid-May–mid-Sept daily 9:00–18:00, closed off-season, at the back end of the narrow wooden lane called Bellgården).

The **Bryggen Walking Tour** is your best bet for seeing Bryggen, the Bryggens Museum, and the Hanseatic Museum (100 kr, June–Aug daily at 11:00 and 12:00, none Sept–May, leaves from Bryggens Museum; for all the details, see "Tours in Bergen," earlier.)

▲▲**Bryggens Museum**—This modern museum explains the 1950s archaeological dig to uncover the earliest bits of Bergen (1050–1500). Brief English explanations are posted. From September through May, when there is no tour, ask to borrow the good museum guidebook (or buy it for 25 kr). The manageable, well-presented permanent exhibit occupies the ground floor. First you'll see foundations from original wooden tenements dating back to the 12th century (displayed right where they were excavated) and a giant chunk of the hull of a 100-foot-long, 13th-century ship that was found here. Then you'll enter an exhibit (roughly shaped like the long, wooden double-tenements outside) that shows off artifacts and explains lifestyles from medieval Bryggen. Behind that is a display of items you might have bought at the medieval market. You'll finish with exhibits about the church in Bergen, the town's role as a royal capital, and its status as a cultural capital. Upstairs are two floors of temporary exhibits (50 kr, included in summer with 100-kr Bryggen Walking Tour described earlier; open May–Aug daily 10:00–16:00; Sept–April Mon–Fri 11:00–15:00, Sat 12:00–15:00, Sun 12:00–16:00; in big modern building just beyond the end of Bryggen and the SAS Radisson Hotel, tel. 55 58 80 10, www.bymuseet.no). The museum has an inexpensive cafeteria with soup-and-bread specials.

▲▲**Hanseatic Museum (Hanseatiske Museum)**—This little museum was founded in the late 1900s to preserve a tenement interior. Its creaky old rooms—with hundred-year-old cod hanging from the ceiling—offer a time-tunnel experience back to Bryggen's glory days. It's located in an atmospheric old merchant house furnished with dried fish, antique ropes, an old oxtail (used for wringing spilled cod-liver oil back into the bucket), sagging steps, and cupboard beds from the early 1700s—one with a medieval pinup girl (50 kr, included in summer with 100-kr Bryggen Walking Tour, open daily June–Aug 9:00–17:00, Sept–May 11:00–14:00, tel. 55 54 46 96, www.museumvest.no).

Admission includes a good 45-minute guided tour (3/day in English, May–mid-Sept only). Even if you tour the museum with the Bryggen Walking Tour, you're welcome to revisit (same ticket) and take this longer tour.

Theta Museum—This small museum highlights Norway's resistance movement (specifically, a 10-person local group called Theta) during the Nazi occupation in World War II. It's housed in Theta's former headquarters—a small room in a wooden Bryggen building (30 kr, mid-May–mid-Sept Tue and Sat–Sun 14:00–16:00, closed Mon, Wed–Fri, and off-season, Enhjørningsgården, tel. 55 31 53 93).

▲▲Fish Market (Fisketorget)—A fish market has thrived here since the 1500s, when fishermen rowed in with their catch and

 haggled with the hungry locals. While it's now become a food circus of eateries selling fishy treats to tourists—no local would come here to actually buy fish— this famous market still offers lots of smelly photo fun and free morsels to taste. Many stands sell pre-made smoked-salmon *(laks)* sandwiches, fish soup, and other snacks ideal for a light lunch (confirm prices before ordering). To try Norwegian jerky, pick up a bag of dried cod snacks *(torsk)*. The red meat is minke whale, caught off the coast of northern Norway. You'll also find local fruit in season and hand-knit sweaters (June–Aug daily 8:00–19:00, less lively on Sun; Sept–May Mon–Sat 8:00–16:00, closed Sun). Watch your wallet: If you're going to get pickpocketed in Bergen, it'll likely be here.

Bergen's Main Square, Torgallmenningen—*Allmenningen* means "for all the people." *Torg* means "square." And, while this is the city's main gathering place, it was actually created as a fire break. The residents of this fire-plagued city—once one of the biggest wooden cities in Europe—knew fires were inevitable. The street plan was designed with breaks, or open spaces like this square, to help contain the destruction. In 1916, it stopped a fire, which is why it has a more modern feel today.

The **Seafarers' Monument** (which locals have nicknamed "the cube of goat cheese" for its shape) dates from about 1950. It celebrates Bergen's contact with the sea and remembers those who worked on it and died in it. Study the faces: All classes are represented. The statues relate to the scenes depicted in the reliefs above. Each side represents a century: 10th century—Vikings with a totem pole recalling the pre-Columbian Norwegian discovery of America; 18th century—equipping Europe's ships; 19th century—whaling; 20th century—shipping and war. For the 21st century, see the real people—a cross-section of today's Norway—sitting at the statue's base. Major department stores (Galleriet, Xhibition, and Telegrafen) are all nearby.

The "blue stone," a popular meeting point at the far end of the square, marks the center of a park-like swath known as **Ole Bulls Plass,** leading from the National Theater (above on right) to a little lake (below on left). The theater, built in Art Nouveau style in 1909, was founded by violinist Ole Bull in 1850, and was the first to host plays in the Norwegian language. After 450 years of Danish and Swedish rule, 19th-century Norway enjoyed a cultural awakening, and Bergen became an artistic power. Ole Bull (a pop idol and heart-throb in his day—women fainted when they heard him play his violin) collaborated with the playwright Henrik Ibsen. Ibsen commissioned Edvard Grieg to write the music for his *Peer Gynt*. These three lions of Norwegian culture all lived and worked together right here in Bergen. The park that spills downhill from the theater has a pleasantly bustling urban ambience. It leads past a popular fountain of Ole Bull (under the trees) to a cast-iron pavilion given to the city by Germans in 1889, and on to the little manmade lake (Lille Lungegårdsvann), which is circled by an enjoyable path. This green zone is considered a park, and is cared for by the local parks department.

▲▲**Fløibanen**—Bergen's popular funicular climbs 1,000 feet in seven minutes to the top of Mount Fløyen for the best view of the town, surrounding islands, and fjords all the way to the west coast. The top is a popular picnic or pizza-to-go dinner spot (a Peppe's Pizza is tucked behind the Hanseatic Museum, a block away from the base of the lift) and also has its own view restaurant in summer (afford-able self-service all day, fancier dinners in evenings; see "Eating in Bergen," later). Sunsets are great here. The top is also the starting point for many peaceful hikes (ask for the *Fløyen Hiking Map* at the Fløibanen ticket window at the base). It's a pleasant but steep walk back down into Bergen. To save your knees, get off at the Promsgate stop halfway down, and then wander through the delightful cobbled and shiplap lanes (note that only the :00 and :30 departures stop at Promsgate). This funicular is regularly used by locals commuting into and out of downtown (70 kr round-trip, daily 7:30–23:00, May–Aug until 24:00, departures generally 4/hr—on the quarter-hour most of the day, tel. 55 33 68 00, www.floibanen.no).

Leprosy Museum (Lepramuseet)—Leprosy is also known as "Hansen's Disease" because in the 1870s a Bergen man named

Armauer Hansen did ground-breaking work in understanding the ailment. This unique museum is in St. Jørgens Hospital, a lep-rosarium that dates back to about 1700. Up until the 19th century, as much as 3 percent of Norway's population had leprosy. This hos-pital—once called "a graveyard for the living" (its last patient died in 1946)—has a meager exhibit in a thought-provoking shell attached to a 300-year-old church. It's really only worth your time and money if you stick around for the free tour (40 kr, mid-May–Aug daily 11:00–16:00, tour gener-ally at top of hour or by request, closed Sept–mid-May, between train station and Bryggen at Kong Oscars Gate 59, tel. 55 96 11 55, www.bymuseet.no).

BERGEN

▲**Wandering**—Bergen is a great strolling town. The harborfront is a fine place to kick back and watch the pigeons mate. Other good areas to explore are over the hill past Klostergate, Marken, Knosesmanet, Ytre Markevei, and the area behind Bryggen.

▲**Aquarium (Akvariet)**—Small, but great fun if you like fish, this aquarium claims to be the second-most-visited sight in Bergen. It's wonderfully laid out and explained in English. Check out the informative exhibit downstairs on Norway's fish-farming industry (150 kr, kids-100 kr, cheaper off-season, open daily May–Aug 9:00–19:00, Sept–April 10:00–18:00, feeding times at the top of most hours in summer, cheery cafeteria with light sandwiches, Nordnesbakken 4, tel. 55 55 71 71, www.akvariet.no). It's at the tip of the peninsula on the south end of the harbor—about a 20-minute walk or short ride on bus #11 from the TI. Or hop on the handy little Vågen "Akvariet" ferry that sails from the fish market to near the aquarium (60 kr round-trip, 2/hr). The lovely park behind the aquarium has views of the sea and a popular swimming beach (described next). The totem pole erected here was a gift from Bergen's sister city in the US—Seattle.

Swimming—Bergen has two seaside public swimming areas: one at the aquarium and the other in Gamle Bergen. Each is a great local scene on a hot sunny day. **Nordnes Sjøbad,** near the aquarium, offers swimmers an outdoor heated pool and a protected area of the sea (25 kr, kids-10 kr, mid-May–Aug Mon–Fri 7:00–19:00, Sat 7:00–14:00, Sun 10:00–14:00, Sat–Sun until 19:00 in good weather, closed off-season, Nordnesparken 30, tel. 55 90 21 70). **Sandviken Sjobad,** at Gamle Bergen (described next), is free. It comes with changing rooms, a roped-off bit of the bay (no pool), a high dive, and lots of sunbathing space.

▲**Gamle Bergen (Old Bergen)**—This Disney-cute gathering of fifty 18th- and 19th-century shops was founded in 1934 to save old buildings from destruction as Bergen modernized. Each of the houses was moved from elsewhere in Bergen and reconstructed here. Together, they create a virtual town that offers a cobbled look at the old life. It's free to wander through the town and park to enjoy the facades of the historic buildings. But to get into the 20 or so museum buildings, you'll need to join a 50-kr English tour, departing on the hour between 10:00–16:00 (open mid-May–early Sept daily 9:00–17:00, closed off-season, tel. 55 39 43 04, www .gamlebergen.museum.no). To get there, take any bus heading west from Bryggen (such as #20, direction: Lonborg) to Gamle Bergen (first stop after the tunnel). You'll get off at a freeway pullout and walk 200 yards, following signs to the museum. Any bus heading back into town takes you to the center (buses come by every few minutes). With the easy bus connection, there's no reason to taxi.

▲**Bergen Art Museum (Bergen Kunstmuseum)**—If you need to get out of the rain (and you enjoyed the National Gallery in Oslo), check out this collection of collections in several neighboring buildings on Rasmus Meyers allé. You'll see works by leading Norwegian painters such as Harriet Backer, J. C. Dahl, Christian Krohg, Edvard Munch, and an interesting modern art section. Small description sheets in English can be found in each room (60 kr, daily 11:00–17:00, closed Mon mid-Sept–mid-May, Rasmus Meyers allé 3, tel. 55 56 80 00, www.bergenartmuseum.no).

▲▲**The Bergen Folklore Show**—Enjoy an intimate and charming hour-long program of traditional music and dance in the historic Schøtstuene (Hanseatic Assembly Rooms). Dancers are accompanied by musicians playing the mouth organ and Hardanger fiddle (100-kr tickets sold by TI and at door, mid-June–late Aug, Tue at 21:00, a few steps below St. Mary's Church, tel. 55 55 20 06, mobile 97 52 86 30).

Near Bergen

▲**Ulriken643 Cable Car**—It's amazingly quick and easy to zip to the 643-meter-high (that's 2,110 feet) summit of Ulriken, the tallest mountain near Bergen. Stepping out of the cable car, you enter a different world, with views stretching to the ocean. A chart clearly shows the many well-marked and easy hikes that fan out over the vast rocky and grassy plateau above the tree line (circular walks of various lengths,

a 40-minute hike down, and a 4-hour hike to the top of the **Fløibanen funicular**). For less exercise, you can simply sunbathe, crack open a picnic, or enjoy the Ulriken restaurant. Summiting involves a 10-minute bus ride (2/hr, departs a block from the fish market) followed by a 5-minute cable-car ride (every 7 minutes, 195 kr round-trip with bus, 145 kr round-trip without bus, 80 kr one-way without bus).

▲▲**Edvard Grieg's Home, Troldhaugen**—Norway's greatest composer spent his last 22 summers here (1885–1907), soaking up inspirational fjord beauty and composing many of his greatest works. Grieg fused simple Norwegian folk tunes with the bombast of Europe's Romantic style. In a dreamy Victorian setting, Grieg's "Hill of the Trolls" is pleasant for anyone and essential for

Grieg fans. The house (which you'll visit on an included 20-min tour) and adjacent museum (with a 20-min video; request an English viewing) are full of memories, including his Steinway. The walls are festooned with photos of the musical and literary superstars of his generation. Hugely popular in his time, Grieg's 1907 funeral

attracted 40,000 mourners. His little studio hut near the water makes you want to sit down and modulate (60 kr, only by tour—departing 2/hr, open daily May–Sept 9:00–18:00, Oct–April 10:00–16:00, tel. 55 92 29 92, www.troldhaugen.com).

Ask the TI about piano concerts in the on-site concert hall—a gorgeous venue, with the fjord stretching out behind the big black

grand piano (220-kr evening concerts, 160-kr matinees, free shuttle bus from TI if you show concert ticket; concerts scheduled roughly mid-June–late Aug Sun and Wed at 18:00, Sat at 14:00). Delightful 30-minute lunch piano concerts (40 kr plus entry ticket) are offered Monday through Friday at 13:00 in June, July, and August.

Getting to Troldhaugen: Public buses drop you a long 20-minute walk from Troldhaugen and a 10-minute walk from the Fantoft Stave Church (described next); just head south on buses #20, #21, #22, #23, or #24 for 15–20 minutes. The three-hour city bus tour promoted by the TI is worthwhile for the informative recorded narration and efficient transportation, getting you within a five-minute walk of Troldhaugen (300 kr,

May–Sept daily at 12:00). If you're driving into Bergen from the east (such as from the Sognefjord), you'll drive right by Troldhaugen on your way into town.

Fantoft Stave Church—This huge, preserved-in-tar stave church burned down in 1992. It was rebuilt and reopened in 1997, but it will never be the same. Situated in a quiet forest next to a mysterious stone cross, this replica of a 12th-century wooden church is bigger, though no better, than

others covered in this book. But it's worth a look if you're in the neighborhood, even after-hours, for its evocative setting (40 kr, mid-May–mid-Sept daily 10:30–14:00 and 14:30–18:00, interior closed mid-Sept–mid-May, no English information, 3 miles south of Bergen on E39 in Paradis; for information on getting here, see the previous listing).

Shopping in Bergen

Most shops are open Mon–Fri 9:00–17:00, Thu until 19:00, Sat 9:00–15:00, and closed Sunday. Many of the tourist shops at the harborfront strip along Bryggen are open daily—even during holidays—until 20:00 or 21:00.

Bryggen is bursting with sweaters, pewter, and trolls. The **Husfliden** shop is popular for its handmade Norwegian sweaters and goodies (good variety and quality but expensive, just off the market square at Vågsalmenning 3).

The **Galleriet** shopping center on Torgalmenningen has six floors of shops, cafés, and restaurants. You'll find a pharmacy, photo shops, clothing, sporting goods, bookstores, and a basement grocery store (Mon–Fri 9:00–20:00, Sat 9:00–18:00, closed Sun).

Sleeping in Bergen

Busy with business travelers and increasingly popular with tourists, Bergen can be jammed any time of year. But with the economic crisis reaching Norway, once proud and pricey hotels may be willing to make deals. You might save a bundle by emailing the bigger hotels and asking for their best price. Otherwise, Bergen has some fine budget alternatives to normal hotels that can save you a bundle.

Hotels

$$$ Hotel Havnekontoret, with the best location in town, fills a grand old shipping headquarters dating from the 1920s. It's an especially fine value on weekends and in the summer, for those who will eat the included dinner. While part of a chain, it has a friendly spirit. Guests are welcome to climb its historic tower (with a magnificent view) or enjoy its free sauna and exercise room downstairs. The hotel's 116 rooms are expensive during weekdays, and half-price on weekends and through most of the summer. If you aren't interested in fancy dining, the room price includes virtually all your food—a fine breakfast, self-service waffles in the afternoon, fruit and coffee all day, and a light dinner buffet each evening. If you take advantage of them, these edible extras are easily worth 600 kr per day per couple,

---

Sleep Code

(6 kr = about $1, country code: 47)

S = Single, **D** = Double/Twin, **T** = Triple, **Q** = Quad, **b** = bathroom, **s** = shower. You can assume credit cards are accepted unless otherwise noted.

To help you sort easily through these listings, I've divided the rooms into three categories, based on the price for a standard double room with bath:

$$$ Higher Priced—Most rooms 1,200 kr or more.
$$ Moderately Priced—Most rooms between 850–1,200 kr.
$ Lower Priced—Most rooms 850 kr or less.

---

making the cost of this fancy hotel little more than a hostel (Db during business peak-2,300 kr, Db Fri-Sun and most of summer-1,200–1,500 kr, extra bed-300 kr, book online to save, free Wi-Fi, facing the harbor across the street from the SAS Radisson Hotel at Slottsgaten 1, tel. 55 60 11 00, www.choicehotels.no, cc.havnekontoret@choice.no).

$$$ Hotel Park Pension is classy, comfortable, and in a fine residential neighborhood a 15-minute uphill walk from the town center (10 min from the train station). It's tinseled in Old World, lived-in charm, yet comes with all of today's amenities (33 rooms—22 in classy old-fashioned hotel, 11 in modern annex across the street; Sb-1,050 kr, Db-1,250 kr, extra bed-350 kr, includes breakfast, winter weekend discounts, free Wi-Fi, Harald Hårfagres Gate 35, tel. 55 54 44 00, fax 55 54 44 44, www.parkhotel.no, booking@parkhotel.no).

$$$ Thon Hotel Rosenkrantz, with 129 rooms, is one block behind Bryggen, between the Bryggens Museum and the Fløibanen funicular station—right in the heart of Bergen's appealing old quarter. However, the next-door nightclub is noisy on Friday and Saturday nights—be sure to request a quiet room (rack rates: Sb-1,295 kr, Db-1,695 kr, these prices include light dinner Mon–Thu; mid-June–Aug: Db-1,200 kr without dinner; includes breakfast, elevator, free Internet access, pay Wi-Fi, Rosenkrantzgate 7, tel. 55 30 14 00, www.thonhotels.no/rosenkrantz, rosenkrantz @thonhotels.no).

$$ P-Hotel, a new, sleek budget hotel, has 43 basic rooms just up from Ole Bulls Plass. While it's not particularly charming and some rooms come with street noise, the price is right (Sb-795 kr, Db-895 kr, credit card only—no cash, box breakfast in your room, elevator, free Wi-Fi, Vestre Torggate, tel. 80 04 68 35, www .p-hotels.no, bergen@p-hotels.no).

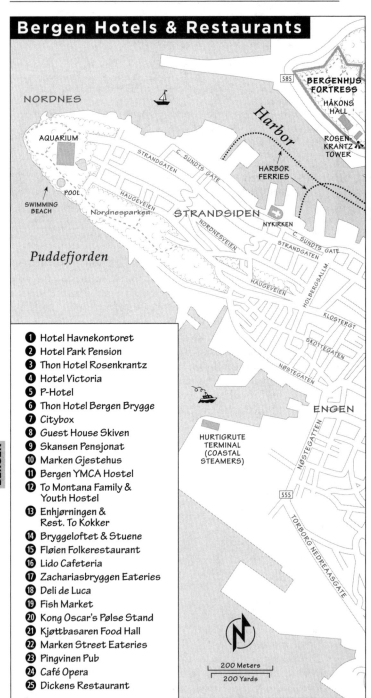

Bergen Hotels & Restaurants

BERGEN

1 Hotel Havnekontoret
2 Hotel Park Pension
3 Thon Hotel Rosenkrantz
4 Hotel Victoria
5 P-Hotel
6 Thon Hotel Bergen Brygge
7 Citybox
8 Guest House Skiven
9 Skansen Pensjonat
10 Marken Gjestehus
11 Bergen YMCA Hostel
12 To Montana Family &
   Youth Hostel
13 Enhjørningen &
   Rest. To Kokker
14 Bryggeloftet & Stuene
15 Fløien Folkerestaurant
16 Lido Cafeteria
17 Zachariasbryggen Eateries
18 Deli de Luca
19 Fish Market
20 Kong Oscar's Pølse Stand
21 Kjøttbasaren Food Hall
22 Marken Street Eateries
23 Pingvinen Pub
24 Café Opera
25 Dickens Restaurant

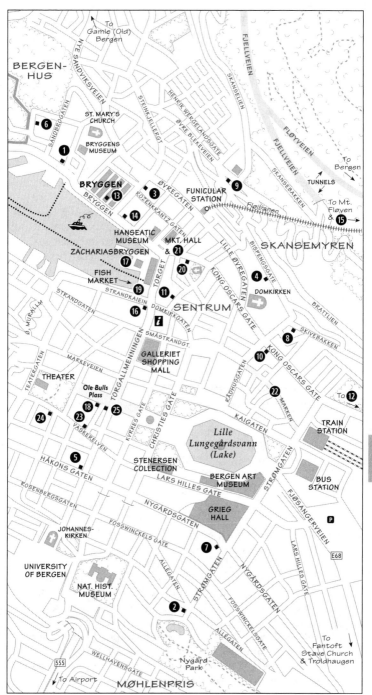

$$ Thon Hotel Bergen Brygge, beyond Bryggen near Håkon's Hall, is part of Thon's cheaper "Budget" chain. However, the 229 rooms are just about as nice as those in its sister hotels. Because of its good prices and great location, it fills up quickly—book ahead (rack rates: Sb-810 kr, Db-1,075 kr, discounts unlikely but you save 7 percent if you book online, skip breakfast to save 65 kr/person, elevator, free Internet access, pay Wi-Fi, Bradbenken 3, tel. 55 30 87 00, fax 55 32 94 14, www.thonhotels.com/bergen brygge, bergenbrygge@thonhotels.no).

$ Hotel Victoria is an old hotel turned into a college dorm that becomes a utilitarian, minimalist budget hotel each summer. There are no public spaces, the tiny reception is open only 9:00–23:00, and you won't get your towels changed. But its 40 modern, bright, simple rooms are plenty comfortable for the price (open June–Aug only, Sb-750 kr, Db-850 kr, Tb-1,150 kr, free Wi-Fi, Kong Oscarsgate 29, tel. 55 31 50 30, www.victoria-hotell.no, booking@victoria-hotell.no).

$ Citybox is a unique, no-nonsense hotel concept: plain, white, clean, and practical. It rents 52 rooms online and provides you with a confirmation number. Check-in is automated—just punch in your number and get your ticket. The reception is staffed daily 9:00–16:00 (S-400 kr, Sb-500 kr, D-600 kr, Db-700 kr, extra bed-150 kr, family room for up to four-1,000 kr, no breakfast, elevator, just away from the bustle in a mostly residential part of town at Nygårdsgate 31, tel. 55 31 25 00, www.citybox.no, post@citybox.no).

Private Homes and Pensions

If you're looking for local character and don't mind sharing a shower, these accommodations—far more quiet, homey, and convenient than hostel beds—might just be the best values in town.

$ Guest House Skiven is a humble little place beautifully situated on a steep, traffic-free cobbled lane called "the most painted street in Bergen." Alf and Elizabeth Heskja (who live upstairs) rent four non-smoking doubles that share a shower, two WCs, and a kitchen (D-500 kr for Rick Steves readers, no breakfast, free Wi-Fi, 4 blocks from station at Skivebakken 17, tel. 55 31 30 30, mobile 90 05 30 30, www.skiven.no, rs@skiven.no). From the station, go down Kong Oscars Gate, uphill on D. Krohns Gate, and up the stairs at the end of the block on the left.

$ Skansen Pensjonat (not to be confused with the nearby Skansen Guest House) is situated 100 yards directly behind the entrance to the Fløibanen funicular. Jannicke Alvær rents seven tastefully decorated rooms with views over town (small non-view S-400 kr, larger S-450 kr, D-650 kr, fancy D on corner with view and balcony-750 kr, includes breakfast, 2 showers on ground floor, 2 WCs, sinks in rooms, family room with TV; all non-smoking, free Wi-Fi, Vetrlidsalmenning 29, tel. 55 31 90 80, www.skansen-pensjonat.no, mail@skansen-pensjonat.no). Follow the switchback road behind the Fløibanen station to the paved plateau with benches, and look for the sign.

Dorms and Hostels

$ Marken Gjestehus is a quiet, tidy, and conveniently positioned 100-bed place between the station and the harborfront. Its rooms, while spartan, are modern and cheery. Breakfast is included, but you'll pay a one-time 65-kr fee for sheets (dorm bed in 8-bed room-175 kr, in 4-bed room-220 kr, S-450 kr, D-550 kr, Db-800 kr, extra bed-135 kr, towels-15 kr, free Wi-Fi, elevator, kitchen, laundry, open all year but with limited reception hours, fourth floor at Kong Oscars Gate 45, tel. 55 31 44 04, fax 55 31 60 22, www.marken-gjestehus.com, post@marken-gjestehus.com).

$ Bergen YMCA Hostel (IYHF), located a block in front of the TI and two blocks from the fish market, is the best location for the price, and its rooms are nicely maintained (bunk in 12- to 32-bed dorm with shared shower and kitchen-180 kr, bunk in 6-bed family room with private bathroom and kitchen-260 kr, Db with kitchen-900 kr, 15 percent cheaper for members June–Aug only, includes sheets, breakfast-60 kr, pay Internet access, free Wi-Fi, roof terrace, fully open June–Aug, no dorm beds off-season, Nedre Korskirkeallmenningen 4, tel. 55 60 60 55, www.bergenhostel.com, ymca@online.no).

Away from the Center: **$$ Montana Family & Youth Hostel (IYHF),** while one of Europe's best, is high-priced for a hostel and way out of town. Still, the bus connections (#31, 15 min from the center) and the facilities—modern rooms, classy living room, no curfew, huge free parking lot, and members' kitchen—are excellent (dorm bed in 20-bed room-200 kr—May–Sept only, bed in Q-265 kr, bed in Tb-300 kr; Sb-650 kr, Db-780 kr; 15 percent cheaper for members, sheets-70 kr, includes breakfast, 30 Johan Blytts Vei, tel. 55 20 80 70, www.montana.no, booking@montana.no).

Eating in Bergen

Bergen has numerous choices: restaurants with rustic, woody atmosphere, candlelight, and steep prices (entrées around 300 kr); chain restaurants that serve pizza, burgers, ribs, and chicken (150–250-kr entrées and pizzas); cafeterias and ethnic eateries with less ambience where you can get quality food at lower prices (100–200 kr); and take-away sandwich shops, bakeries, and cafés for a light bite (50–100 kr). You can always get a glass or pitcher of water for free, and fancy places give you seconds on potatoes for free—just ask. Remember, if you get your food to go, it's taxed at a lower rate and you'll save 12 percent.

Splurges in Bryggen

You'll pay a premium to eat at these three restaurants, but you'll have a memorable meal in a pleasant setting. If it's beyond your budget, remember that you can fill up on potatoes and drink tap water to dine for exactly the price of the dinner plate.

Enhjørningen Restaurant ("The Unicorn") is *the* place in Bergen for fish. With thickly painted walls and no right angles, this dressy-yet-old-time wooden interior wins my "Bryggen Atmosphere" award. The dishes, while not hearty, are close to gourmet and beautifully presented (275–320-kr main dishes, 500–600-kr multi-course meals, nightly 16:00–22:30, #29 on Bryggen harborfront—look for anatomically correct unicorn on the old wharf facade and dip into the alley and up the stairs, tel. 55 30 69 50).

Restaurant To Kokker, down the alley from Enhjørningen (and with the same owners), serves more meat and game. The prices and quality are equivalent, but even though it's also in an elegant old wooden building, I like the Unicorn's atmosphere much better (most main dishes around 300 kr, 500–650-kr multi-course meals, Mon–Sat 17:00–23:00, closed Sun, tel. 55 30 69 55).

Bryggeloftet & Stuene Restaurant, in a brick building just before the wooden stretch of Bryggen, is a vast eatery serving seafood and traditional meals. To dine memorably yet affordably, this is your best Bryggen bet. Upstairs feels more elegant and less touristy than the main floor—if there's a line downstairs, just head on up (100–150-kr lunches, 200–300-kr dinners, Mon–Sat 11:00–23:30, Sun 13:00–23:30, #11 on Bryggen harborfront, try reserving a view window upstairs, tel. 55 30 20 70).

Atop Mount Fløyen, at the Top of the Funicular

Fløien Folkerestaurant offers meals with a panoramic view. The cheaper cafeteria section has a light menu, with coffee, cake, and sandwiches for around 50 kr and a 115-kr soup buffet (May–Aug daily 10:00–22:00, Sept–April Sat–Sun only 12:00–17:00). The restaurant section has decent, expensive dinners with an emphasis on locally caught fish for about 250–350 kr (130–150-kr lighter dishes, May–Aug daily 17:00–23:00, restaurant closed Sept–April, tel. 55 33 69 99).

Cafeteria Overlooking the Fish Market

Lido offers basic, affordable food with great harbor and market views, better ambience than most self-serve places, and a

BERGEN

museum's worth of old town photos on the walls. For cold items (such as open-face sandwiches and desserts, 50–80 kr), grab what you want, pay the cashier, and find a table. For hot dishes (120–170-kr Norwegian standards, including one daily special discounted to 105 kr), grab a table, order and pay at the cashier, and they'll bring your food to you (June–Aug Mon–Fri 10:00–21:00, Sat–Sun 13:00–20:00; Sept–May Mon–Fri 10:00–19:00, Sat 10:00–18:00, Sun 13:00–18:00; second floor at Torgalmenningen 1a, tel. 55 32 59 12).

Good Chain Restaurants

You'll find these tasty chain restaurants in Bergen and throughout Norway. All of these are open long hours daily (shorter off-season). Several are located at **Zachariasbryggen,** a modern restaurant complex lining a pier at the head of the harbor (on Torget), which also has an overpriced Tex-Mex restaurant.

Peppe's Pizza has cold beer and good pizzas (medium size for 1–2 people-175–200 kr, large for 2–3 people-200–250 kr, take-out possible; consider the Moby Dick, with curried shrimp, leeks, and bell peppers). There are six Peppe's in Bergen, including one behind the Hanseatic Museum near the Fløibanen funicular station and another inside the Zachariasbryggen harborfront dining complex, with views over the harbor.

Baker Brun makes 50–70-kr sandwiches, including wonderful shrimp baguettes, and pastries such as *skillingsbolle*—cinnamon rolls—warm out of the oven (open from 9:00, seating inside or take-away; locations include facing the fish market at Zachariasbryggen and in Bryggen).

Bon Appétit sells 60-kr baguette sandwiches and wraps, plus ice cream (locations include near Baker Brun at Zachariasbryggen and in Bryggen). Restaurant desserts run 100 kr; strolling with an ice-cream cone can save plenty.

Deli de Luca is a cut above other take-away joints, adding sushi and calzones to the normal lineup of sandwiches. While a bit more expensive than the others, the variety and quality are appealing (open long hours daily, on corner of Engen and Vaskerelven—a block off Ole Bulls Plass). With good weather, enjoy your meal with sun-worshipping locals in the great Theater Park across the street.

Budget Bets

The **Fish Market** has lots of stalls bursting with salmon sandwiches, fresh shrimp, fish-and-chips, and fish cakes. For a tasty, memorable, and inexpensive Bergen meal, assemble a seafood picnic here (ask for prices first; June–Aug daily 7:00–19:00, less lively Sun; Sept–May Mon–Sat 7:00–16:00, closed Sun).

Kong Oscar's Pølse Stand, your classic hot-dog stand, sells a wide variety of sausages (various sizes and flavors—including reindeer). The well-described English menu makes it easy to order your choice of artery-clogging guilty pleasures (15-kr tiny weenie, 45-kr medium-size weenie, 65-kr jumbo, open daily 11:00–5:00 in the morning, you'll see the little hot-dog shack a block up Kong Oscar Gate from the harbor, Kenneht is the boss).

Kjøttbasaren, the restored meat market of 1887, is a genteel-feeling food hall with stalls selling groceries such as meat, cheese, bread, and olives—a great opportunity to assemble a bang-up picnic (Mon–Fri 10:00–17:00, Thu until 18:00, Sat 9:00–16:00, closed Sun).

Marken Pedestrian Street Eateries

This cobbled lane, leading from the train station to the harbor, is lined with creative little restaurants and trendy cafés. Strolling along here, you can choose from cheap chicken and burgers, Vietnamese at **Bambus 33** (elegant, seating indoors and out, daily 14:00–23:00, Marken 33, tel. 55 56 00 60), the **Indian Palace** (with 70-kr lunch special, Marken 32), and the **Aura Café** (classy sandwiches and salads, indoors and out, daily until 20:00, weekends until 19:00, Marken 9).

From Ole Bulls Plass up to the Theater

Bergen's "in" cafés are stylish, cozy, small, and open very late—a great opportunity to experience the local yuppie scene. Around the cinema on Neumannsgate, there are numerous ethnic restaurants, including Italian, Middle Eastern, and Chinese.

Pingvinen Pub ("The Penguin") is a homey place in a charming neighborhood, serving traditional Norwegian home cooking to an enthusiastic local clientele. The pub has only indoor seating, with a long row of stools at the bar and five charming, living-room-cozy tables. After the kitchen closes, the place stays open very late as a pub. For unpretentious Norwegian cooking in a completely untouristy atmosphere, this is your best budget value (daily plates-120–150 kr, Sun–Thu 14:00–22:45, Fri–Sat 12:00–20:45, Vaskerelven 14 near the National Theater, tel. 55 60 46 46).

Café Opera, with a playful-slacker vibe, is the hip budget choice for its loyal, youthful following. With two floors of seating, and tables out front across from the theater, it's a winner (light 30–40-kr sandwiches until 16:00, 100–130-kr dinners, daily 11:00–24:00, occasional live music, live locals nightly, English newspapers in summer, chess, around the left side of the theater at Engen 18, tel. 55 23 03 15).

Dickens is a lively, checkerboard, turn-of-the-century–feeling place serving fish, chicken, and steak. The window tables in the atrium are great for people-watching, as is the fine outdoor terrace

(150-kr lunches, 250-kr dinners, Mon–Sat 11:00–24:00, later on Fri and Sat, Sun 13:00–24:00, reservations smart, Kong Olav V's Plass 4, tel. 55 36 31 30).

Bergen Connections

Bergen is conveniently connected to **Oslo** by plane and train (trains depart Bergen daily at 7:58, 10:28, 15:58, and 22:58—but no night train on Sat, arrive at Oslo seven scenic hours later, additional departures in summer and fall, confirm times at station, 50-kr seat reservation required—but free with first-class railpass, book well in advance if traveling mid-July–Aug). From Bergen, you can take the Norway in a Nutshell train/bus/ferry route; for information, see the Norway in a Nutshell chapter. Train info: tel. 81 50 08 88.

To get to **Stockholm** or **Copenhagen,** you'll go via Oslo (see "Oslo Connections" on page 68)...unless you fly. Before buying a ticket for a long train trip from Bergen, look into cheap flights.

By Express Boat to Balestrand and Flåm (on Sognefjord): The handy Fylkesbaatane express boat links Bergen with Balestrand (4 hrs) and Flåm (5.5 hrs).

By Bus to Kristiansand: If you're heading to Denmark on the ferry from Kristiansand, catch the Haukeli express bus (departing Bergen daily at 7:30). After a nearly two-hour layover in Haukeli, take the bus at 14:40, arriving at 18:50 in Kristiansand in time for the overnight ferry to Denmark (for boat details, see the South Norway chapter).

By Boat to Stavanger: Flaggruten catamarans sail to Stavanger (2–4/day, 4 hrs, 720 kr one-way, 950 kr round-trip; nearly half-price for students and railpass-holders; tel. 55 23 87 00 or 05505, www.hsd.no). From Stavanger, trains run to Kristiansand and Oslo, and ships sail to Denmark (for Stavanger's transportation connections, see the South Norway chapter).

By Boat to Denmark: Fjordline runs a boat from Bergen to Hirtshals, Denmark (17 hours; departs Mon, Wed, Fri generally at 12:30; boat from Hirtshals runs Sun, Tue, and Thu; seat in reclining chair-around 1,500 kr, tel. 81 53 35 00, www.fjordline.com).

By Boat to the Arctic: Hurtigruten coastal steamers depart nearly daily (mid-April–mid-Sept at 20:00, mid-Sept–mid-April

at 22:00) for the seven-day trip north up the scenic west coast to Kirkenes on the Russian border.

This route was started in 1893 as a postal and cargo delivery service along the west coast of Norway. Although no longer delivering mail, their ships still fly the Norwegian postal flag by special permission and deliver people, cars, and cargo from Bergen to Kirkenes. A lifeline for remote areas, the ships call at 34 fishing villages and cities.

For the seven-day trip to Kirkenes, allow from $1,599 and up per person based on double occupancy (includes three meals per day, taxes, and port charges). Prices vary greatly depending on the season (highest June–July), cabin, and type of ship. Their fleet includes those with a bit of brass built in the 1960s, but the majority of the ships were built in the mid-1990s and later. Shorter voyages are possible (including even just a day trip to one of the villages along the route). Cabins should be booked well in advance. Ship services include a 24-hour cafeteria, a launderette on newer ships, and optional port excursions ($28–170). Check online for senior and off-season (Oct–March) specials at www .hurtigruten.com.

Call Hurtigruten in New York (US tel. 800-323-7436) or in Norway (tel. 81 00 30 30). For most travelers, the ride makes a great one-way trip, but a flight back south is a logical last leg (rather than returning to Bergen by boat—a 12-day round-trip).

SOUTH NORWAY

Stavanger • Setesdal Valley • Kristiansand

South Norway is not about must-see sights or jaw-dropping scenery—it's simply pleasant and pretty. Spend a day in the harborside town of Stavanger. Delve into your Scandinavian roots at the Norwegian Emigration Center or into the oil industry at the surprisingly interesting Petroleum Museum. Window-shop in the old town, cruise the harbor, or hoof it up Pulpit Rock for a fine view.

A series of time-forgotten towns stretch across the Setesdal Valley, with sod-roofed cottages and locals who practice fiddles and harmonicas, rose painting, whittling, and gold- and silver-work. The famous Setesdal filigree echoes the rhythmical designs of the Viking era and Middle Ages. Each town has a weekly rotating series of hikes and activities for the regular, stay-put-for-a-week visitor. The upper valley is dead in the summer but enjoys a bustling winter.

In Kristiansand, Norway's answer to a seaside resort, promenade along the strand, sample a Scandinavian zoo, or set sail to Denmark.

Planning Your Time

Even on a busy itinerary, Stavanger warrants a day. If you are an avid genealogist, consider two. The port town is connected by boat to Bergen (and Hirtshals, Denmark) and by train to Kristiansand.

Frankly, without a car, the Setesdal Valley is not worth the trouble. There are no trains in the valley, bus schedules are as sparse as the population, and the sights are best for joyriding. If you're in Bergen with a car, and want to get to Denmark, this route is more interesting than repeating Oslo. On a three-week Scandinavian trip, I'd do it in one long day, as follows: 7:00-Leave

Bergen; 9:00—Catch Kvanndal ferry to Utne; 10:00—Say good-bye to the last fjord at Odda; 13:00—Lunch in Hovden at the top of Setesdal Valley; 14:00—Frolic south with a few short stops in the valley; 16:30—Arrive in Kristiansand for dinner. Spend the night and catch the 9:00 boat to Denmark the next morning.

Kristiansand is not a destination town, but rather a place to pass through, conveniently connecting Norway to Denmark by ferry.

Stavanger

This burg of about 117,000 feels more cosmopolitan than most Norwegian cities. This is thanks in part to the oil industry, with its multinational workers and the money they bring into the city. Known as Norway's festival city, Stavanger hosts several lively events, including jazz in May (www.maijazz.no), chamber music in August (www.icmf.no), and a wooden boats festival in early September. With all of this culture, it's no surprise that Stavanger was named a European Capital of Culture for 2008.

Orientation to Stavanger

The most scenic and interesting parts of Stavanger surround its harbor. Here you'll find the Norwegian Emigration Center, lots of shops and restaurants, the indoor fish market, and a produce market (Mon–Fri 9:00–16:00, Sat 9:00–15:00, closed Sun). The artificial Lake Breiavatnet—bordered by Kongsgaten on the east and Olav V's Gate on the west—separates the train and bus stations from the harbor.

Tourist Information

The helpful staff at the TI can help you plan your time in Stavanger, and can also give you hiking tips and day-trip information. Pick up a free city guide and map (June–Aug daily 9:00–18:00; Sept–May Mon–Fri 9:00–16:00, Sat 9:00–14:00, closed Sun; Domkirkeplassen 3, tel. 51 85 92 00, www.regionstavanger.com).

Arrival in Stavanger

By Boat: Express boats from Bergen dock at Fiskepiren. From here, it's a five-minute walk to the center of town or to the train station. A taxi to a downtown hotel costs about 100 kr (tel. 51 90 90 90 or 51 90 90 50).

By Train and Bus: Stavanger's train and bus stations are a five-minute walk around Lake Breiavatnet to the harbor (train

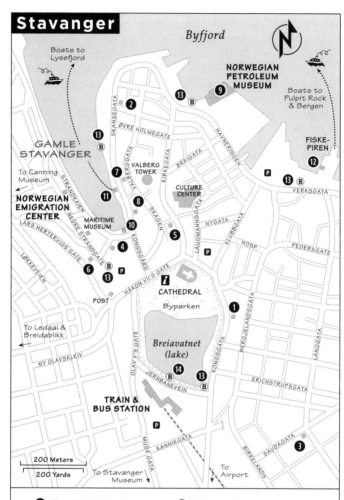

Stavanger

Byfjord

Boats to Lysefjord

NORWEGIAN PETROLEUM MUSEUM

Boats to Pulpit Rock & Bergen

GAMLE STAVANGER

FISKE-PIREN

To Canning Museum

NORWEGIAN EMIGRATION CENTER

VALBERG TOWER

MARITIME MUSEUM

CULTURE CENTER

POST

CATHEDRAL

Byparken

To Ledaal & Breidablikk

Breiavatnet (lake)

TRAIN & BUS STATION

200 Meters
200 Yards

To Stavanger Museum

To Airport

SKANSEGATA · ØVRE HOLMEGATE · KIRKEGATA · BREIGATA · HAVNERINGEN · VERKSGATA · VALBERGGATA · SKAGEN · LAUGMANNSGATE · NYGATA · KLUBBGGA · HOSP · PEDERSGATE · STRANDKAIEN · NEDRE STRANDGATE · LARS HERTERVIGS GATE · LØKKEVEIEN · KONGSGGARD · HAKON VII'S GATE · BERGJELANDSGATA · KONGSGATA · LANGGATA · NY OLAVSKLEIV · OLAV'S GATE · JERNBANEVEIN · ERICHSTRUPSGATA · MUSE GATA · KANNIKGATA · BIRKELANDS · SAUDAGATA

Legend

1. Thon Hotel Maritim
2. Skansen Hotell & Gjestehus
3. Stavanger B&B
4. Nye La Piazza Rest.
5. Vertshuset Mat & Vin Restaurant
6. Meny Supermarket
7. N. B. Sorensen's Dampskibsexpedition Pub & Rest.
8. Sjøhuset Skagen Rest.
9. Bølgen og Moi Rest.
10. Fish Market
11. Boats to Lysefjord
12. Boats to Pulpit Rock & Bergen
13. Flybussen (Airport Bus) Stops
14. Bus to Fjordline Terminal (Ferries to Hirtshals, Denmark)

SOUTH NORWAY

ticket and reservation office Mon–Thu 6:30–17:45, Fri 6:30–19:45, Sat 9:00–16:45, Sun 10:30–17:45). Luggage lockers and Norway-wide train timetables are available at the train station.

By Plane: Stavanger's Sola Airport, about nine miles outside the city, is connected to downtown by the Flybussen (85 kr, buy ticket on bus, Mon–Fri 7:45–24:15, 3–4/hr, less Sat–Sun, 30 min, tel. 51 59 90 60, www.flybussen.no). This airport bus shuttles travelers to the bus station (Byterminalen) and train station (next to each other), the city center, and the boat terminal (Fiskepiren). To get to the airport from the city center, catch the shuttle at any of these stops.

Sights in Stavanger

▲▲Norwegian Petroleum Museum (Norskolje Museum)—
This entertaining, informative museum—dedicated to the discovery of oil in Norway's North Sea in 1969 and the industry built up around it—offers something for everyone. With half of Western Europe's oil reserves, Norway is the Arabia of the North. Since the discovery of oil here in 1969, the formerly poor agricultural nation has been transformed into a world-class player. It's ranked third among the world's top oil exporters, producing 3.2 billion barrels a day.

This museum describes how oil was formed, how it's found and produced, and what it's used for. There are interactive exhibits covering everything from the "History of the Earth" (4.5 billion years displayed on a large overhead globe, showing how our planet has changed—stay for the blast that killed the dinosaurs), to day-to-day life on an offshore platform, to petroleum products in our lives. Kids love the model drilling platform that they can climb on. The museum's architecture was designed to echo the foundations of the oil industry—bedrock (the stone building), slate and chalk deposits in the sea (slate floor of the main hall), and the rigs (cylindrical platforms). While the museum has its fair share of propaganda, it also has several good exhibits on the environmental toll of drilling and consuming oil (80 kr; June–Aug daily 10:00–19:00; Sept–May Mon–Sat 10:00–16:00, Sun 10:00–18:00; tel. 51 93 93 00, www.norskolje.museum.no). The small museum shop sells various petroleum-based products.

Eating at the Museum: The **Bølgen og Moi** restaurant has an inviting terrace over the water for thirsty museum-goers. They also serve lunch (from 150 kr) and dinner (480–600 kr), with a fantastic view over the harbor (daily 11:00–17:00 and 16:00–22:00, reservations recommended for dinner, tel. 51 93 93 53).

▲Norwegian Emigration Center (Det Norske Utvandrer-senteret Ble)—This fine museum, in an old warehouse near the wharf where the first boats sailed with emigrants to "Amerika" in 1825, is worth ▲▲▲ for anyone seeking his or her Norwegian roots. On the second floor, you'll find a study center and library. It's free to use the computers and microfilm viewers to look up your relatives. The library is lined with shelves of *bygdebøker*— books from farm districts all over Norway, documenting the history of landowners and local families. For 300 kr per hour, the staff will give you a step-by-step consultation. Otherwise, they'll help answer questions and steer you in the right direction at no charge. The third floor has a small exhibit everyone will enjoy: It tells the story of the first emigrants who left for America—why they left, the journey, and what life was like in the New World (library—free, museum—20 kr, Mon–Fri 9:00–15:00, closed Sat-Sun, Standkaien 31, tel. 51 53 88 60, www.emigrationcenter.com). If you want to look up relatives, do some homework ahead of time and bring at least two or three of the following: family surname, farm name, birth year, and emigration year.

Stavanger Museum—This "museum" is actually five different buildings/museums covered by one 60-kr ticket: the **Stavanger Museum,** featuring the history of the city and a zoological exhibit (Muségate 16); Stavanger **Sjøfartsmuseum,** the maritime museum (Nedre Strandgate 17–19); **Norsk Hermetikkmuseum,** the Norwegian canning museum (*brisling*—herring—is smoked mid-June–mid-Aug Tue and Thu, Øvre Strandgate 88A); **Ledaal,** a royal residence and manor house (Eiganesveien 45); and **Breidablikk,** a wooden villa from the late 1800s (Eiganesveien 40A). Pick up the handy brochure and buy your ticket from the TI (museums open mid-June–mid-Aug daily 11:00–16:00; off-season Tue–Sun 11:00–16:00, closed Mon, except Ledaal and Breidablikk—open Sun only; www.stavanger.museum.no).

Gamle Stavanger—Stavanger's "old town" centers on Øvre Strandgate, on the west side of the harbor. Wander the narrow, winding back lanes and peek into a workshop or gallery to find ceramics, glass, jewelry, and more (free, shops and galleries open roughly daily 10:00–16:00, coinciding with the arrival of cruise ships).

Stavanger Cathedral (Domkirke)—The cathedral was originally built in 1125 in a Norman style, with basket-handle Romanesque arches. After a fire badly damaged the church in the 13th century, a new chancel was added in the pointy-arched Gothic style. Have a look inside and see where the architecture changes about three-quarters of the way up the aisle (free; June–Aug daily 11:00–19:00; Sept–May Tue–Thu and Sat–Sun 11:00–16:00, closed Mon and Fri; tel. 51 84 04 00).

SOUTH NORWAY

Day Trips to Lysefjord and Pulpit Rock

The nearby Lysefjord is an easy day trip. Those with more time (and strong legs) can hike to the top of the 1,800-foot-high Pulpit Rock (Preikestolen). The dramatic 270-square-foot plateau atop the rock gives you a fantastic view of the fjord and surrounding mountains. The TI has brochures for several boat tour companies and sells tickets.

Boat Tour of Lysefjord—Rodne Clipper Fjord Sightseeing offers 3.5-hour round-trip excursions from Stavanger to Lysefjord (including a view of Pulpit Rock). Boats depart from the east side of the harbor, in front of Skansegaten, along Skagenkaien. Buy your ticket on board or at the TI (380 kr; July–Aug daily at 10:30 and 14:30, Thu–Sat also at 12:00; May–June and Sept daily at 12:00; Oct–April Fri–Sun only at 12:00; tel. 51 89 52 70, www.rodne.no).

Ferry and Bus to Pulpit Rock—The Pulpit Rock trail's starting point, about an hour from Stavanger by a ferry-and-bus combination, is easily reached in summer by public transit or tour. Then comes the hard part: the two-hour hike to the top. The total distance is 4.5 miles and the elevation gain is roughly 1,000 feet. Pack a lunch and plenty of water and wear good shoes.

Tide Reiser offers ferry-and-bus tours to the trailhead from Stavanger. The following are approximate departures—reconfirm all times at the TI before you go: Ferries leave from the Fiskepiren boat terminal to Tau (200-kr combo-ticket includes bus, mid-May–mid-Sept daily at 8:00 and 9:45, mid-April–mid-May and late Sept daily at 9:45 only; no tours Oct–mid-April, tel. 55 23 87 00, www.tide reiser.com). After you cross the fjord to Tau, buses meet the incoming ferries and head to Pulpit Rock cabin or to Preikestolen Fjellstue, the local youth hostel. Be sure to time your hike so that you can catch the last bus leaving Pulpit Rock cabin for the ferry (mid-May–mid-Sept last bus leaves daily at 18:15, mid-April–mid-May and late Sept last bus leaves at 15:45). Cheaper public transit options are also available; pick up the helpful leaflet and confirm details at the TI. They can also give you details about more strenuous hikes.

Sleeping in Stavanger

$$$ Thon Hotel Maritim, about two blocks from the train station, near the artificial Lake Breiavatnet, can be a good deal for a big-business class hotel (Sb-1,222 kr, Db-1,472 kr; weekends Sb-775 kr, Db-1,020 kr; includes breakfast, elevator, Kongsgaten 32, tel. 51 85 05 00, fax 51 85 05 01, www.thonhotels.no/maritim, maritim@thonhotels.no).

$$$ Skansen Hotell & Gjestehus splits 28 rooms between its hotel (newer, more expensive rooms) and guest house (less

---

Sleep Code

(6 kr = about $1, country code: 47)
S = Single, **D** = Double/Twin, **T** = Triple, **Q** = Quad, **b** = bathroom, **s** = shower. All of these places accept credit cards.

To help you sort easily through these listings, I've divided the rooms into three categories, based on the price for a standard double room with bath:

$$$ **Higher Priced**—Most rooms 1,000 kr or more.
$$ **Moderately Priced**—Most rooms between 600–1,000 kr.
$ **Lower Priced**—Most rooms 600 kr or less.

---

expensive for essentially the same quality). Most of the rooms are on the street and can be noisy, but you're just off the harbor in a great location (hotel: Sb-1,130 kr, Db-1,290 kr; guest house: Sb-1,030 kr, Db-1,190 kr; about 400 kr cheaper on Fri–Sun nights, includes breakfast, non-smoking floors, elevator to most floors, Skansengate 7, tel. 51 93 85 00, fax 51 93 85 01, www.skansenhotel .no, post@skansenhotel.no).

$$ Stavanger B&B is your best home-away-from-home in Stavanger. This large red house among a sea of white houses has 14 tidy rooms, each with its own shower (but the toilet's down the hall). Waffles, coffee, and friendly chatter are served up every evening at 21:00 (Ss-790 kr, Ds-890 kr, Ts-990 kr, extra bed-150 kr, includes breakfast, 10-min walk behind train station in residential neighborhood, Vikedalsgate 1A, tel. 51 56 25 00, fax 51 56 25 01, www.stavangerbedandbreakfast.no, peck@online.no). If you let them know in advance, they may be able to pick you up or drop you off at the boat dock or train station.

Eating in Stavanger

Casual Dining

Nye La Piazza, just off the harbor, has an assortment of pasta and other Italian dishes, including pizza, for 125–200 kr (Mon 13:00–24:00, Tue–Sat 12:00–24:00, Sun 12:00–22:00, Rosenkildettorget 1, tel. 51 52 02 52).

Vertshuset Mat & Vin, in an elegant setting, serves up big portions of traditional Norwegian food and pricier contemporary fare (200–270 kr, light meals-90–150 kr, open daily 11:00–22:00, a block behind main drag along harbor at Skagen 10 ved Prostbakken, tel. 51 89 51 12).

Meny is a large supermarket with a good selection and a fine deli for super-picnic shopping (Mon–Fri 9:00–20:00, Sat until 18:00, closed Sun, in Straen Senteret shopping mall, Lars Hertervigs Gate 6, tel. 51 50 50 10).

Dining Along the Harbor with a View

The harborside street of Skansegata is lined with lively restaurants and pubs, and most serve food. Here are a couple options:

N. B. Sorensen's Dampskibsexpedition consists of a lively pub on the first floor (150–200 kr for pasta, fish, meat, and vegetarian dishes, Mon–Sat 11:00–24:00, Sun 13:00–23:00) and a fine-dining restaurant on the second floor, with tablecloths, view tables overlooking the harbor, and entrées from 300 kr (Mon–Sat 18:00–23:00, closed Sun, Skagenkaien 26, tel. 51 84 38 20). The restaurant is named after an 1800s company that shipped from this building, among other things, Norwegians heading to the US. Passengers and cargo waited on the first floor, and the manager's office was upstairs. The place is filled with emigrant-era memorabilia.

Sjøhuset Skagen, with a woodsy interior, invites diners to its historic building for lunch or dinner. The building, from the late 1700s, housed a trading company. Today, you can choose from local seafood specialties with an ethnic flair, as well as plenty of meat options (100–150-kr lunches, 200–300-kr dinners, Mon–Sat 11:30–24:00, Sun 13:00–22:00, Skagenkaien 16, tel. 51 89 51 80).

Stavanger Connections

From Stavanger by Train to: Kristiansand (4–7/day, 3.5 hrs), **Oslo** (5/day, 8–9 hrs, overnight possible).

By Boat to Bergen: Flaggruten catamarans sail between Bergen and Stavanger (2–4/day, 4 hrs, 720 kr one-way, 950 kr round-trip; nearly half-price for students and railpass-holders; tel. 55 23 87 00, www.hsd.no).

By Boat to Hirtshals, Denmark: For details on this boat, see the "Sailing Between Norway and Denmark" sidebar.

The Setesdal Valley

Welcome to the remote, and therefore very traditional, Setesdal Valley. Probably Norway's most authentic cranny, the valley is a mellow montage of sod-roofed water mills, ancient churches, derelict farmhouses, yellowed recipes, and gentle scenery.

The Setesdal Valley joined the modern age with the construction of the valley highway in the 1950s. All along the valley you'll see the unique two-story storage sheds called *stabburs* (the top floor was used for storing clothes; the bottom, food) and many sod roofs.

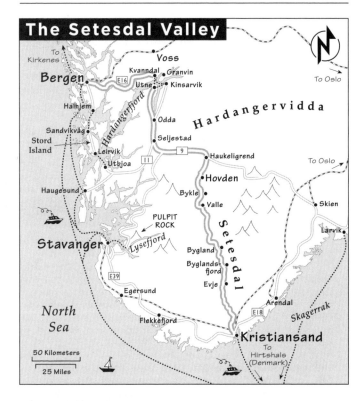

The Setesdal Valley

Even the bus stops have rooftops the local goats love to munch.

In the high country, just over the Sessvatn summit (3,000 feet), you'll see herds of goats and summer farms. If you see an *ekte geitost* sign, that means genuine, homemade goat cheese is for sale. (It's sold cheaper and in more manageable sizes in grocery stores.) To some, it looks like a decade's accumulation of earwax. I think it's delicious. Remember, *ekte* means all-goat—really strong. The more popular and easier-to-eat regular goat cheese is mixed with cow's-milk cheese.

For more information on the Setesdal Valley, see www.setesdal.com.

Sailing Between Norway and Denmark

Two companies sail between the tips of Norway and Denmark. **Color Line** and **Fjordline** sail fast boats between Kristiansand, Norway, and Hirtshals, Denmark (2.25–3.5 hours). In addition, Fjordline boats connect Stavanger, Norway, and Hirtshals (12 hours, covered below). They also link Bergen with Hirtshals, though at 17 hours, it's a long haul.

Both Color Line and Fjordline offer car packages (covering up to 5 people and the car) and have various on-board amenities such as restaurants, coffee bars, duty-free shops, and several classes of travel.

Sailing Between Kristiansand and Hirtshals, Denmark: Color Line ships generally sail twice daily, all year, with a few more sailings added during summer, but mysteriously they sail only once a day in mid-April. Sailing from Norway to Denmark, Color Line boats usually leave Kristiansand at 8:00 and 16:30, arriving in Hirtshals at 11:15 and 19:45. Going from Denmark to Norway, the boats leave Hirtshals at 12:15 and 20:45, arriving in Kristiansand at 15:30 and midnight. Fares vary with day of week and season (cheaper weekdays and off-season). During the summer, passenger fares are €56/person mid-week, €62/person on weekends; car packages start at €204 mid-week and €237 on weekends.

Fjordline's seasonal ferry makes the crossing three times a day from late June to mid-August in a speedy 2.25 hours. The schedule is cut back to twice a day in late spring and early fall, with no ferries from October to April. In high season, sailing from Norway to Denmark, Fjordline boats leave Kristiansand at 7:00, 13:30, and 19:45, arriving in Hirtshals at 9:15, 15:45, and 22:00. Going from Denmark to Norway, the boats leave Hirtshals at 10:15, 16:45, and 22:45, arriving in Kristiansand at 12:30, 19:00,

From Odda to Hovden

Attractions from here to Kristiansand are listed roughly from north to south.

Odda—At the end of the Hardanger Fjord, just past the huge zinc and copper industrial plant, you'll hit the industrial town of Odda (well-stocked **TI** for whole region and beyond; in summer Mon–Fri 7:30–19:00, Sat–Sun 11:00–17:00; off-season Mon–Fri 7:30–15:00, closed Sat–Sun; on market square at Torget 2–4, tel. 53 65 40 05, www.visitodda.com). Odda brags that Kaiser Wilhelm

and 1:00 in the morning. Passenger fares start at €79/person mid-week; car packages start at €165 mid-week.

Sailing Between Stavanger and Hirtshals, Denmark: Fjordline ships sailing from Norway to Denmark travel overnight, which can save you the cost of a hotel. Enjoy an evening in Stavanger, then sleep (or vomit) as you sail to Denmark. The boat generally sails four times a week (usually Mon, Wed, Fri, and Sat; departing Stavanger at either 19:00, 20:30, or 21:00; arriving in Hirtshals at either 7:00, 8:00, or 8:30 the next day). Ships sailing from Denmark to Norway leave Hirtshals in the morning or afternoon, arriving in Stavanger at night, not as desirable an option. These boats also sail four days a week (typically Tue, Thu, Sat, and Sun; departing Hirtshals at either 8:30, 12:30, or 14:30; arriving in Stavanger at either 20:30, 00:15, or 02:30 in the morning).

Fares vary, depending on how far in advance you book, the time of year, the day of the week, and the type of accommodation you want. Basic fares range from €13 to €102, plus the cost of meals (€14 breakfast, €38 dinner) and accommodations (an airline-type seat or cabin). A seat, referred to as a "sleeperette," starts at €8.50. But if you're efficient enough to spend a night traveling, you owe yourself the comfort of a private room. Cabins start at €71 for a basic, two-berth, inside cabin, and go up to €420 for a "Fjord Class" cabin with a double bed and ocean view. Car packages range from €38 to €438.

Reservations: To get the best fare, book online and early—as soon as you can commit to a firm date (http://fjordline.no and www.colorline.com). This is especially true for Fjordline. Many cheaper fares are non-refundable and non-changeable, so be sure to check the details carefully when you book. Days of the week and departure/arrival times can vary, so confirm specific schedules when you make your reservations.

Discounts: Color Line gives a discount off its regular fares to Eurailpass-holders, but you must call Color Line directly to book (Norway tel. 81 50 08 11 or 22 94 42 00; Denmark tel. 99 56 19 77). Fjordline doesn't offer discounts to Eurailers.

came here a lot, but he's dead and I'd drive right through. If you want to visit the tongue of a glacier, drive to Buar and hike an hour to Buarbreen. From Odda, drive into the land of boulders. The many mighty waterfalls that line the road seem to have hurled huge rocks (with rooted trees) into the rivers and fields. Stop at the giant double waterfall (on the left, pullout on the right, drive slowly through it if you need a car wash).

Røldal—Continue over Røldalsfjellet and into the valley below, where the old town of Røldal is trying to develop some tourism. Drive on by. Its old church isn't worth the time or money. Lakes are like frosted mirrors, making desolate huts come in pairs. Haukeliseter, a group of sod-roofed buildings filled with cultural clichés and tour groups, offers pastries, sandwiches, and reasonable hot meals (from 100 kr) in a lakeside setting. Try the traditional *rømmegrøt* porridge.

Haukeligrend—Haukeligrend is a bus/traffic junction, with daily bus service to/from Bergen and to/from Kristiansand (TI inside the café, open daily all year 10:00–19:00, brochures available all the time, TI staff available periodically, Internet access, tel. 35 07 03 67).

Hovden

Hovden is a ski resort at the top of the Setesdal Valley (2,500 feet). It's barren in the summer and painfully in need of charm. Still, it makes a good home base if you want to explore the area for a couple of days. Locals come here to walk and relax for a week.

Tourist Information: The TI is open all year (Mon–Fri 9:00–16:00, summer Sat 9:00–14:00, July also Sun 9:00–14:00, otherwise closed Sat–Sun, tel. 37 93 93 70, www.hovden.com, post@hovden .com).

Sights and Activities in Hovden

Canoe Rental—Hegni Center, on the lake at the south edge of town, rents canoes (230 kr/day, 120 kr/half-day, hourly rentals also possible, cash only, mid-June–mid-Aug daily 10:00–20:00, mid-Aug–early Sept daily 11:00–18:00, mid-Sept–mid-Oct Sat–Sun only 11:00–16:00, closed mid-Oct–mid-June, tel. 91 32 25 81).

Hikes near Hovden—Good walks offer you a chance to see reindeer, moose, arctic fox, and wabbits—so they say. The TI and most hotels stock brochures, maps, and other information about moderate to strenuous hikes in the area. Berry picking is popular in late August, when small, sweet blueberries are in season. A chairlift sometimes takes sightseers to the top of a nearby peak, with great views in clear weather (90 kr, July daily 11:00–14:00, Aug–mid-Oct Wed and Sat–Sun only). Hunting season starts in late August for reindeer (only in higher elevations) and later in the fall for grouse and moose.

Moose Safari—Per Johanson offers a 2.5-hour *Elg Safari* (that's Norwegian for "moose"). Learn more about this "king of the forest" during a late-night drive through Setesdal's back roads with a stop for moose-meat soup (340 kr, June–mid-Sept only; generally Tue, Fri, and Sun at 22:00—more often based upon demand; 50 percent money-back guarantee if you don't see a moose, tel. 37 93 93 70).

Museum of Iron Production (Jernvinnemuseum)—Learn about iron production from the late Iron Age (about 1,000 years ago) with the aid of drawings, exhibits, and recorded narration from a "Viking" (available in English; free, mid-June–mid-Aug daily 11:00–17:00, otherwise ask for the key at the TI or Hegni Center). The museum is about 100 yards behind the Hegni Center (look for the sign from the road to *Jernvinnemuseum*).

Swimming Pool—A super indoor spa/pool complex, the Hovden Badeland, provides a much-needed way to spend an otherwise dreary and drizzly early evening here (155 kr for 3 hours or more, cheaper for shorter visits, daily 10:00–19:00 in summer, shorter hours off-season, tel. 37 93 93 93).

Sleeping and Eating in Hovden

$$ Hovden Fjellstoge is a big, old ski chalet renting Hovden's only cheap beds. Even if you're just passing through, their café is a good choice for lunch or an early dinner. Check out the mural in the balcony overlooking the lobby—an artistic rendition of this area's history. Behind the mural is a frightening taxidermy collection (hotel: Sb-750 kr, bunk-bed Db-990 kr, includes breakfast; cabins: from 650 kr for 2–4 people with bathroom and kitchen; dorms: dorm bed-200 kr, D-500 kr, 25 kr extra if you're not a hostel member, breakfast-70 kr, sheets-100 kr, towel-20 kr; tel. 37 93 95 43, www.hovdenfjellstoge.no, post @hovdenfjellstoge.no).

From Hovden to Kristiansand

▲**Dammar Vatnedalsvatn**—Nine miles south of Hovden is a two-mile side-trip to a 400-foot-high rock-pile dam (look for the *Dammar* signs). Enjoy the great view and impressive rockery. This is one of the highest dams in northern Europe. Read the chart. Sit out of the wind a few rows down the rock pile and ponder the vastness of Norwegian wood.

▲**Bykle**—The most interesting folk museum and church in Setesdal are in the teeny town of Bykle. The 17th-century church has two balconies—one for men and one for women (free, late June–mid-Aug daily 11:00–17:00, tel. 37 93 85 00). Drivers should note that the Bykle toll booth accepts only exact change.

Grasbrokke—On the east side of the main road (at the *Grasbrokke* sign) is an old water mill (1630). A few minutes farther south, at the sign for *Sanden Såre Camping*, exit onto a little road to stretch your legs at another old water mill with a fragile, rotten-log sluice.

Flateland—The **Setesdal Museum** (Rygnestadtunet) offers more of what you saw at Bykle (30 kr, two buildings; late June–Aug daily

11:00–17:00; closed off-season; 1 mile east of the road, tel. 37 93 63 03, www.setesdalsmuseet.no). Unless you're a glutton for culture, I wouldn't do both.

Honneevje—Past Flateland is a nice picnic and WC stop, with a dock along the water for swimming...for hot-weather days or polar bears.

▲**Valle**—This is Setesdal's prettiest village (but don't tell Bykle). In the center, you'll find fine silver- and gold-work, homemade crafts next to the TI, and old-fashioned *lefse* cooking demonstrations (in the small log house by the Valle Motell). The fine suspension bridge attracts kids of any age (b-b-b-b-bounce) and anyone interested in a great view over the river to strange mountains that look like polished, petrified mudslides. European rock climbers, tired of the over-climbed Alps, often entertain spectators with their sport. Is anyone climbing? (TI tel. 37 93 75 27.)

Sleeping in Valle: **$$ Valle Motell** rents basic rooms (Sb-625 kr, Db-690 kr, includes breakfast, cabins with kitchen and bath but no breakfast-690–750 kr, tel. 37 93 77 00, www.valle-motell .no, post@valle-motell.no).

Nomeland—The Sylvartun silversmith shop sells Setesdal silver in a 17th-century log cabin (May–Sept daily 10:00–17:00, closed Oct–April, tel. 37 93 63 06).

Grendi—The Ardal Church (1827) has a rune stone in its yard. Three hundred yards south of the church is a 900-year-old oak tree.

Evje—A huge town by Setesdal standards (3,500 people), Evje is famous for its gems and mines. Fancy stones fill the shops here. Rock hounds find the nearby mines fun; for a small fee, you can hunt for gems. The TI is by Route 9 in the center of Evje (daily 10:00–15:00; tel. 37 93 14 00). The **Setesdal Mineral Park** is on the main road, two miles south of town (100 kr; July–mid-Aug daily 10:00–18:00, mid-Aug–Sept Mon–Sat 10:00–16:00, Sun 10:00–17:00; May–June Mon–Sat 10:00–16:00, Sun 10:00–17:00, closed Oct–April; tel. 38 00 30 70, www.mineralparken.no).

Kristiansand

This "capital of the south" has 80,000 inhabitants, a pleasant Renaissance grid-plan layout (Posebyen), a famous zoo with Norway's biggest amusement park (6 miles toward Oslo on the main road), a daily bus to Bergen, and lots of big boats going to Denmark. It's the closest thing to a beach resort in Norway. Markensgate is the bustling pedestrian market street—a pleasant place for good browsing, shopping, eating, and people-watching.

Stroll along the Strand Promenaden (marina) to Christiansholm Fortress.

Orientation to Kristiansand

The **TI** is at Rådhusgata 6, a few blocks south of the boat, bus, and train station (mid-June–mid-Aug Mon–Fri 9:00–18:00, Sat 10:00–18:00, Sun 12:00–18:00; mid-Aug–mid-June Mon–Fri 9:00–15:30, closed Sat–Sun; tel. 38 12 13 14, www.sorlandet.com). The bank at the Color Line terminal opens for each arrival and departure (even the midnight ones). The Fønix Kino cinema complex is within two blocks of the ferry and TI (70–100 kr, seven screens, movies shown in English, schedules at the entrance, tel. 38 10 42 00).

Sleeping in Kristiansand

(6 kr = about $1, country code: 47)
Kristiansand hotels are expensive and nondescript.

$$$ Rica Hotel Norge is a modern option (rack rates: Sb-1,375 kr, Db-1,575 kr; mid-June–mid-Aug: Sb-1,295 kr, Db-1,495 kr; weekend rates year-round: Sb-795 kr, Db-995 kr; Dronningensgate 5, tel. 38 17 40 00, fax 38 17 40 01, www.hotel -norge.no, firmapost@hotel-norge.no).

$$$ Thon Hotel Wergeland is inviting for a large chain hotel. It's within earshot of the church bells and busy Kirkegate, but quieter rooms away from the street are available (Sb-1,095, Db-1,395, includes breakfast, non-smoking rooms, no elevator, Internet access and Wi-Fi, Kirkegate 15, tel. 38 17 20 40, fax 38 02 73 21, www.thonhotels.no/wergeland, wergeland@thonhotels.no).

$$ At Frobusdalen Rom, Arild and Inger Nilssen rent seven clean, bright rooms and two apartments in a beautiful guest house. You'll have access to the garden, a full kitchen, and a large sitting room filled with lovely antiques and wooden wainscoting (Sb-400–500 kr, Db-600–800 kr, Db with balcony-1,200 kr, apartment for 4–6 people-1,200–2,400 kr, higher prices are for slightly larger room, no breakfast, laundry service available, free parking; 5-min walk from the boat, bus, and train terminals at Frobusdalen 2; tel. 91 12 99 06, www.gjestehus.no, imsan@start.no).

Eating in Kristiansand

The otherwise uninteresting harbor area has a cluster of wooden buildings called **Fiskebasaren** ("Fish Bazaar"). The indoor fish market is only open during the day, but numerous restaurants (serving fish, among other dishes) provide a nice atmosphere for dinner.

Follow Vester Strandgate past the Fønix movie theater to Østre Strandgate, take a right, and follow the signs to Fiskebrygga.

Kristiansand Connections

From Kristiansand by Train to: Stavanger (4–7/day, 3.5 hrs), **Oslo** (4/day, 4.5 hrs).

Route Tips for Drivers
Bergen to Kristiansand via the Setesdal Valley (10 hrs): Your first key connection is the Kvanndal–Utne ferry (departures hourly 6:00–23:00, less on weekends, reservations not possible or even necessary if you get there 20 min early, breakfast in cafeteria, www.hsd.no). If you make the 9:00, your day will be more relaxed. Driving comfortably, with no mistakes or traffic, it's two hours from your Bergen hotel to the ferry dock. Leaving Bergen is a bit confusing. Pretend you're going to Oslo on the road to Voss (Route E16, signs for *Nestune, Landås, Nattland*). About a half-hour out of town, after a long tunnel, leave the Voss road and take Route 7 heading for Norheimsund, and then Kvanndal. This road, treacherous for the famed beauty of the Hardanger Fjord it hugs as well as for its skinniness, is faster and safer if you beat the traffic (which you will with this plan).

The ferry drops you in Utne, where a lovely road takes you to Odda and up into the mountains. From Haukeligrend, turn south and wind up to Sessvatn at 3,000 feet. Enter the Setesdal Valley. Follow the Otra River downhill for 140 miles south to the major port town of Kristiansand. Skip the secondary routes. South of Valle, you'll have to pass a 25-kr tollbooth. The most scenic stretch is between Hovden and Valle. South of Valle, there is a lot more logging (and therefore less scenic). As you enter Kristiansand, pay a 10-kr toll and follow signs for Denmark.

PRACTICALITIES

This section covers just the basics on traveling in this region (for much more information, see *Rick Steves' Scandinavia*). You'll find free advice on specific topics at www.ricksteves.com/tips.

Money

Norway uses the Norwegian kroner: 1 krone equals about $0.17. To roughly convert prices in kroner to dollars, divide prices by 6 (100 kr = about $16). Check www.oanda.com for the latest exchange rates.

The standard way for travelers to get kroner is to withdraw money from a cash machine (ATM) using a debit or credit card, ideally with a Visa or MasterCard logo. Before departing, call your bank or credit-card company: Confirm that your card will work overseas, ask about international transaction fees, and alert them that you'll be making withdrawals in Europe.

Most Norwegian merchants and automated machines accept payment using the European chip-and-PIN system, which requires users to type in their PIN (Personal Identification Number) when using the card for purchases. Your non-European credit card will usually work in these machines, provided you know the PIN. However, since your card might not always work, you can avoid hassles by making withdrawals from ATMs and paying for purchases with cash.

To keep your valuables safe, wear a money belt. But if you do lose your credit or debit card, report the loss immediately to the respective global customer-assistance centers. Call these 24-hour US numbers collect: Visa (410/581-9994), MasterCard (636/722-7111), and American Express (623/492-8427).

Phoning

Smart travelers use the telephone to reserve or reconfirm rooms, reserve restaurants, get directions, research transportation connections, confirm tour times, phone home, and lots more.

To call Norway from the US or Canada: Dial 011-47 and then the local number. (The 011 is our international access code, and 47 is Norway's country code.)

To call Norway from a European country: Dial 00-47 followed by the local number. (The 00 is Europe's international access code.)

To call within Norway: Dial the local number.

Tips on Phoning: To make calls in Norway, you can buy two different types of phone cards—international or insertable—sold locally at newsstands. Cheap international phone cards, which work with a scratch-to-reveal PIN code, allow you to call home to the US for pennies a minute, and also work for domestic calls. You can use these cards from any phone, including the one in your hotel room, but some hotels charge for calls to the "toll-free" access line (ask before you dial). Insertable phone cards, which must be inserted into public pay phones, are reasonable for calls within Norway (and work for international calls as well, though not as cheaply as the international phone cards). Note that insertable phone cards—and most international phone cards—work only in the country where you buy them. Calling from your hotel-room phone *without* using an international phone card is usually expensive.

A mobile phone—whether an American one that works in Europe, or a European one you buy when you arrive—is handy, but can be pricey. For more on phoning, see www.ricksteves.com /phoning.

Emergency Telephone Numbers: To summon the **police** or an **ambulance**, call 112. For passport problems, call the **US Embassy** (in Oslo; tel. 22 44 85 50; passport services available Mon–Fri 9:00–12:00, www.norway.usembassy.gov). For other concerns, get advice from your hotelier.

Making Hotel Reservations

To ensure the best value, I recommend reserving rooms in advance, particularly during peak season. Email the hotelier with the following key pieces of information: number and type of rooms; number of nights; date of arrival; date of departure; and any special requests. (For a sample form, see www.ricksteves.com/reservation.) Use the European style for writing dates: day/month/year. For example, for a two-night stay in July, you could request: "1 double room for 2 nights, arrive 16/07/10, depart 18/07/10." Hoteliers typically ask for your credit-card number as a deposit.

In these times of economic uncertainty, some hotels are willing to deal to attract guests—try emailing several to ask their best price. In general, hotel prices can soften if you do any of the following: offer to pay cash, stay at least three nights, or travel off-season. You can also try asking for a cheaper room (for example, with a bathroom down the hall), or offer to skip breakfast. In Oslo, business-class hotels drop prices to attract tourists with summer rates (from July through mid-August) and weekend rates (Friday and Saturday, but not Sunday). You need to ask about these discounts. Any time of year, the TI's Oslo Package is a good deal for couples and great for families with young children; see www.visitoslo.com.

Eating

Restaurants are often expensive. Alternate between picnics (outside or in your hotel or hostel); cheap, forgettable, but filling cafeteria or fast-food fare ($20 per person); and atmospheric, carefully chosen restaurants popular with locals ($35 per person and up). Ethnic eateries—Indian, Turkish, Greek, Italian, and Asian—offer a good value and a break from Norwegian fare.

The *smörgåsbord* (known in Norway as the *store koldt bord*) is a revered Scandinavian culinary tradition. Seek it out at least once during your visit. Begin with the fish dishes, along with boiled potatoes and *knekkebrød* (crisp bread). Then move on to salads, egg dishes, and various cold cuts. Next it's meatball time! Pour on some gravy as well as a spoonful of lingonberry sauce. Still hungry? Make a point to sample the Nordic cheeses and the racks of traditional desserts, cakes, and custards.

Hotel breakfasts are a huge and filling buffet, generally included but occasionally a $10-or-so option. It usually features fruit, cereal, various milks, breads and crackers, cold cuts, pickled herring, caviar paste, and boiled eggs. The brown cheese with the texture of earwax and a slightly sweet taste is *geitost* ("goat cheese").

In Norway, alcohol is sold only at state-run liquor stores called Vinmonopolet (though weak beer is also sold at supermarkets). To avoid extremely high restaurant prices for alcohol, many Norwegians—and tourists—buy their wine, beer, or spirits at a store and then drink at a public square; this is legal and openly practiced. One local specialty is *akvavit*, a strong, vodka-like spirit distilled from potatoes and flavored with anise, caraway, or other herbs and spices—then drunk ice-cold.

Service: Good service is relaxed (slow to an American). When you want the bill, say, *"Regningen, takk."* Throughout Norway, a service charge is included in your bill, so there's no need to leave an additional tip. In fancier restaurants or for great service, round up the bill (about 5 percent of the total check).

Transportation

By Train and Bus: Trains cover many of my recommended Norwegian destinations. To see if a railpass could save you money, check www.ricksteves.com/rail. If you're buying tickets as you go, note that prices can fluctuate. To research train schedules and fares, visit the Norwegian train website: www.nsb.no. Nearly any long-distance train ride requires you to make a reservation before boarding (the day before is usually fine). If you're taking the Norway in a Nutshell route in mid-July or August, it's smart to make reservations at least a week in advance for the Oslo–Bergen train and the Flåm-Gudvangen fjord cruise.

Don't overlook long-distance buses, which are usually slower than trains but have considerably cheaper and more predictable fares. On certain routes (e.g., Oslo-Stockholm), the bus is less expensive and only slightly slower than the train. Norway's biggest bus carrier is Nor-Way Bussekspress (www.nor-way.no).

By Car: It's cheaper to arrange most car rentals from the US. For tips on your insurance options, see www.ricksteves.com/cdw, and for route planning, consult www.viamichelin.com. Bring your driver's license. Local road etiquette is similar to that in the US. Use your headlights day and night; it's required in most of Scandinavia. A car is a worthless headache in any big city—park it safely (get tips from your hotelier).

By Boat: Boats are both a necessary and spectacular way to travel through Norway's fjords or along its coast (for various routes, see www.fjordtours.no, www.fjord1.no, and www.hsd.no). Reserve ahead if you're planning on taking overnight boats in summer or on weekends to link Oslo and Copenhagen (www.dfdsseaways.com). Other worthwhile ferry routes connect Norway and northern Denmark; see www.fjordline.com and www.colorline.com.

Helpful Hints

Time: Europe uses the 24-hour clock. It's the same through 12:00 noon, then keep going: 13:00, 14:00, and so on. Norway is six/nine hours ahead of the East/West Coasts of the US.

Holidays and Festivals: Europe celebrates many holidays, which can close sights and attract crowds (book hotel rooms ahead). For information on holidays and festivals in Norway, check the Scandinavia Tourist Board website: www.goscandinavia.com. For a simple list showing major—though not all—events, see www.ricksteves.com/festivals.

Numbers and Stumblers: What Americans call the second floor of a building is the first floor in Europe. Europeans write dates as day/month/year, so Christmas is 25/12/10. Commas are decimal points and vice versa—a dollar and a half is 1,50, and there are 5.280 feet in a mile. Europe uses the metric system: A kilogram is 2.2 pounds; a liter is about a quart; and a kilometer is six-tenths of a mile.

Resources from Rick Steves

This Snapshot guide is excerpted from *Rick Steves' Scandinavia*, which is one of more than 30 titles in my series of guidebooks on European travel. I also produce a public television series, *Rick Steves' Europe*, and a public radio show, *Travel with Rick Steves*. My website, www.ricksteves.com, offers free travel information, free vodcasts and podcasts of my shows, free audio tours of major sights in Europe (for you to download onto an iPod or other MP3 player), a Graffiti Wall for travelers' comments, guidebook updates, my travel blog, an online travel store, and information on European railpasses and our tours of Europe.

Additional Resources

Tourist Information: www.goscandinavia.com
Passports and Red Tape: www.travel.state.gov
Packing List: www.ricksteves.com/packlist
Cheap Flights: www.skyscanner.net
Airplane Carry-on Restrictions: www.tsa.gov/travelers
Updates for This Book: www.ricksteves.com/update

How Was Your Trip?

If you'd like to share your tips, concerns, and discoveries after using this book, please fill out the survey at www.ricksteves.com/feedback. Thanks in advance—it helps a lot.

Norwegian Survival Phrases

Norwegian can be pronounced quite differently from region to region. These phrases and phonetics match the mainstream Oslo dialect, but you'll notice variations. Vowels can be tricky: *å* sounds like "oh," *æ* sounds like a bright "ah" (as in "apple"), and *u* sounds like the German *ü* (purse your lips and say u). Certain vowels at the ends of words (such as *d* and *t*) are sometimes barely pronounced (or not at all). In some dialects, the letters *sk* are pronounced "sh." In the phonetics, Ī / ī sounds like the long i in "light."

Hello. (*formal*)	**God dag.**	goo dahg
Hi. / Bye. (*informal*)	**Hei. / Ha det.**	hī / hah deh
Do you speak English?	**Snakker du engelsk?**	SNAHK-kehr dew ENG-ehlsk
Yes. / No.	**Ja. / Nei.**	yah / nī
Please.	**Vær så snill.**	vayr soh sneel
Thank you (very much).	**(Tusen) takk.**	(TEW-sehn) tahk
You're welcome.	**Vær så god.**	vayr soh goo
Can I help you?	**Kan jeg hjelpe deg?**	kahn yī YEHL-peh dī
Excuse me.	**Unnskyld.**	EWN-shuld
(Very) good.	**(Veldig) fint.**	(VEHL-dee) feent
Goodbye.	**Farvel.**	fahr-VEHL
one / two	**en / to**	ayn / toh
three / four	**tre / fire**	treh / FEE-reh
five / six	**fem / seks**	fehm / sehks
seven / eight	**syv / åtte**	seev / OH-teh
nine / ten	**ni / ti**	nee / tee
hundred	**hundre**	HEWN-dreh
thousand	**tusen**	TEW-sehn
How much?	**Hvor mye?**	voor MEE-yeh
local currency: (Norwegian) crown	**(Norske) kroner**	(NORSH-keh) KROH-nehr
Where is...?	**Hvor er...?**	voor ehr
..the toilet	**...toalettet**	toh-ah-LEH-teh
men	**menn** Or: **herrer**	mehn / HEHR-rehr
women	**damer**	DAH-mehr
water / coffee	**vann / kaffe**	vahn / KAH-feh
beer / wine	**øl / vin**	uhl / veen
Cheers!	**Skål!**	skohl
The bill, please.	**Regningen, takk.**	RĪ-ning-ehn tahk

Rick Steves ®

EUROPEAN TOURS

ADRIATIC • ATHENS & THE HEART OF
GREECE • BARCELONA & MADRID • BELGIUM
& HOLLAND • BERLIN, VIENNA & PRAGUE
BEST OF EUROPE • BEST OF ITALY
BEST OF TURKEY • BULGARIA • EASTERN
EUROPE • ENGLAND • FAMILY EUROPE
GERMANY, AUSTRIA & SWITZERLAND
HEART OF ITALY • IRELAND • ISTANBUL
LONDON • PARIS • PARIS & HEART OF
FRANCE • PARIS & SOUTH OF FRANCE
PORTUGAL • PRAGUE & BUDAPEST • ROME
SAN SEBASTIAN & BASQUE COUNTRY
SCANDINAVIA • SCOTLAND • SICILY
SOUTH ITALY • SPAIN & MOROCCO
ST. PETERSBURG, TALLINN & HELSINKI
VENICE, FLORENCE & ROME • VILLAGE
FRANCE • VILLAGE ITALY • VILLAGE TURKEY

VISIT **TOURS.RICKSTEVES.COM**

Great guides, small groups, no grumps

Start your trip at

Free information and great gear to

▸ Plan Your Trip

Browse thousands of articles and a wealth of money-saving tips for planning your dream trip. You'll find up-to-date information on Europe's best destinations, packing smart, getting around, finding rooms, staying healthy, avoiding scams and more.

▸ Eurail Passes

Find out, step-by-step, if a rail pass makes sense for your trip—and how to avoid buying more than you need. Get a bunch of free extras!

▸ Graffiti Wall & Travelers' Helpline

Learn, ask, share—our online community of savvy travelers is a great resource for first-time travelers to Europe, as well as seasoned pros.

Rick Steves' Europe Through the Back Door, Inc.

ricksteves.com

turn your travel dreams into affordable reality

▶ Free Audio Tours & Travel Newsletter

Get your nose out of this guide-book and focus on what you'll be seeing with Rick's free audio tours of the greatest sights in Paris, Rome, Florence and Venice.

Subscribe to our free *Travel News* e-newsletter, and get monthly articles from Rick on what's happening in Europe.

▶ Great Gear from Rick's Travel Store

Pack light and right—on a budget—with Rick's custom-designed carry-on bags, roll-aboards, day packs, travel accessories, guidebooks, journals, maps and DVDs of his TV shows.

Rick Steves

www.ricksteves.com

TRAVEL SKILLS
Europe Through the Back Door

EUROPE GUIDES
Best of Europe
Eastern Europe
Europe 101
European Christmas
Postcards from Europe

COUNTRY GUIDES
Croatia & Slovenia
England
France
Germany
Great Britain
Ireland
Italy
Portugal
Scandinavia
Spain
Switzerland

CITY & REGIONAL GUIDES
Amsterdam, Bruges & Brussels
Athens & The Peloponnese
Budapest
Florence & Tuscany
Istanbul
London
Paris
Prague & The Czech Republic
Provence & The French Riviera
Rome
Venice
Vienna, Salzburg & Tirol

PHRASE BOOKS & DICTIONARIES
French
French, Italian & German
German
Italian
Portuguese
Spanish

RICK STEVES' EUROPE DVDs
Austria & The Alps
Eastern Europe
England
Europe
France & Benelux
Germany & Scandinavia
Greece, Turkey, Israel & Egypt
Ireland & Scotland
Italy's Cities
Italy's Countryside
Rick Steves' European Christmas
Spain & Portugal
Travel Skills & "The Making Of"

PLANNING MAPS
Britain, Ireland & London
Europe
France & Paris
Germany, Austria & Switzerland
Ireland
Italy
Spain & Portugal

JOURNALS
Rick Steves' Pocket Travel Journal
Rick Steves' Travel Journal

NOW AVAILABLE

RICK STEVES APPS FOR THE iPHONE OR iPOD TOUCH

With these apps you can:

▶ Spin the compass icon to switch views between sights, hotels, and restaurant selections—and get details on cost, hours, address, and phone number.

▶ Tap any point on the screen to read Rick's detailed information, including history and suggested viewpoints.

▶ Get a deeper view into Rick's tours with audio and video segments.

Go to iTunes to download the following apps:

Rick Steves' Louvre Tour

Rick Steves' Historic Paris Walk

Rick Steves' Orsay Museum Tour

Rick Steves' Versailles

Rick Steves' Ancient Rome Tour

Rick Steves' St. Peter's Basilica Tour

Once downloaded, these apps are completely self-contained on your iPhone or iPod Touch, so you will not incur pricey roaming charges during use overseas.

Rick Steves books and DVDs are available at bookstores and through online booksellers.
Rick Steves guidebooks are published by Avalon Travel, a member of the Perseus Books Group.
Rick Steves apps are produced by Übermind, a boutique Seattle-based software consultancy firm.

Avalon Travel
a member of the Perseus Books Group
1700 Fourth Street
Berkeley, CA 94710

Printed in the USA by Worzalla
Second printing July 2010

ISBN 978-1-59880-592-5

For the latest on Rick's lectures, guidebooks, tours, public radio show, and public television series, contact Europe Through the Back Door, Box 2009, Edmonds, WA 98020, 425/771-8303, fax 425/771-0833, www.ricksteves.com, rick@ricksteves.com.

Europe Through the Back Door Reviewing Editor: Cameron Hewitt
ETBD Editors: Jennifer Madison Davis, Tom Griffin, Cathy McDonald, Cathy Lu, Gretchen Strauch, Sarah McCormic
ETBD Managing Editor: Risa Laib
Research Assistance: Gretchen Strauch, Lauren Mills, Cathy McDonald
Avalon Travel Senior Editor and Series Manager: Madhu Prasher
Avalon Travel Project Editor: Kelly Lydick
Copy Editor: Jennifer Malnick
Proofreader: Janet Walden
Production and Layout: McGuire Barber Design
Cover Design: Kimberly Glyder Design
Graphic Content Director: Laura VanDeventer
Maps and Graphics: David C. Hoerlein, Laura VanDeventer, Brice Ticen, Lauren Mills, Barb Geisler, Pat O'Connor, Mike Morgenfeld
Front Cover Photo: Neist Point © Cameron Hewitt
Additional Photography: Rick Steves, Cameron Hewitt, Gene Openshaw, Bruce VanDeventer, Lauren Mills, David C. Hoerlein, Jennifer Hauseman, Jennifer Schutte, Ken Hanley, Sarah Murdoch, Darbi Macy, Dominic Bonuccelli

ABOUT THE AUTHOR

RICK STEVES

 Rick Steves is on a mission: to help make European travel accessible and meaningful for Americans. Rick has spent four months every year since 1973 exploring Europe. He's researched and written more than 30 travel guidebooks, writes and hosts the public television series *Rick Steves' Europe*, and also produces and hosts the weekly public radio show *Travel with Rick Steves*. With the help of his hardworking staff of 70 at Europe Through the Back Door, Rick organizes tours of Europe and offers an information-packed website (www.ricksteves.com). Rick calls Edmonds, just north of Seattle, home.